MW00910217

We at IDG Books Worldwide created *Creating Cool Navigator Gold Web Pages* to meet your growing need for quick access to the most complete and accurate computer information available. Our books work the way you do: They focus on accomplishing specific tasks — not on learning random functions. Our books are not long-winded manuals or dry reference tomes. In each book, expert authors tell you exactly what you can do with new technology and software and how to evaluate its usefulness for your needs. Easy to follow information, comprehensive coverage, and convenient access in language and design — it's all here.

The authors of our books are uniquely qualified to give you expert advice as well as to provide insightful tips and techniques not found anywhere else. Our authors maintain close contact with end users through feedback from articles, training sessions, e-mail exchanges, user group participation, and consulting work. Because our authors know the realities of daily computer use and are directly linked to the reader, our books have a strategic advantage.

Our experienced authors know how to approach a topic in the most efficient manner, and we know that you, the reader, will benefit from a "one-on-one" relationship with the author. Our research shows that readers make computer book purchases because they want expert advice. Because readers want to benefit from the author's experience, the author's voice is always present in an IDG Books Worldwide book.

In addition, the author is free to include or recommend useful software in an IDG Books Worldwide book. The software that accompanies each book is not intended to be a casual filler but is linked to the content, theme, or procedures of the book. We know that you will benefit from the included software.

You will find what you need in this book whether you read it from cover to cover, section by section, or simply one topic at a time. As a computer user, you deserve a comprehensive resource of answers. We at IDG Books Worldwide are proud to deliver that resource with *Creating Cool Navigator Gold Web Pages*.

Brenda McLaughlin
Senior Vice President and Group Publisher

Internet: YouTellUs@idgbooks.com

CREATING COOL™ NAVIGATOR GOLD WEB PAGES

Ron Wodaski

CREATING COOL™
NAVIGATOR GOLD WEB PAGES

Ron Wodaski

IDG Books Worldwide, Inc.
An International Data Group Company

Foster City, CA ♦ Chicago, IL ♦ Indianapolis, IN ♦ Southlake, TX

Creating Cool™ Navigator Gold Web Pages

Published by
IDG Books Worldwide, Inc.
An International Data Group Company
919 E. Hillsdale Blvd, Suite 400
Foster City, CA 94404
www.idgbooks.com (IDG Books Worldwide Web Site)

Library of Congress Catalog Card No.: 96-77081

ISBN: 0-7645-3021-6

Printed in the United States of America

10 9 8 7 6 5 4 3 2 1

1B/RU/RQ/ZW/FC

Distributed in the United States by IDG Books Worldwide, Inc.

Distributed by Macmillan Canada for Canada; by Contemporanea de Ediciones for Venezuela; by Distribuidora Cuspide for Argentina; by CITEC for Brazil; by Ediciones ZETA S.C.R. Ltda. for Peru; by Editorial Limusa SA for Mexico; by Transworld Publishers Limited in the United Kingdom and Europe; by Academic Bookshop for Egypt; by Levant Distributors S.A.R.L. for Lebanon; by Al Jassim for Saudi Arabia; by Simron Pty. Ltd. for South Africa; by Pustak Mahal for India; by The Computer Bookshop for India; by Toppan Company Ltd. for Japan; by Addison Wesley Publishing Company for Korea; by Longman Singapore Publishers Ltd. for Singapore, Malaysia, Thailand, and Indonesia; by Unalis Corporation for Taiwan; by WS Computer Publishing Company, Inc. for the Philippines; by WoodsLane Pty. Ltd. for Australia; by WoodsLane Enterprises Ltd. for New Zealand. Authorized Sales Agent: Anthony Rudkin Associates for the Middle East and North Africa.

For general information on IDG Books Worldwide's books in the U.S., please call our Consumer Customer Service department at 800-762-2974. For reseller information, including discounts and premium sales, please call our Reseller Customer Service department at 800-434-3422.

For information on where to purchase IDG Books Worldwide's books outside the U.S., please contact our International Sales department at 415-655-3172 or fax 415-655-3295.

For information on foreign language translations, please contact our Foreign & Subsidiary Rights department at 415-655-3021 or fax 415-655-3281.

For sales inquiries and special prices for bulk quantities, please contact our Sales department at 415-655-3200 or write to the address above.

For information on using IDG Books Worldwide's books in the classroom or for ordering examination copies, please contact our Educational Sales department at 800-434-2086 or fax 817-251-8174.

For authorization to photocopy items for corporate, personal, or educational use, please contact Copyright Clearance Center, 222 Rosewood Drive, Danvers, MA 01923, or fax 508-750-4470.

is a trademark under exclusive license to IDG Books Worldwide, Inc., from International Data Group, Inc.

About the Author

Ron Wodaski lives on the quiet shores of Puget Sound, north of Seattle. A former freelance correspondent for National Public Radio, Ron joined the personal computer revolution more than 15 years ago. He has worked at every level of the industry, from programmer to MIS Manager, and with many different languages.

He has written for many magazines, including Multimedia World, Technique, CD-ROM World, and others. He is president of Multimedia Madness, Inc., a company that provides consulting services related to the Web and multimedia production.

Welcome to the world of IDG Books Worldwide.

IDG Books Worldwide, Inc., is a subsidiary of International Data Group, the world's largest publisher of computer-related information and the leading global provider of information services on information technology. IDG was founded more than 25 years ago and now employs more than 8,500 people worldwide. IDG publishes more than 270 computer publications in over 75 countries (see listing below). More than 90 million people read one or more IDG publications each month.

Launched in 1990, IDG Books Worldwide is today the #1 publisher of best-selling computer books in the United States. We are proud to have received eight awards from the Computer Press Association in recognition of editorial excellence and three from *Computer Currents'* First Annual Readers' Choice Awards. Our best-selling ...*For Dummies*® series has more than 25 million copies in print with translations in 30 languages. IDG Books Worldwide, through a joint venture with IDG's Hi-Tech Beijing, became the first U.S. publisher to publish a computer book in the People's Republic of China. In record time, IDG Books Worldwide has become the first choice for millions of readers around the world who want to learn how to better manage their businesses.

Our mission is simple: Every one of our books is designed to bring extra value and skill-building instructions to the reader. Our books are written by experts who understand and care about our readers. The knowledge base of our editorial staff comes from years of experience in publishing, education, and journalism — experience which we use to produce books for the '90s. In short, we care about books, so we attract the best people. We devote special attention to details such as audience, interior design, use of icons, and illustrations. And because we use an efficient process of authoring, editing, and desktop publishing our books electronically, we can spend more time ensuring superior content and spend less time on the technicalities of making books.

You can count on our commitment to deliver high-quality books at competitive prices on topics you want to read about. At IDG Books Worldwide, we continue in the IDG tradition of delivering quality for more than 25 years. You'll find no better book on a subject than one from IDG Books Worldwide.

John J. Kilcullen

John Kilcullen
President and CEO
IDG Books Worldwide, Inc.

Dedication

This book is dedicated to my family, who make all things worthwhile.

Credits

Senior Vice President and Group Publisher
Brenda McLaughlin

Acquisitions Manager
Walter Bruce

Acquisitions Editor
Gregory S. Croy

Software Acquisitions Editor
Tracy Lehman Cramer

Marketing Manager
Melisa M. Duffy

Managing Editor
Andy Cummings

Editorial Assistant
Timothy J. Borek

Development Editors
Pat O'Brien
Peggy Watt

Copy Edit Coordinator
Barry Childs-Helton

Technical Reviewer
Stephen Pedrick

Media Archive Coordination
Leslie Popplewell

Production Director
Andrew Walker

Supervisor of Page Layout
Craig A. Harrison

Production Associate
Christopher Pimentel

Project Coordinator
Phyllis Beaty

Graphics & Production Specialists
Diann Abbott
Mario Amador
Vincent F. Burns
Tom Debolski
Ritchie Durdin
Andreas F. Schueller
Mark Schumann

Quality Control Specialist
Mick Arellano

Proofreader
Deb Kaufmann

Indexer
Steve Rath

Book Design
Theresa Sánchez-Baker

Cover Design
three 8 Creative Group

Acknowledgments

I had a lot of help in writing this book. Some of it was direct, and much of it was indirect. I want to thank my son, Justen, who reviewed each chapter in detail. He identified numerous ways that I could improve the manuscript, and the book would not be nearly as useful without his help.

I want to thank my assistant, Robin Comforto, who handled most of the administrative burdens during the writing of the book. Robin also spent many hours huddled over the computer creating the many, many graphic variations you'll find on the CD-ROM.

I'm also grateful to the folks at IDG Books Worldwide who put so much effort into making this a quality book. I'd like to thank, in particular, Pat O'Brien, who once again provided assistance above and beyond the call of duty. A big thank-you to my editor, Greg Croy, whose long experience in the industry is invaluable. Thanks also to Super Speedster and Editor Extraordinaire Peggy Watt, who helped whip the book into final shape.

Thanks again to the crew at the Bayview Restaurant, who so graciously allowed me to write while the seals, otters, gulls, and great blue herons cavorted outside by the water.

And special thanks to everyone who ever asked me a question about Navigator Gold on CompuServe or the Internet. Such questions helped to shape the book, and to direct it at the real needs of real people. My family has supported my work from the beginning and deserves my thanks. My lifetime partner and mate, Pat Golden Dieter, helped edit the book. My kids, Blue, Jesse, Deja, Chrystal, and Dustin, all contributed by demonstrating how to enjoy life and still get the job done. My parents, Earl and Evelyn McCullough, brought me up believing in myself. Thanks for being in my life.

Contents at a Glance

Table of Contents

Striking Gold

Introduction

When I started creating web pages, I did it the hard way. I used HTML tags, which look like a cross between a bad college term paper and the darker depths of computer programming. It was a little like writing a letter with both hands tied behind your back while an evil troll tickles your feet. In other words, it was tedious and utterly lacking in pizzazz.

In 1995, software began to appear that promised to make creating web pages easier. Some of them did, in fact, make it easier. The problem was that the software didn't make it easy enough. HTML, the very foundation of web pages, was growing more and more complex. It was a terrible quandary: It was getting easier and easier to put your web page on the Web, but it was getting harder and harder to create that web page.

Throughout this time, by far the most popular web browser was Netscape's Navigator. When the word hit the streets that Netscape planned to add web page creation tools to Navigator, you could hear the collective sigh of relief all over the Web. Everyone expected that Navigator Gold would do for web page creation what Navigator did for web browsing: make it simple, and make it powerful.

With version 3.0 of Navigator Gold, Netscape did indeed strike gold. Nowhere else will you find the same combination of features:

➡ A top-notch web browser

➡ An easy-to-use web page creation tool

➡ Newsgroup support

➡ Internet mail

➡ One-button web publishing

By stuffing all of the functionality into one software package — and offering it at a ridiculously low price, Netscape staked out the territory before anyone else could even get started. If you want to create web pages with a minimum of fuss, and a maximum of power, Netscape's Navigator Gold is the place to start.

If you do not already have a copy of Netscape Navigator Gold, you can download the latest version from Netscape. To find the link for downloading, visit the web site for this book, located at

```
http://www.olympus.net/biz/mmad/ng/index.htm
```

Note: Web page references often change. I have included numerous URLs for web pages throughout this book. If you ever have trouble finding a web page referenced in the book, visit the above page to find out where the page has moved. If you find a page has moved, and it's not listed on the above page, send e-mail to ronw@olympus.net to let me know, and I'll update the book's home page. You can also use that e-mail address to let me know what you think about the book, any problems you encounter, and so on.

Features of This Book

This book is dedicated to the proposition that the best way to learn stuff is by doing it yourself. That's why you'll find hands-on tutorials in every chapter. Every tutorial makes use of material that I have provided on the CD-ROM, so you won't have to waste your time typing in unnecessary material.

You'll find several different icons haunting the book's margins:

When you see this icon, you know that some friendly help is available. I will expand on ideas in the text, or offer some shortcuts or fancy tricks that you can try.

This icon marks potential rough spots in the road. Whenever possible, I'll not only offer a warning, but also some ideas for how to minimize the risk.

Whenever you face a really big piece of trouble, you'll see this icon. Check this material carefully; it will help you avoid all kinds of serious trouble.

A lot of the material in the book is also available on the CD-ROM. For example, if I show a picture of a web page that I created, you will almost always be able to find the web page on the CD-ROM. You can learn a lot about how to create good web pages from exploring these on-disc pages with the right mouse button while in Edit mode.

About the CD-ROM

The CD-ROM that comes with this book contains material that is referenced throughout the book, as well as useful graphics and utility software to make your life easier. It also contains many, many sample web pages that you can use as templates to create your own pages. For a complete list of CD-ROM contents, see the Appendix.

Mining for Gold

Surfin' with Style

There are now millions of web pages on the Internet, and the number of pages is growing every second. Netscape Gold combines all of the tools you need for surfing the net and for making your own waves, too. With Netscape Navigator Gold, you have the best of both worlds: You can browse the Web and create your own home pages using a single tool.

Netscape Navigator Gold is a very efficient way to combine all of your web activity under a single umbrella. In this chapter, you'll learn how the World Wide Web works, how you can best make use of it, and how to surf the Web effectively with Navigator Gold. You'll learn how to create your own web pages with Gold starting in Chapter 2.

Web Basics

The heart of the World Wide Web is the web page (see Figure 1-1). Unlike a printed page, which can hold mere text and images, a web page can contain **hyperlinks** and **objects**. A hyperlink is a link to another web page, to a picture, to a video clip — in short, a link to anything that can exist on the Web. An object is a computer program that you can place on the page. When you click on the object, the program runs. You don't have to be able to write programs to use objects on your web pages — you can download useful objects from many, many web locations. Objects are an exciting advance in web technology, and I'll reveal the secrets you need to know in Chapter 5.

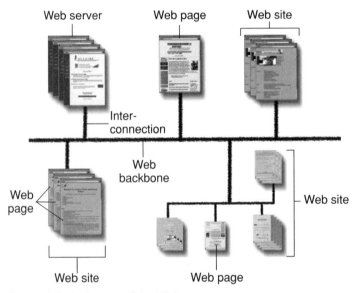

Figure 1-1: A diagram of the Web.

TIP

Don't be confused by terminology! The **Web** and **World Wide Web** are the same thing. "Internet" refers to everything that has anything to do with the computers linked around the world into a single loose network. The Web is just a part of the Internet — the most interesting part, the part with images and videos and games and those lovely, expressive, delicious web pages.

A collection of one or more web pages is called a web site (see Figure 1-1). Typically, a web site resides on one or more web servers. A web server is simply a computer that is accessible to web browsers. You might also see the word **node** used to describe a web site, or a web server. These words have shades of meaning that are important to the people who administer web sites, but the term web server is probably the most useful, and that's what I'll use throughout the book to describe a single physical computer on the Internet.

Each web server is connected to the Internet, usually by some kind of direct, full-time connection (see Table 1-1). This means that most web servers are available to you any time of the day or night. Most web surfers use a dial-up connection — you only connect to the Web when you use your modem to call the web server of your Internet Service Provider.

Web servers are connected to each other, usually by high-capacity phone lines. Information travels from server to server along these connections. There are various grades of connections, ranging from simple modems just like the one you probably use (14,400 or 28,800 bits per second), all the way up to major telephone trunk lines (many megabits per second). Each kind of connection can carry only so much traffic. If you ever experience a slowdown in Web activity, it usually means that a connection between your computer and the source of the web page you are waiting for has reached its carrying capacity, and you are waiting for your turn to use the connection.

The highest-capacity lines of all are often referred to as the web backbone (see Figure 1-1), and they carry the long-distance and high-volume web traffic. The backbone can carry huge amounts of data in very short portions of time, but the average user can't readily connect to the backbone. As a rule, the faster the connection, the higher its capacity, and the more it costs. Table 1-1 shows some of the more common kinds of connections.

To see current pricing and connection types, visit the UUNET web page at http://www.uunet.com and the NorthWestNet home page at http://www.nwnet.net. The web site for NorthWestNet is also a nice example of the right way to do a business web site; check it out!

In addition to web servers, other kinds of servers are on the Internet. FTP servers are used for file copying, for example. E-mail also uses the Internet, traveling across the same connection as web pages and other files. It's no wonder that you sometimes have to wait for something to come to you across the Internet: With so much traffic, the various kinds of connections get loaded to capacity fairly often.

Table 1-1: Typical Kinds of Web Connections

Type	Connection	Max Capacity**	Typical Provider Charges*		
			Local ISP	UUNET	NorthWestNet
Dial-up	14.4 modem	14.4 Kbps	$20/month	***	***
Dial-up	28.8 modem	28.8 Kbps	$20/month	***	***
Dial-up	ISDN line	64–128 Kbps	$30-100/month, $50 startup	***	***
Direct	56K frame relay	56 Kbps (DS0)	****	$600/month, $500 setup	***
Direct	128K frame relay	128 Kbps	****	$1,000/month, $3,000 setup	$500/month, $3,000 setup
Direct	Fractional T1	256 or 512 Kbps	****	$1,000 to $2,000/month; $5,000 setup	$800+/month, $5,995 setup
Direct	T1 (DS1)	1.54 Mbps	****	$2,000+/month; $5,000 setup	$1,595/month frame relay; $2195/month std. $3,500-6,000 setup
Direct	Multi T1	3, 4.5, or 6 Mbps	****	$4,000 to $5,000/month, $6,000 setup	Multiply by number of T1 lines
Direct	T3 (DS3)	45 Mbps	****	$49,000/month, $6,000 setup	$27,000/month, $6,000 setup

* Charges shown vary considerably from one provider to the next, and equipment charges and special options are not included.

** Under many conditions, and especially with dial-up connections, you will not get the maximum capacity available on the connection. Other, lower-capacity connection may be involved, or the server may be too busy to take full advantage of connection capacity.

*** These services are not always offered by large national providers.

**** These services are not often offered by local Internet Service Providers.

The web page: more than a document

Because a web page can contain objects and hyperlinks, it is a dynamic, living thing. Book pages (see Figure 1-2) are static: you see the text, you see the picture, and you read on to the next page. A book lives and dies by the content on the page. You can't interact with a book, unless you count tossing the book into the trash if you don't like it!

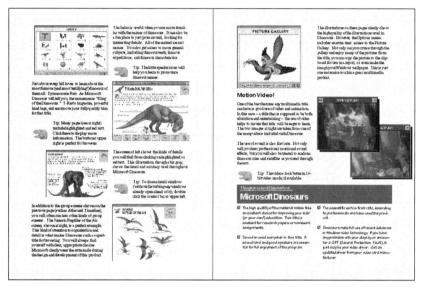

Figure 1-2: A book is a static means of communicating.

Web pages (see Figure 1-3) are alive. You can read a web page on a computer in Spain, and click on a link that will take you to your neighbor's computer. You might look up some information about the recent price fluctuations of Russian potatoes on a web server in Moscow, and then traipse over to the Philippines to compare that to the price history of sugar cane in Manila.

Figure 1-3: A web page is a dynamic communication tool.

The capability to include objects and hyperlinks is what distinguishes a web page from any other kind of publishing. Web publishing is also fast and responsive. It can take from three months to two years for a book to be published (and that is *after* someone writes it!), but you can publish a web page the very same day you create it. Using tools like Java, you can even create web pages that update themselves every few seconds.

Books versus the Web

All that a book has is its content. That might be words, that might be pictures, but a book is never anything more than what lies between the front and back covers. Even text content can be powerful — Moby Dick comes to mind — but a book is a book is a book (with the usual apologies to Gertrude Stein).

Web pages are radically different from books. A clever web page might have very little content of its own. It might point to other web pages; it might allow you to search for information on other web pages. It might even contain an interactive game written in Java, or display a form asking for reader input.

The differences between books and web pages are huge and many. You probably won't be curling up in bed with a nice web page anytime soon — or if you do, it will probably be to get work done, or to play a game. A book is still a book, and perhaps it will turn out that books are the best way to tell a good story.

When you create a web page, remember that web pages and books have even less in common that books and movies. To understand the potential of a web page, you have to learn to think of new ways of communicating. These include such things as interaction between the reader and the page, linking separate pages for instant access, and searching for information.

The bottom line is that the web page is almost always much more than what it seems at first glance. A book blossoms in the imagination; a web page blossoms as you interact with it.

Web publishing goes beyond any form of publishing that came before it. The potential for a revolution in communication is as great as the revolution that followed the invention of the printing press. When Gutenburg printed books in the mid-1400s, he put important documents into the hands of the average person. Since that simple beginning, we have come to a time when the onslaught of information is nearly overwhelming. The web allows the average person to decide which slices of that onslaught to pay attention to, and it also allows the average person to participate by publishing at a very low cost.

But all the hype and all the excitement in the world won't put you on the web, or help you publish your own web pages. You need practical advice, and that's what we'll be pursuing for the rest of this chapter. Buckle up your safety belt, because we're going on a tour of the Web universe at hyperspeed.

When you see a web page in your browser, you see text and images, and perhaps a few other goodies like hyperlinks and objects. Figure 1-3b shows a typical web page. Listing 1-1 shows what the page *really* looks like. All that "stuff" in the listing is called **HTML** (HyperText Markup Language).

There are HTML tags mixed in with the text that you see in Figure 1-3b. Keep in mind that Listing 1-1 shows just a very small portion of the HTML required to build the page shown in Figure 1-3b.

Figure 1-3b: A sample web page.

An HTML tag is simply legal HTML "stuff" that sits between angle brackets. For example, the following text contains tags for turning bold text on, and off:

```
<B>This text would appear in bold because it sits between
HTML tags for bold.</B>
```

The whole idea of using Netscape Gold to create web pages is to avoid having to mess with HTML tags. This means that you do not have to learn HTML to create web pages; you can simply use Netscape Gold to create them visually. There are some fun things you can do with HTML tags that you cannot do with Netscape Gold, and you'll learn about that in Chapter 6. For now, it's only important that you know what's behind every web page you see: HTML. You won't see very many references to HTML tags, but HTML will be behind everything that you do in Netscape Gold.

For example, if you select some text and give it the italic attribute, what's really happening is that Netscape Gold is adding the tags for the start and end of italic.

Listing 1-1: Some sample HTML

```
<HTML>
<HEAD>
<TITLE>
Virtual Reality News and Views
</TITLE>
<META NAME="AUTHOR" CONTENT="Ron Wodaski">
</HEAD>
<BODY BACKGROUND="jpg/weave.jpg">
<TABLE border=0 cellpadding=12 width=100%>
  <tr>
    <TD colspan=1 valign=top>
      <A HREF="audio/jungle.wav"><IMG SRC="gif/sound.gif"
ALIGN="LEFT" border=0></a>
    </TD>
    <td align="left" colspan=2>
      <br>
    </td>
    <td align="right" colspan=1>
      <h4><i>December 11, 1995</i></h4>
    </td>
  </tr>
  <tr>
    <TD colspan=1>
<embed src="vrml/mmad.wrl" border=none align=center
width=150 height=150>
<p>
<font size="+1">Click and drag in this <b>VRML
image.</b></font><br>
<i>Right click for options.</i>
    </TD>
    <td colspan=3 align="center">
      <center><IMG SRC="gif/constr.gif" ALIGN="LEFT"
```

(continued)

Listing 1-1: *(continued)*

```
border=0>
        <H1><i>Virtual Reality News and Views</i></H1>
        <h3><i>Your gateway to all things VR on the
web</i></h3>
        <hr>
        <font size="-1"><i>Designed for use with <A
href="http://www.netscape.com">
Netscape 1.2</a> or
        MS <a href="http://www.msn.com">Internet Explorer
2.0</a>.<br>
        <b>VRML objects</b> require <a
href="http://www.paperinc.com/wfxwin32.html">WebFX Netscape
2.0 Plugin</a>.</i></font>
        <p><A href="vr.htm">Back to non-VRML version.</a>
        </center>
    </td>
  </tr>
```

[Note: much more HTML code follows in the original file.]

Web page = URL

The smallest unit on the Web is the web page. Every page has a unique address. This address is called a **URL** (Uniform Resource Locator). Your browser can use a URL to find any web page. Figure 1-4 shows a typical URL for a web page.

Protocol   Server   Path   Filename

Figure 1-4: A typical URL, containing protocol, domain name, path, and a filename.

From left to right, a URL contains up to four different kinds of elements: protocol, server, path, and filename.

A protocol simply defines how the information at a URL should be handled by the browser. For web pages, the standard protocol is called **HTTP** (HyperText Transfer Protocol). Other protocols include **FTP** (File Transfer Protocol) and **Gopher** (a search mechanism). Most of the time, your browser will sort through protocols for you automatically. Figure 1-5 shows the protocol portion of a URL highlighted. A protocol is always required to have a valid URL.

http://www.olympus.net/biz/mmad/index.htm

Figure 1-5: The protocol portion of a URL.

Although a protocol is required, some browsers will add the protocol for you. For example, if you try to enter a URL such as

```
ftp.mycompany.download
```

Netscape Gold will automatically convert it to

```
ftp://ftp.mycompany.download
```

The server portion of the URL specifies a particular Web server somewhere out on the Web. This is also often referred to as a **domain name**. Domain names are unique — every server has its own domain name. Figure 1-6 shows the server portion of the URL highlighted. A server or domain name is always required to have a valid URL.

http://www.olympus.net/biz/mmad/index.htm

Figure 1-6: The domain name or server identifies the computer containing the web page.

A server need not be referred to by its domain name. Servers are also specified by numerical entries that look like this: 198.133.237.1. To turn this into a complete URL, simply add the other elements: http://198.133.237.1/biz/mmad/index.htm. Most of the time, however, you will use domain names for servers. Occasionally, you may see a numerical entry.

The path portion of the URL is just like a path specification on your local computer. It simply tells where to find a page in the server's directory structure. It always begins with a slash. If a filename is included, the path must also end with a slash. If no filename is specified, the ending slash is optional. If no filename is specified in the URL, then the server will look for a default filename at the path location. These usually have names like index.htm or default.htm. Figure 1-7 shows the path portion of a URL highlighted.

http://www.olympus.net/biz/mmad/index.htm

Figure 1-7: The path specification locates the file on the server.

The filename is just that: the name of a file on the server. Although some operating systems, such as Windows 95, allow spaces in filenames, filenames on a server should never have a space. Figure 1-8 shows the filename portion of a URL highlighted.

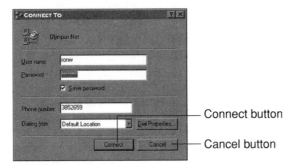

http://www.olympus.net/biz/mmad/index.htm

Figure 1-8: The filename follows the last slash.

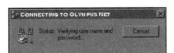

— Connect button

— Cancel button

Figure 1-8b: The connection dialog box, which appears whenever you start Netscape Gold without an existing connection.

Figure 1-8c: The connection dialog box while a connection is pending.

Figure 1-8d: The connection dialog box shows that a connection is complete.

You may have noticed that a URL uses forward slashes between various parts of the URL. You are probably used to using the backslash (\) instead. However, a backslash will not work as part of a URL! Always remember to type a forward slash when you are constructing a URL.

Given a URL, you can find the web page it refers to. In fact, URLs are the key to unlocking the power of the web. By putting a URL into a hyperlink on a web page, you can jump to the URL. Since pictures, text, and objects can be used for hyperlinks, almost anything on a web page can point to almost anywhere on the web!

Text and images

By far the most common elements of a web page are text and images. You can create a web page with just text, or just images, but that would be rare. A little text, a little imagery— presto! You've got the ingredients for a web page. Figure 1-9 shows a simple web page, created with Netscape Gold.

This web page is available on the CD-ROM. This is the first of many files located on the CD-ROM that I use to illustrate important points. You'll see this CD-ROM icon every time there is a file on the CD-ROM related to the text. The file can be found at:

```
\tutorial\chap01\sample page 01.htm
```

Double-click on the file to open it in Browse mode. When you see the connection dialog box (see Figure 1-8b), you can either click on the Connect button to connect to your Internet Service Provider (ISP), or you can click Cancel because, after all, you are just opening a local file. This assumes you already have set up a connection for your ISP, and that your User name and Password are set. If not, you can still proceed with many of the tutorials — just click the Cancel button to dismiss the Connect dialog box.

If you choose to connect, it may take from a few seconds to a few minutes, depending on the nature of your Internet connection. While the connection is pending, you'll see a dialog box like the one shown in Figure 1-8c, with various messages as the connection progresses. When the connection is complete, you'll see the dialog box shown in Figure 1-8d.

The background color of some of your web pages may differ from the white background you will see in most of the Netscape Gold images in this book. To make sure that all of the images are as clear as possible, I changed the default background color for Netscape Gold. If you want to change the default background color to white, like I did, so that your work matches mine as closely as possible, use the Options I General Preferences menu selection to open the preferences dialog box. Click the Colors tab, click the Custom radio button for the background, and then click the Choose Color button for the background. This opens the Standard Windows Color dialog box. Click on the white square to choose white as the background color. Click OK, then OK again, to save the change.

To edit the file (that is, to make changes to it), you must enter Edit mode. Click the Edit button in the Netscape Gold toolbar (see margin) to change to Edit mode. When in Edit mode, you'll see different tools on the toolbar. The Netscape Gold toolbar is shown in Figure 1-8e. Table 1-2 lists the buttons in the toolbar and their functions.

Font size   Text styles   Advanced
            and hyperlinks features   Properties

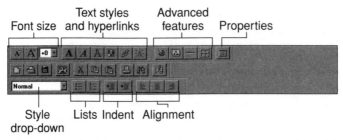

Style   Lists Indent Alignment
drop-down

Figure 1-8e: The Netscape Gold Edit mode toolbar; see Table 1-2 for details.

TIP

You'll need a folder on your hard disk to save the various web pages that you create. I suggest that you create a folder on your C: (or other) hard drive, and call it Gold Pages. You can create a new folder by

➡ Double-clicking the My Computer icon on your Windows 95 desktop.

➡ Double-clicking the icon for the C: drive (or any other hard drive on your computer).

This opens a window showing the folders on the C: drive. Use the File|New|Folder menu choice to create a new folder.

The new folder has the default name New Folder. Type a new name for the folder:

Gold Pages

Press the Enter key to save the name change.

That's all there is to it. You now have a folder where you can save all of the files you create while working with this book.

Table 1-2: Netscape Gold Edit Mode Toolbar

Button	Name	Description
A⁻	Font smaller	Makes the font size of selected text smaller.
A⁺	Font larger	Makes the font size of selected text larger.
+3 ▾	Font size	Allows you to specify the font size for selected text. Expressed in terms of amount larger or smaller than default font size, not in absolute font size.
A	Bold	Applies bold formatting to the selected text.

Table 1-2: Netscape Gold Edit Mode Toolbar

Button	Name	Description
	Italic	Applies italic formatting to the selected text.
	Fixed width	Applies a fixed-width font to the selected text (usually displayed as Courier)
	Font color	Applies a color you specify to the selected text.
	Hyperlink	Allows you to specify a hyperlink for the selected text or image.
	Clear styles	Removes all styles from the selected text.
	Target	Creates a named target, which you can jump to from any web page.
	Picture	Adds a picture at the cursor location.
	Horizontal rule	Adds a horizontal rule at the cursor location.
	Table	Adds a table at the cursor location. You can specify such things as number of rows, number of colums, table width, and so on in a dialog box before the table is actually created.
	Properties	Displays a dialog box showing the properties of the currently selected item. You can edit the properties if desired.
	New document	Creates a new, empty web page in its own Edit window.
	Open	Opens an existing web page in a new Edit window.
	Save	Saves the current web page to the hard disk.
	Browse	Displays the current web page in Browse mode. If the file has been changed, but not saved, you will be asked to save the file in order to switch to Browse mode.
	Cut	Cuts the selected item(s) to the clipboard.
	Copy	Copies the selected item(s) to the clipboard.

(continued)

Table 1-2: Netscape Gold Edit Mode Toolbar *(continued)*

Button	Name	Description
	Paste	Pastes the contents of the clipboard. Note that you cannot paste an image, because all images must be either .GIF or .JPG image files.
	Print	Prints the current page.
	Find	Allows you to search for a text string on the current page.
	Publish	If you are connected to your Internet Service Provider (ISP), uploads the page and its images to your web server.
Normal	Paragraph format	Used to apply paragraph formats to selected text.
	Bulleted list	Converts the currently selected line(s) of text into a bulleted list.
	Numbered list	Converts the currently selected line(s) of text into a numbered list.
	Decrease indent	Shifts the currently selected paragraph(s) to the left, but no farther than the left margin of the page or table cell.
	Increase indent	Shifts the currently selected paragraph(s) to the right.
	Left	Aligns the currently selected paragraph(s) to the left margin of the page or table cell.
	Center	Aligns the currently selected paragraph(s) between the left and right margins of the page or table cell.
	Right	Aligns the currently selected paragraph(s) to the right margin of the page or table cell.

The web page in Figure 1-9 isn't very interesting. All of the text looks the same, and it's just about impossible to see how the page is organized. We can use Netscape Gold to apply text formatting, which will make the page's organization much clearer.

Since the file was loaded from a CD-ROM, and changes you make will have to be saved to your hard disk. Do not try to save changes to the CD-ROM, as it is read-only.

Figure 1-9: A sample of a web page with text and image.

Headings

Three paragraphs are intended as headings on this sample web page:

```
Welcome to my sample web page!
This is a headline for a section of the web page
This is a second headline for a new section of the web
page.
```

There are six available levels of HTML headings. Heading level 1 (HTML tags: <H1></H1>) is the largest and boldest, while heading level 6 (HTML tags: <H6></H6>) is the smallest and lightest. The first paragraph, just under the picture of a cornfield, gets a level 1 heading, and the other two get a level 2 heading. To apply a heading style to a paragraph, click to place the cursor in the paragraph, and then choose the Heading style from the Style drop-down list shown in Figure 1-10. Figure 1-11 shows the three headings as they appear on the web page.

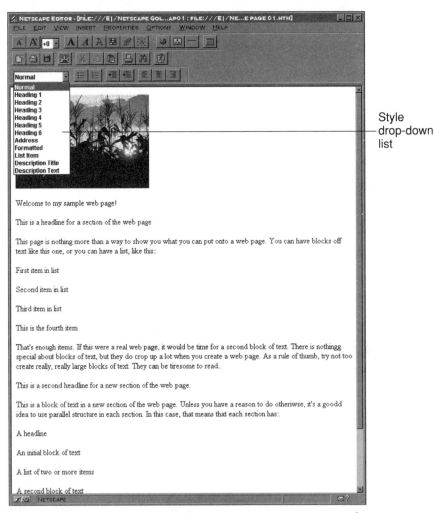

Style drop-down list

Figure 1-10: Choosing a format for a paragraph.

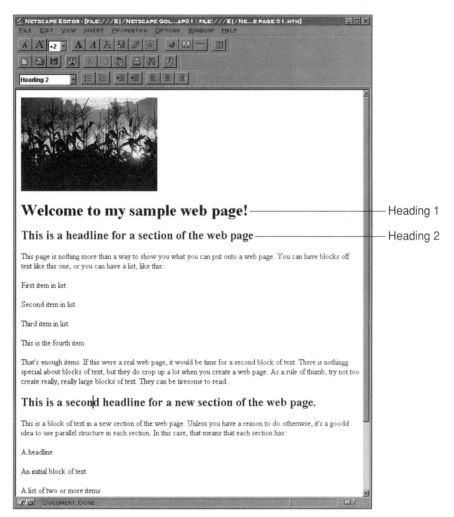

Figure 1-11: The sample web page with headings applied.

That's all you need to do to apply a heading to a line of text. The most important use of headings is to make the organization of the web page as clear as possible.

Rules

As you can see in Figure 1-11, headings do make the organization of the page clearer. However, you can do more. HTML includes tags for horizontal rules. Use the Horizontal Rule tool (shown in the margin, and found in the

Netscape Gold toolbar) to add a rule. Simply click to position the cursor at the start or end of a line, and click the rule tool. If the cursor was at the end of a line of text, the rule will appear below the line of text. If the cursor was at the start of a line of text, the rule will be above that point. Figure 1-12 shows where you can add rules to the sample web page.

Figure 1-12: Adding rules to a web page.

Using a combination of headings of different sizes and rules, you can easily make the organization of your web pages crystal clear.

Lists

If you read the text on the sample web page, you know that there are two lists on the page. However, it's not immediately clear that these are lists, because the text in the lists is identical to the other text on the page. There is nothing to call attention to the lists. Since lists are commonly used on web pages, there are HTML tags that makes lists look like, well, lists! To convert standard text into list text, select the text for the list by clicking and dragging (see Figure 1-13). Then click on the drop-down list on the toolbar, and select List Item (Figure 1-14).

Selected text for list

Figure 1-13: *Selecting lines for a list.*

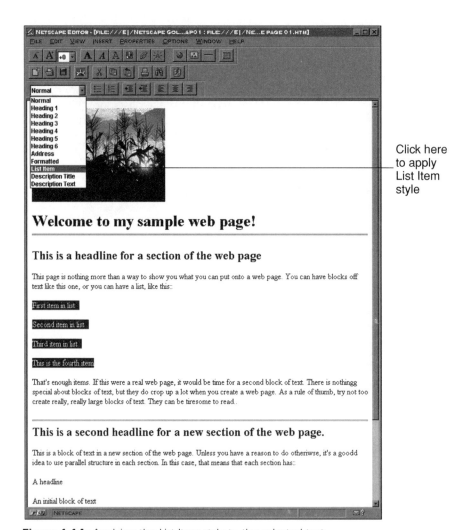

Click here
to apply
List Item
style

Figure 1-14: Applying the List Item style to the selected text.

The result is shown in Figure 1-15. Notice that the list items have a small bullet at the left, and that the style List Item appears in the Style drop-down box. The space between list items is also reduced. Both of these steps make it very clear that the text is actually a list, and make the purpose of this part of the page much clearer to a visitor.

There is a second list on the sample web page, and you can apply List item to it, too.

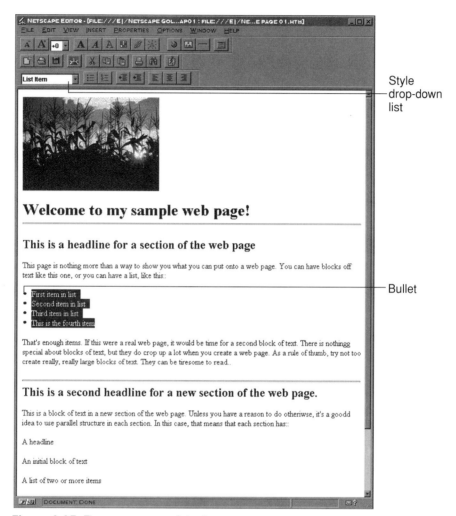

Style drop-down list

Bullet

Figure 1-15: The appearance of the list.

To see the result in a browser, you must first save the changes to your hard disk. The file you opened was on the CD-ROM. Use the File I Save As menu selection to save the file to your hard disk, in the C:\Gold Pages folder. Use the same filename (Sample page 01.htm). Then click on the View in Browser tool on the Netscape Gold toolbar. Figure 1-16 shows what the file should look like. In the future, you can move back and forth between Browse and Edit mode. The easiest way to do this is to keep both windows open. Make changes in the Edit window, save to disk, and then click the Reload button (see margin) in the Browse window.

Figure 1-16: Viewing the result of the changes in Browse mode.

Text formatting

Headings and lists are actually kinds of text formatting, but more kinds of text formatting are available to you for your web pages. Text formatting falls into two broad categories: character formatting and paragraph formatting. Character formatting is applied to one or more individual characters, while paragraph formatting is applied to an entire paragraph. Headings and lists are both paragraph formats.

For examples of character formatting, you can double-click the file

```
\tutorial\chap01\character formatting.htm
```

on the CD-ROM (see Figure 1-17) to view it in your browser. Table 1-3 provides additional information about the kinds of character formatting supported in Netscape Gold.

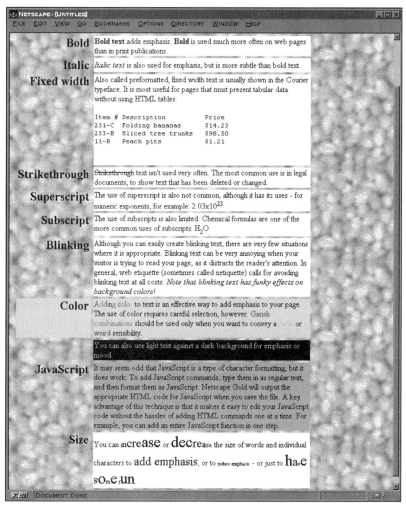

Figure 1-17: Examples of character formatting.

Table 1-3: Character Formatting

Formatting type	Example
Bold	**Bold text** adds emphasis. **Bold** is used much more often on web pages than in print publications.
Italic	*Italic text* is also used for emphasis, but is more subtle than bold text.
Fixed width	`Also called preformatted, fixed width text is usually shown in the Courier typeface. It is most useful for pages that must present tabular data without using HTML tables.`
Strikethrough	~~Strikethrough~~ text isn't used very often. The most common use is in legal documents, to show text that has been deleted or changed.
Superscript	The use of superscript is also not common, although it has its uses— for numeric exponents, for example: 2.03^{23}
Subscript	The use of subscripts is also limited. Chemical formulas are one of the more common uses of subscripts: H_2O
Blinking	Although you can easily create blinking text, there are very few situations where it is appropriate. Blinking text can be very annoying when your visitor is trying to read your page, as it distracts the reader's attention. In general, web etiquette (sometimes called **netiquette**) calls for avoiding blinking text at all costs.
Color	Adding color to text is an effective way to add emphasis to your page. The use of color requires careful selection, however. Garish combinations should be used only when you want to convey a punk or weird sensibility. You can also use light text against a dark background for emphasis or mood.
JavaScript	It may seem odd that JavaScript is a type of character formatting, but it does work. To add JavaScript commands, type them in as regular text, and then format them as JavaScript. Netscape Gold will output the appropriate HTML code for JavaScript when you save the file. A key advantage of this technique is that it makes it easy to edit your JavaScript code without the hassles of adding HTML commands one at a time. For example, you can add an entire JavaScript function in one step.

Table 1-3: Character Formatting

Formatting type	Example
Size	You can increase or decrease the size of words and individual characters to add emphasis, or to reduce emphasis – or just to have some fun.

For examples of paragraph formatting, you can double-click the file

`\tutorial\chap01\paragraph formatting.htm`

on the CD-ROM (see Figure 1-18) to view it in your browser. Table 1-4 provides additional information about the kinds of paragraph formatting supported in Netscape Gold.

Table 1-4: Paragraph Formatting

Formatting type	Example
Normal	Normal text is, well, normal text. It is what you get when you enter text without any special formatting. Normal is the default text format: If you don't apply a paragraph format to new text that you add to a page, it appears in normal format.
Headings 1–6	These six levels of headings are used to add organization to your web page. Heading level 1 is the largest, and heading level 6 is the smallest.
Address	This is really just italic formatting, but it applies to an entire paragraph, not just the selected text. You can use it for anything, not just addresses.
Formatted	This is similar to fixed-width character formatting, but it applies to an entire paragraph. It is very useful for tabular data, too.
List Item	Applies to any one item in a list. There are numbered and bulleted lists, as well as specialized lists that are discussed in detail in Chapter 2.
Description Title	This paragraph format is combined with Description Text to create definition lists. A definition list consists of the definition term, which gets a Description Title format, and the definition itself, which gets a Description Text format.

(continued)

Table 1-4: Paragraph Formatting *(continued)*

Formatting type	Example
Description Text	This paragraph format is combined with Description Title to create definition lists. A definition list consists of the definition term, which gets a Description Ttle format, and the definition itself, which gets a Description Text format.

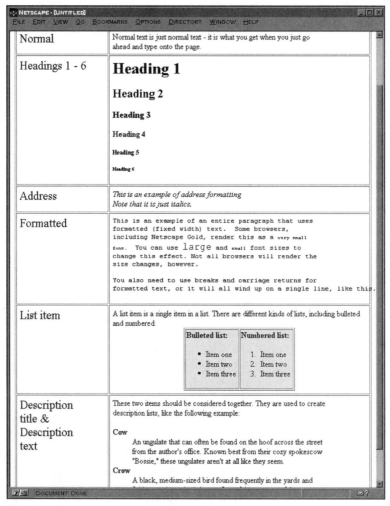

Figure 1-18: Examples of paragraph formatting.

You can create serviceable web pages using nothing more than character and paragraph formatting, as shown in Figure 1-19. You can view this web page yourself by double-clicking the file

```
\tutorial\chap01\sample page 02.htm
```

on the CD-ROM.

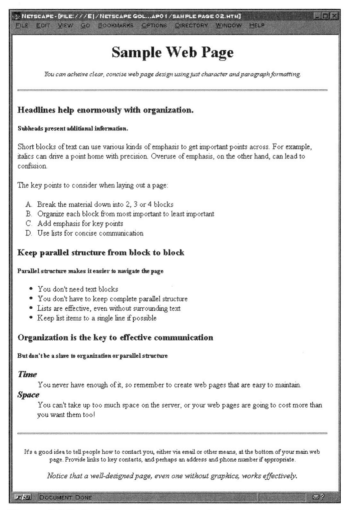

Figure 1-19: A web page that uses only character and paragraph formatting to present information.

Images

You have already seen several examples of web pages with images (see Figure 1-9). Netscape Gold makes it easy to add images to a web page. Once added, you can define where on the page you want to place the image. The two most common placements are **in-line** and **independent**. In-line images act like a single text character. They flow with the text. A large image acts like a large character, pushing the lines further apart. Figure 1-20 shows examples of several in-line images.

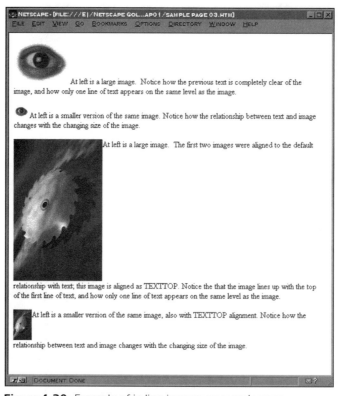

Figure 1-20: Example of in-line images on a web page.

You can view this web page yourself by double-clicking the file

`\tutorial\chap01\sample page 03.htm`

on the CD-ROM.

The top two images in Figure 1-20 use default alignment with text. The second two images use TEXTTOP alignment, aligning the top of the image with the top of the line of text. There are several other alignment options, and they are discussed in detail in Chapter 2.

An independent image floats on the page, at the right or left margin, and text flows around the image. Figure 1-21 shows examples of independent images. You can view this web page yourself by double-clicking the file

```
\tutorial\chap01\sample page 04.htm
```

on the CD-ROM.

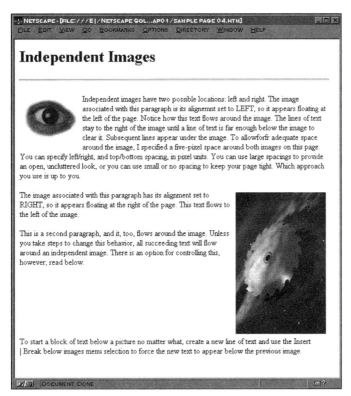

Figure 1-21: Example of independent images on a web page.

When working with large images, you can put just an image in-line inside a paragraph, and then center, left, or right align the paragraph. This is the only way to center an image. However, you will almost always get more attractive results for left and right alignment by using an independent image with alignment set to RIGHT or LEFT.

NETSCAPE
NAVIGATOR
GOLD

For example, start Netscape Gold by double-clicking the Netscape Gold icon (see margin) to run the program. Click the File | New Document | Blank menu selection to create a new document.

To add an image to a web page, click the Picture tool on the toolbar (see margin).

If you see the dialog box shown in Figure 1-22, click the Save button and save the document to your hard disk, in the `C:\Gold Pages` folder. Use the original filename (`sample page 04.htm`). You can't add pictures — or perform many other actions — until you have saved your new web page to disk.

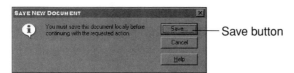

Figure 1-22: If you see this dialog box, you didn't save the file first.

CD-
ROM

This opens a dialog box allowing you to specify the image, and the image's properties (see Figure 1-23). Use the Browse button to locate the file `\tutorial\chap01\eye01.gif` on the CD-ROM (see Figure 1-24). Click the Open button to indicate that you have selected the correct image file.

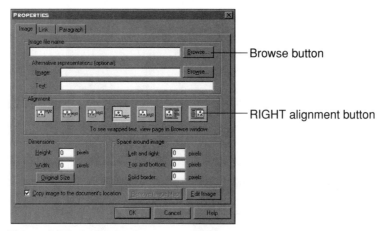

Figure 1-23: Adding an image to a web page.

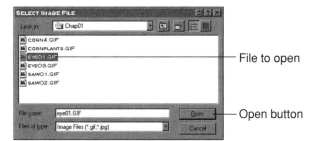

Figure 1-24: Selecting the image file.

 Make the image right aligned by clicking on the RIGHT Alignment button (refer to Figure 1-25 for location). Set the left/right and top/bottom spaces to 5 pixels. Click the OK button to add the picture (see Figure 1-26). Notice that the image appears on the left; it won't appear at the right in Edit mode, but it will be properly positioned when you view it in Browse mode. Save your work again (File | Save menu selection), and click the View in Browser tool on the toolbar (see margin). In Browse mode, the image is where it should be, at the right of the page.

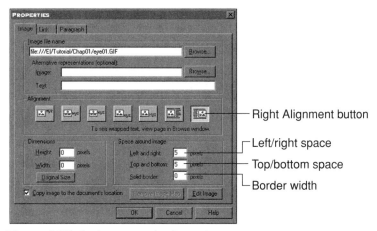

Figure 1-25: Setting properties for an image.

If you want, experiment with adding more images, or with adding text. Try using an alignment of LEFT instead of RIGHT, and note the differences. Remember to save your work so you can view it in Browse mode; Edit mode will not reveal all of your changes.

Figure 1-26: The image added to the page.

Netscape Gold is, by and large, a WYSIWYG web page editor — What You See Is What You Get. However, certain things are not the same in Browse and Edit modes. Image alignment, some features of tables, and all features of forms are completely different in the two modes. Always save your work and check its appearance in Browse mode before you decide what works, and what doesn't.

Hyperlinks

Hyperlinks are the heart of a web page. When you click on a hyperlink, your browser will display the web page that the hyperlink points to. There are three kinds of hyperlinks:

Text hyperlinks: By default, a text hyperlink shows up in a different color (usually blue), and is underlined (see the left example in Figure 1-27). You can define different colors for a hyperlink (and other kinds of text) using Netscape Gold (see the right example in Figure 1-27). The file \tutorial\chap01\links.htm shows the actual color changes created with Netscape Gold.

Figure 1-27: A text hyperlink is normally underlined.

Image hyperlinks: By default, an image hyperlink appears with a blue border around the image (see Figure 1-28). You can change the width and color of the border using Netscape Gold, or remove it entirely. The file `\tutorial\chap01\links.htm` shows an example of an image used as a hyperlink.

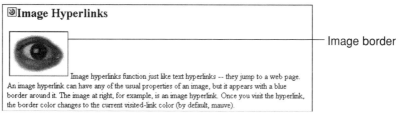

Figure 1-28: An image hyperlink, by default, has a blue border.

JavaScript/Java hyperlinks: You can create button hyperlinks using JavaScript, and the Java programming language enables you to get creative about hyperlinks. Even an animation could be a hyperlink with Java. Figure 1-29 shows a web page that uses a vertically scrolling bar to display hyperlinks.

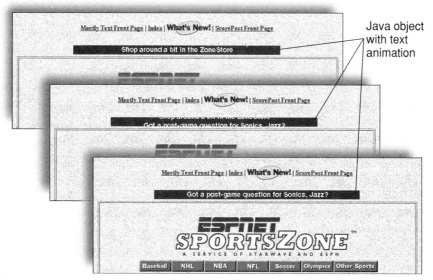

Figure 1-29: Three frames from an animation with hyperlinks.

Using hyperlinks

Text and image hyperlinks are easy to find, even if they don't use the default settings (blue and underlined for text, thin blue border for images). Whenever you pass the cursor over a hyperlink, it changes to a hand. Figure 1-30 shows an example.

─── Hand cursor

Figure 1-30: The cursor changes to a hand when it passes over a hyperlink (text or image).

If the hyperlink is part of a Java applet, the cursor will not change to a hand — most Java applets will do their best to make it obvious that they are a hotspot. You can even add a text caption that tells the reader to click on the applet to jump to a hyperlink.

The default colors (or even custom colors) apply only to a hyperlink that you have not visited recently. For example, assume that you click on a hyperlink on page A, and jump to page B. If you then click the Back button (far left of the Netscape Gold toolbar) to return to page A, the color of the hyperlink changes to indicate that you have already visited page B (see Figure 1-31). Some web pages may have dozens of hyperlinks, and the color change means that you do not have to keep track of where you have visited — the changing colors does it for you.

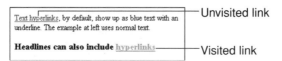

─── Unvisited link

─── Visited link

Figure 1-31: The color of previously visited hyperlinks is different from the color of unvisited hyperlinks.

Not all text and image hyperlinks will take you to a web page. There are two common kinds of links that behave differently when clicked: *mailto* links, and *download* links. A mailto link will run your mail program, and usually the To: address will be filled in for you. Figure 1-32 shows a typical mailto link. A download link will give you the option of downloading a file from a distant web server to your local hard disk. When you click a download link, you will see a dialog box that allows you to specify the filename, and where to put the file on your hard disk. Unless you have a specific reason not to, accept the default filename for downloads.

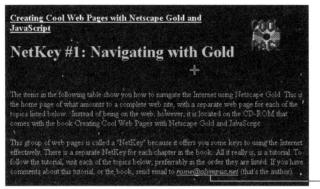
——— mailto link

Figure 1-32: A typical mailto link.

Creating hyperlinks

It's easy to create hyperlinks with Navigator Gold. I have included a file on the CD-ROM with text and images. Run Navigator Gold if it is not already running. Use the File | Open File in Editor menu selection to open the file

```
\tutorial\chap01\hyperlinks.htm
```

Figure 1-33 shows the appearance of the file in Netscape Gold (Edit mode).

 If Netscape Gold is your default web browser, you can use another method to open web page files. Double-click the file's icon to browse the file, and then click the Edit icon (see figure in margin) to go to Edit mode.

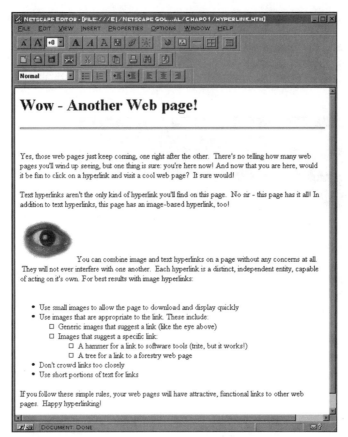

Figure 1-33: The sample file before hyperlinks are added.

 To create a hyperlink with text, select the text by clicking and dragging the mouse. Figure 1-34 shows the text to select: "cool web page." Now click the hyperlink tool (see margin) to display the Properties dialog box. Note that the Link tab is automatically selected (see Figure 1-35).

To add a hyperlink, simply type the URL of the web page into the text box labeled "Link to a page location or local file." For this example, type the home page for this book:

```
http://www.olympus.net/biz/mmad/ng/index.htm
```

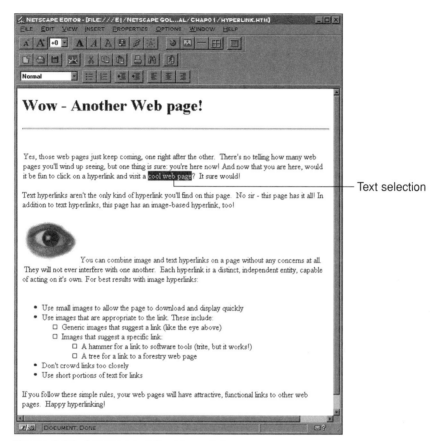

— Text selection

Figure 1-34: Selecting text for a hyperlink.

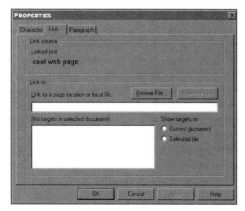

Figure 1-35: The Properties dialog box, with the Link tab selected.

You can also enter a simple filename if the file will be located in the same folder/directory on the web server as the currently open file. Click OK to create the hyperlink. Click anywhere in the window to remove the selection highlight, and your text hyperlink should now be in blue, and underlined (see Figure 1-36).

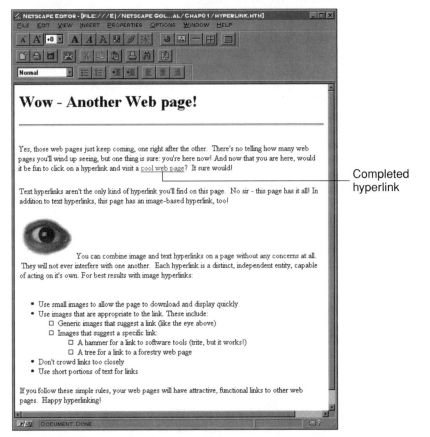

Completed hyperlink

Figure 1-36: The completed text hyperlink.

To create a hyperlink with the eye image, click on the eye image to select it (see Figure 1-37). You could click the hyperlink tool, but instead right-click on the image to display the context menu shown in Figure 1-38. Click on "Create link using selected" to open the Properties dialog box.

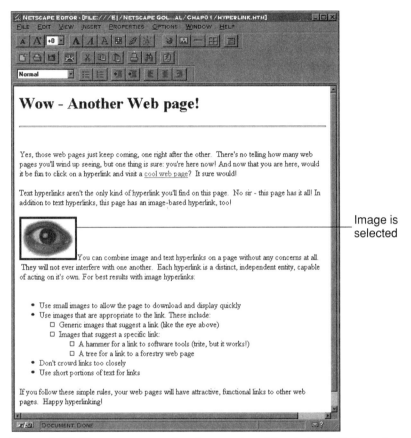

Image is
selected

Figure 1-37: The appearance of an image when it is selected in Edit mode.

Many menu operations can be accessed using the right mouse button. Simply right-click on an object — text, image, bookmark, whatever — and then select your action from the pop-up context menu.

Once again, the Link tab of the Properties dialog box is active. Simply type in a hyperlink in the usual "Link to a page location or local file" text box (see Figure 1-39). This time, the hyperlink text is

```
http://espnet.sportszone.com
```

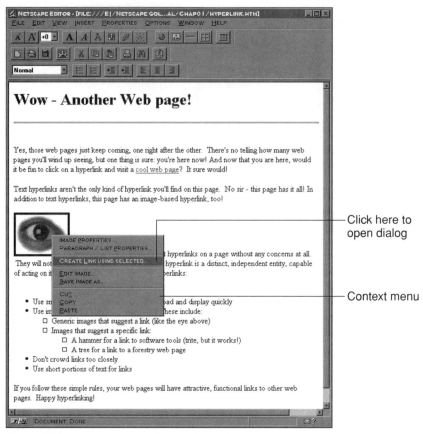

Figure 1-38: A context menu for a selected image.

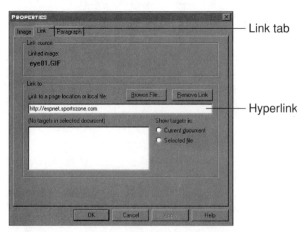

Figure 1-39: Adding the hyperlink to the Properties dialog box.

Click OK to create the hyperlink. Click anywhere in the window to remove the selection highlight, and your image hyperlink should now be outlined in blue (see Figure 1-40). Before you can view the changes in your browser, save the file to your hard disk, in the `C:\Gold Pages` folder (remember, you can't save a file to the CD-ROM!). Netscape Gold will not switch to Browse mode unless the file is saved first. Use the File | Save As menu selection to save the file. You can use the original name, `hyperlink.htm`, as the Save filename. Click OK to complete the Save operation, then click the Browse mode button in the toolbar (see margin) to open a browse window (see Figure 1-41). Note the appearance of the image hyperlink in Browse mode.

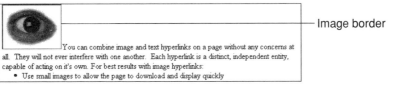

Image border

Figure 1-40: The image hyperlink has a blue border.

Figure 1-41: The appearance of an image hyperlink in Browse mode.

A version of the file `\tutorial\chap01\hyperlinks.htm` with the hyperlinks already added is available on the CD-ROM. The filename is

```
\tutorial\chap01\hyperlink.htm
```

If you are a sports enthusiast, and haven't yet visited SportsZone, you're missing out on what is probably not only the best sports site on the Web, but perhaps the best-designed web pages anywhere on the Web.

Image maps

There will be many times when you are content to have a complete image dedicated to a single hyperlink. But there will also be times when you would like to have different parts of an image jump to different URLs. For example, you could use an image like the one shown in Figure 1-42 as a menu. The buttons at the bottom of the image would jump to specific URLs, while the rest of the image would do nothing.

— Button for hyperlink

Figure 1-42: A sample image to use as an image map.

Image maps require special tools. I have included an excellent image map builder on the CD-ROM. It is called Map This!, and you can find out how to install it in the Appendix, and how to use it in Chapter 4.

Technically speaking, you could create an image map entirely by hand. However, that is both arduous and unnecessary. There are a number of good tools for creating image maps readily available. From a practical point of view, there is every reason to use tools to create image maps: It takes less time, it takes less work, and the results are much more likely to work the first time.

Tables

I mentioned earlier in this chapter that it's important to have well-organized web pages. The new user can find what's needed quickly, and the experienced user can jump right to the most interesting portion of your web site — but only if each page is well organized. Headings and lists help, but the absolute best tool for organizing a web page is the table.

Figure 1-43 shows a web page that uses not just a single table, but tables within tables, to organize information. Not all browsers support tables. If you use them, you run the risk that some people will not be able to make sense out of your web site. As more and more browsers are updated to support tables, this is becoming less and less of a problem. Given the powerful results you can get using tables, they are a compelling tool for creating web pages.

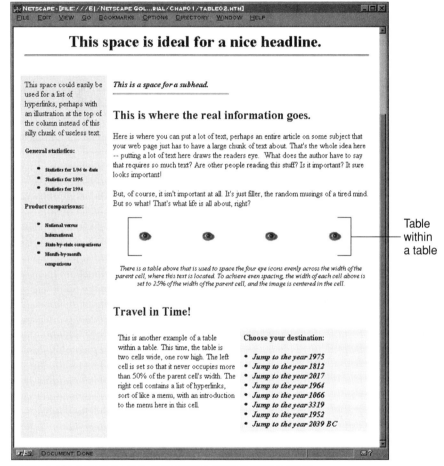

Figure 1-43: A sample web page with a table within a table.

If you want to alert visitors that their browser must support tables in order to view your pages properly, a simple line of text above the table will do the job. For example, the top line of text on a page that uses tables might read

This page requires a browser that supports tables

That's all it takes. If you really like Netscape Navigator as a browser, you might provide a text hyperlink like the one shown in Figure 1-44, which allows the visitor to jump right to a download site for Netscape products.

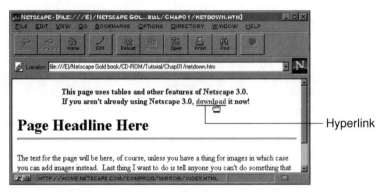

Hyperlink

Figure 1-44: A hyperlink for downloading Netscape Navigator.

Forms

So far, all of the web page goodies I have described are meant to make the web page more interactive for the visitor. Forms allow the visitor to interact with you, the creator of a web page. Figure 1-45 shows a sample form. Note that there are areas for user input, and buttons at the bottom of the form for sending the contents of the form to you.

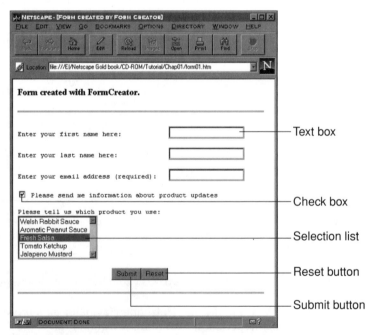

Text box

Check box

Selection list

Reset button

Submit button

Figure 1-45: A web page that uses a form for user input.

Now for the bad news: Version 3.0 of Netscape Gold doesn't directly support forms. This is not an obstacle, however. You can add a simple form to a web page, and I have included Form Creator software on the CD-ROM that you can use to create forms. Figure 1-45b shows what a form created in Form Creator looks like in Edit mode. The small tags indicate where unsupported HTML tags are located in a web page. (Unsupported means unsupported in this version of Netscape Gold.) Double-clicking on the little tags allows you to edit a form element. You'll learn more about forms, and how to create them, in Chapter 6.

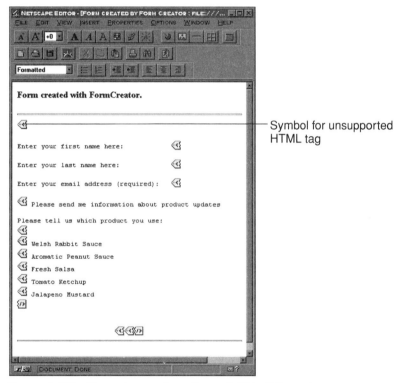

Symbol for unsupported HTML tag

Figure 1-45b: The web page from Figure 1-45 in Edit mode.

NetKey #1: Navigating with Gold

Before we move on to the next chapter, I want to provide some insights into the Netscape Gold functions that have nothing to do with creating web pages. Much of the functionality built into Netscape Gold is for navigating (okay, surfing) the Web. Most of these features are also included in the standard edition of Netscape Navigator. During the rest of this chapter, I have been referring to these features using the phrase "Browse mode."

Figure 1-46 shows the appearance of Netscape Gold when in Browse mode. Working down from the top of the program window, you see a menu bar, a toolbar, a text box that shows the URL of the current web page, a row of buttons called the Directory buttons, an image area that displays the current web page, and, at the bottom, a status bar.

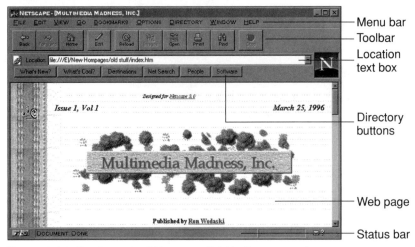

Menu bar
Toolbar
Location text box
Directory buttons
Web page
Status bar

Figure 1-46: The features of Netscape Gold in Browse mode.

When you use Browse mode, you won't go about learning it item by item. You want to do something. That's exactly how I'm going to describe the Browse mode features: in the order in which you can use them.

To begin, I suggest that you double-click on the file

```
/tutorial/index.htm
```

which will automatically start Netscape Gold in Browse mode. As usual, if you do not want to connect, click the Cancel button when the connection dialog box appears (refer back to Figure 1-8b). The file /tutorial/index.htm is shown in Figure 1-47.

The file /tutorial/index.htm contains hyperlinks to the NetKeys for every chapter in the book. To learn how to explore the navigational abilities of Netscape Gold, click the hyperlink for Chapter 1, *Mining for Gold*. The first NetKey page for this chapter is shown in Figure 1-48. To explore this NetKey, simply click on any and every hyperlink (usually underlined text) that strikes your fancy.

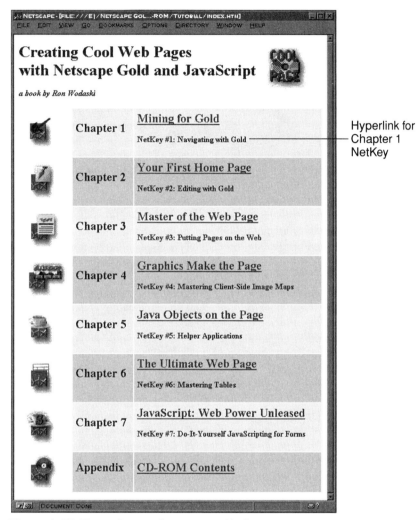

Hyperlink for Chapter 1 NetKey

Figure 1-47: The web page for access to NetKey pages.

This NetKey doesn't cover *every* aspect of navigation, just those skills that you need to get up and surfing comfortably. You can get more detailed information about Internet navigation with the Help | Handbook menu selection, which is really a hyperlink to the web page at the URL

```
http://home.netscape.com/eng/mozilla/3.0/handbook/
```

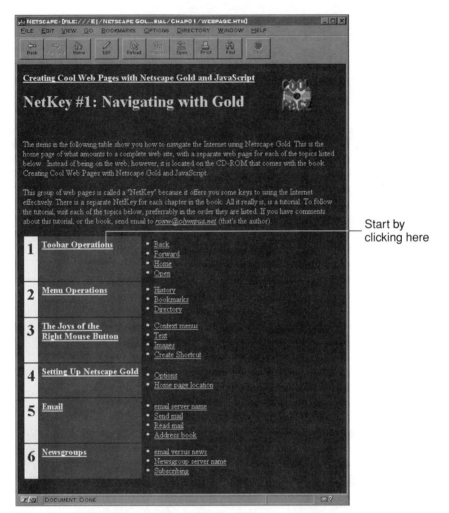

Figure 1-48: The NetKey page for Chapter 1.

I have set up the web pages for this NetKey just like a typical web site. You can learn a lot about organizing information for a multipage web site by looking at how these pages are laid out. The easiest way to do this is to open each of the files in Edit mode (or click on the Edit button when in Browse mode) and right-click on everything you can find to examine item properties.

Your First Home Page

Creating a New Page

Netscape Gold provides three ways to create a web page. They range from very easy to totally customized. The method you choose will depend on the kind of web page you want to create.

Wizard: To create a page with Netscape's Wizard, you simply pick selections from a list. This gives you limited options to customize the appearance of your page, but the content will be completely customized. The culinary equivalent is buying a frozen dinner: It's easy, and it doesn't take a lot of time.

Template: Templates provide you with a selection of different web pages to use as a basis for your own page. You substitute your own text and images for the text and images you find in the template. The content is customized, and you select from a limited range of templates to get the look you prefer. The culinary equivalent is cooking a meal from a recipe, and throwing in a seasoning packet instead of individual herbs.

Blank: By starting with a blank page, you have total control over both content and appearance of your web page. This option is covered in detail in Chapter 3. The culinary equivalent is a home-cooked gourmet meal.

Each method has advantages and disadvantages. When you create a page with the Wizard, you don't have a large number of options, but you also have a guaranteed path to successfully creating a web page. Templates offer a wider range of choices, but you still are using someone else's design. When you start with a blank page, you have total freedom, but you also have to know what you are doing to accomplish anything. A good cook knows that a little bit of basil goes a long way — just as a good web page designer knows that too many images spoil the broth — oops! — the page.

In this chapter, you'll experience the first two techniques for creating a web page. You'll learn the basic skills needed for working with web pages. In the following chapter, you'll get a chance to put all your skills to work creating a web page from scratch.

You have probably seen two different phrases used to describe web pages: "home page" and "web page." A home page is the main page for a web site. It is usually a starting page that serves as a stepping stone to the other web pages on the site. The phrase "web page" describes any web page at all, including home pages, pages created by automatic programs, and so on.

Creating Pages with the Wizard

NETSCAPE
NAVIGATOR
GOLD

To create a new web page using the Netscape Wizard, start Netscape Gold in Browse mode. You can use the Windows Start menu (Start | Programs | Netscape Gold | Netscape Gold 3.0), or you can double-click the Netscape Gold icon on your desktop (see margin). If you see the connection dialog box (see Figure 2-1), click the Connect button to connect to the Internet. The Wizard is located on Netscape's web server (in other words, it is physically located on a computer at Netscape's web site), and you must be connected to the Internet to access the Wizard.

As part of the process of creating a web page with the Wizard, you will be asked to provide URLs for your favorite web pages. You may want to make a list of your favorite sites, and have the URLs handy as you create your Wizard web page.

Once the connection is made, Netscape Gold will display whatever home page you have chosen to use. Figure 2-2 shows my home page, ESPN's SportsZone. Click the File | New Document | From Wizard menu selection (see Figure 2-3) to launch the Wizard.

Figure 2-1: The connection dialog box.

Figure 2-2: An atypical home page.

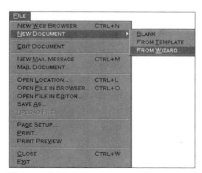

Figure 2-3: Launching the Wizard.

Using the Wizard

It may take a few moments for the Wizard to appear (see Figure 2-4). The Wizard doesn't look like much to start with, but it gets better. This first screen has three frames, but only one frame is in use so far. Read the introductory information, then click the Start button to go to the real Wizard.

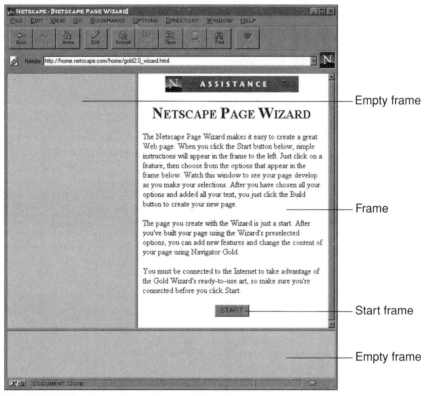

Figure 2-4: The Netscape web page Wizard.

Figure 2-5 shows the actual web page Wizard. The left frame now has some content. It looks like simple text, but notice that there are a number of hyperlinks embedded in the text. By clicking each hyperlink in sequence, you will build a web page step by step. The frame on the right is the Preview frame. It contains a sample of the page you are creating; it will change appearance each time you add something to the page. The bottom frame will be used to enter information for your page, or to make choices about what to include on your page.

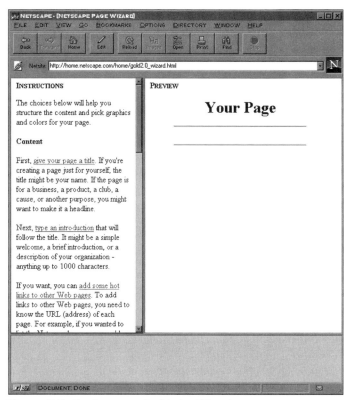

Figure 2-5: Getting started with the Wizard.

Because the Wizard is a web page itself, it's possible that Netscape may make changes to the Wizard after this book is published. The steps shown here should therefore be used as a guide. If you encounter different steps, more options, or anything else not shown here, use the information presented here to adapt to the changes.

Wizard tutorial

The following tutorial describes how to work with the Netscape Gold Wizard. The basic process involves:

➥ Creating page elements, one at a time

➥ Setting page color and background

➥ Copying the web page to your computer

➥ Publishing the page on the Web

The tutorial covers all of the steps except publishing, which is covered in detail in the NetKey at the end of this chapter.

1. Page title

To begin creating your page, click the hyperlink text "give your page a title." (see Figure 2-5.) This displays a text box in the bottom frame where you can enter the title for your page (see Figure 2-6). The text "Type your title here." appears in the text box. Delete it, and replace it with the title for your page. For this tutorial, I suggest you type the text "Zen and the Art of the Web Page". When you have the text entered, click the Apply button. Note that the image of the page in the right-hand frame changes to display your title (see Figure 2-7).

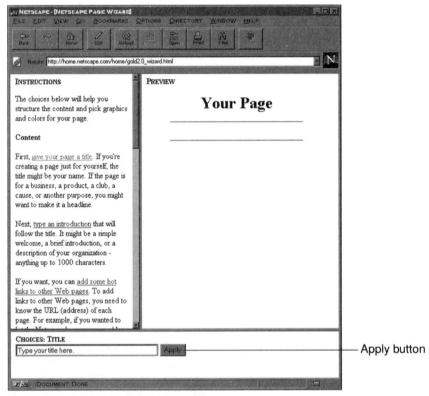

Figure 2-6: Adding a title to your page.

If you make a mistake with the page title, and click the Apply button, you can retype the page title, and click the Apply button again. This is true of all of the steps in this tutorial. Simply repeat any action to place your change on the page. For example, to change the page title to "There are a million web pages on the Naked Internet" (with apologies to Jack Webb), simply delete the contents of the text box in the bottom frame, and type the new text into the text box. Then click the Apply button, and — presto! — the page title is changed.

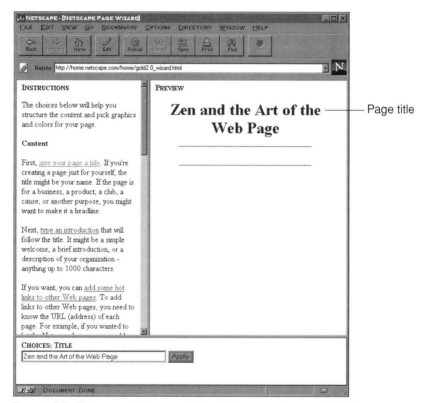

Figure 2-7: The new title appears on the sample web page at right.

2. Page description

The next step is to add a page description. Click on the hyperlink text "type an introduction" (refer to Figure 2-7). This displays a text area in the bottom frame (see Figure 2-8) where you type the page description.

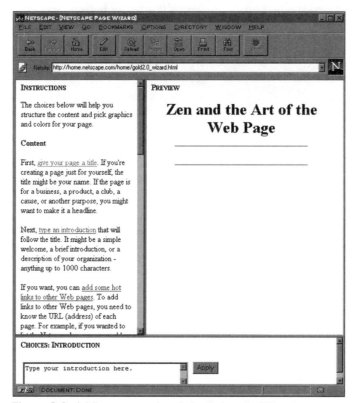

Figure 2-8: *Adding a page description using the Wizard.*

Be sure to select and delete the text instructions that initially appear in the text area. Then type in the page description:

```
Welcome to my web page. Here, you will learn to
understand the true nature of the web page.
```

Click the Apply button to apply the description text to the page. The result will appear in the right-hand frame (see Figure 2-9). If you want to add a longer description, you can use up to 1,000 characters in the text area.

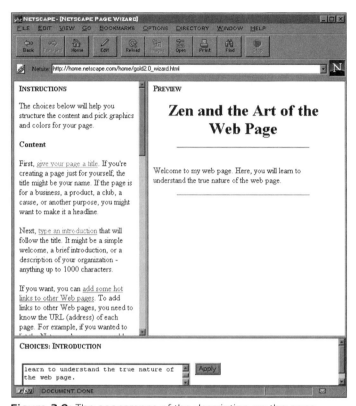

Figure 2-9: The appearance of the description on the page.

The bottom frame in Figure 2-8 is hiding part of the text area. To increase the space available for the bottom frame, move your cursor carefully to the boundary at the top edge of the bottom frame. The cursor changes to the form shown in the margin. Drag the boundary up or down until you have the bottom frame the size you want it (see Figure 2-10, which shows a very large bottom frame).

So far, I've referred to a text box and a text area. A text box, shown in Figure 2-6, allows you to enter a single line of text. A text area, shown in Figure 2-8, allows you to enter multiple lines of text. You can enter text wider than a text box; the text will scroll when you enter more text than the text box can hold. You can also enter more lines of text than the vertical size of a text area allows. The text area will scroll to allow entry of additional text.

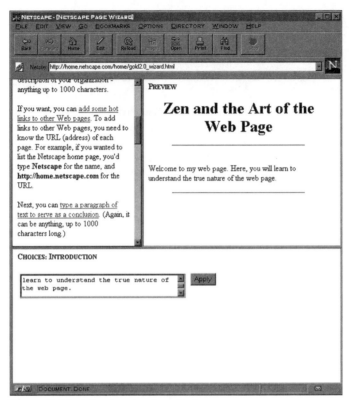

Figure 2-10: Adjusting the size of a frame.

3. Hyperlinks

The Wizard now allows you to add hyperlinks to one or more web pages. If you haven't already done so, make a list of your favorite web sites. During this step, you will add the URLs for these sites to your Wizard web page. Visitors to your page can click on the hyperlinks to visit your favorite web pages.

Click on the text "add some hot links to other web pages" in the left frame of the Wizard (see Figure 2-11). "Hot links" is another (and slightly cooler) way to refer to hyperlinks. The bottom frame changes to display two text boxes (see Figure 2-11). The top text box is for the name or description of a web page, and the bottom text box is for the URL for that web page.

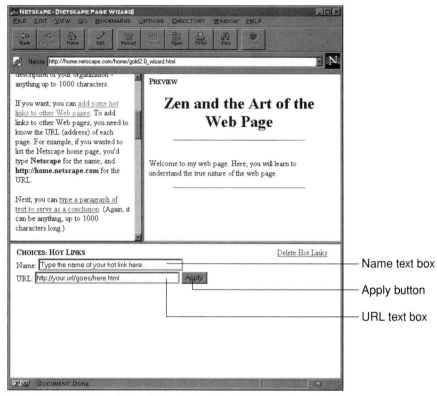

Figure 2-11: Adding hyperlinks to your favorite web pages.

To add a hyperlink, type the name

```
Cool Web Pages with Netscape Gold
```

in the top text box, and the URL

```
http://www.olympus.net/biz/mmad/ng
```

in the bottom text box. This is the home page for this book. Check your typing (a URL has to be exactly right) and click the Apply button to add the hyperlink to your web page. Check the right frame (see Figure 2-12) to verify that the hyperlink is present.

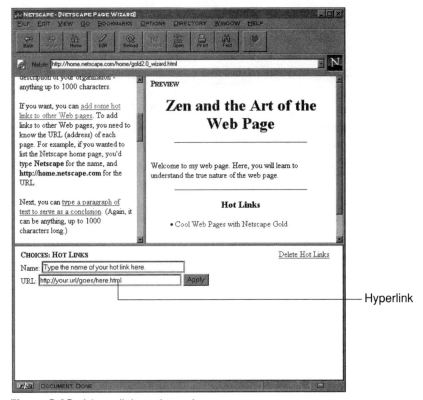

Figure 2-12: A hyperlink on the web page.

To add another hyperlink, type the name

```
Netscape home page
```

in the top text box, and the URL

```
http://www.netscape.com
```

in the bottom text box. This is the home page for Netscape, the company that created Netscape Gold. You can find hyperlinks to all kinds of Netscape-related products and information on that page. Most important, you'll find information about future beta releases of Netscape Gold.

If you cannot see the entire sample web page in the right frame, simply click and drag the mouse on the boundary between the right frame and the bottom frame, and drag it lower (see Figure 2-13).

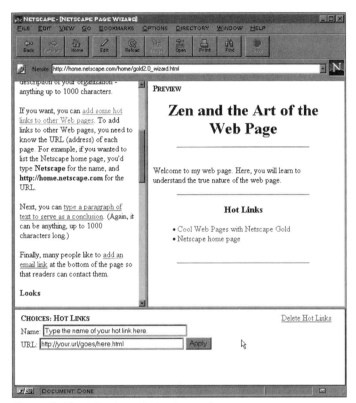

Figure 2-13: Adjusting relative frame sizes.

4. Page conclusion

To add a concluding paragraph to your web page, click the text hyperlink "type a paragraph of text to serve as a conclusion" in the left frame. If this text is not visible, scroll downward in the frame using the scroll bar at the right of the frame. This displays a text area in the bottom frame (see Figure 2-14) where you can type up to 1,000 characters for a concluding paragraph(s). For this example, type

```
If you cannot reach a state of true understanding of the
Web's nature from these hot links, then try sitting down
with a hot dog on a sunny day and contemplate the nature
of having your computer on, off, on, off, on, …
```

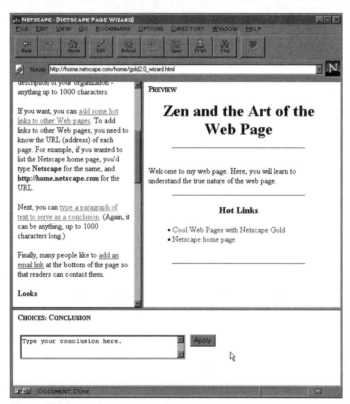

Figure 2-14: Adding a concluding paragraph.

Of course, if you have even more Zen-like comments of your own, feel free to express your creativity! When you have the text as you like it, click the Apply button to add the text to the sample web page in the right frame (see Figure 2-15).

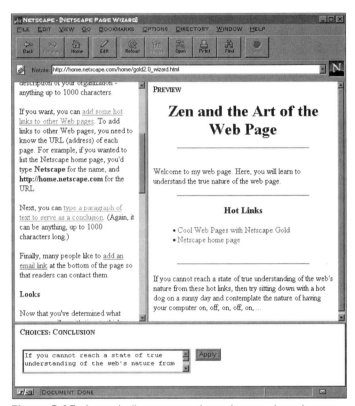

Figure 2-15: A concluding paragraph on the sample web page.

5. E-mail link

Most web pages have an e-mail link at the bottom of the primary page. The Wizard allows you to add an e-mail link to your page. Click the text "add an e-mail link" in the left frame, which puts a single text box in the bottom frame (see Figure 2-16). Add your e-mail address in the text box, and click the Apply button to add the e-mail link.

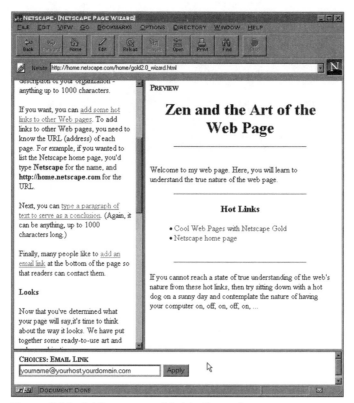

Figure 2-16: Adding an e-mail link to the web page.

Figure 2-17 shows what a typical e-mail link looks like. That's my e-mail address; you should see your own e-mail address in the Preview frame of the Netscape window.

6. Background color

Scroll down in the left frame to see your options for changing the colors used on your page. The default colors for the sample web page are the Netscape default colors: gray or white background, black text, blue hyperlinks, and so on. You can change the color of these elements individually (background color, background pattern, text color, link color, visited link color), or you can choose from a list of preset color combinations.

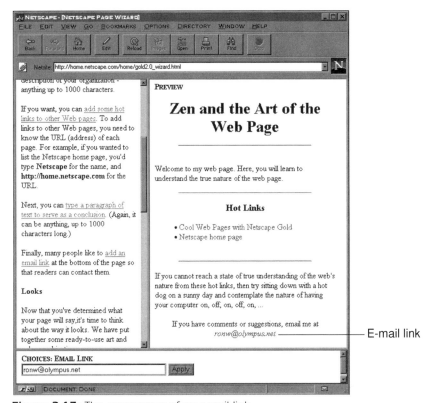

Figure 2-17: The appearance of an e-mail link.

To select a preset color combination, click on the text "a preset color combination" in the left frame (see Figure 2-18). The bottom frame displays the available color combinations; scroll right to see additional combinations.

The little hand in Figure 2-18 shows the color combination I chose: a blue-gray background with light green text, yellow hyperlinks, and light blue for visited links. You may select the same choice, or any color combination you find pleasing.

As you pass the cursor over the various combinations, the hex codes for the combination appear in the status line at the bottom of the window. For example, the color combination I choose uses the hex codes ('006699', 'CCFFCC', 'FFFF00', '00FFFF').

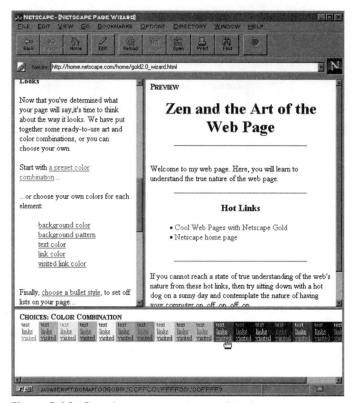

Figure 2-18: Choosing a preset color combination.

To apply the color combination, click anywhere in that color combination. You will see the combination applied to the sample web page. If you don't like it, simply click on a different combination. Figure 2-19 shows (in black and white) the combination I chose.

You can see this combination in color by viewing the file

```
\tutorial\chap02\wizard.htm
```

on the CD-ROM.

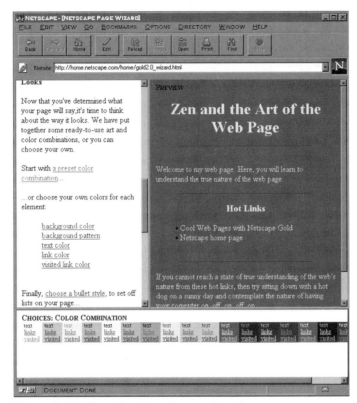

Figure 2-19: Changing the colors used on the page.

7. Adding a bullet style

The hot links you added are shown on the sample web page as bullets. You can change the bullet style used on your page by clicking the text "choose a bullet style" in the left frame. This displays several different bullet styles in the bottom frame (see Figure 2-20). Point to the style you like, and click on it to add it to your page. I picked the bullet style second from the left (an animated square pyramid), and the result is shown in Figure 2-21.

Figure 2-20: Selecting a bullet style.

Hot Links

▶ Cool Web Pages with Netscape Gold
▶ Netscape home page

Figure 2-21: A new bullet style on the web page.

8. Adding horizontal rules

There are several thin horizontal lines on the web page. These are the default separations that the Wizard uses to divide your page into sections. You can also choose alternate horizontal lines. Click on the text "choose a horizontal rule style" in the left frame. This displays a number of different horizontal line styles in the bottom frame. In Figure 2-22, I have moved the frame boundary to show a larger number of the available selections. To change the horizontal lines, click on any of the available styles shown.

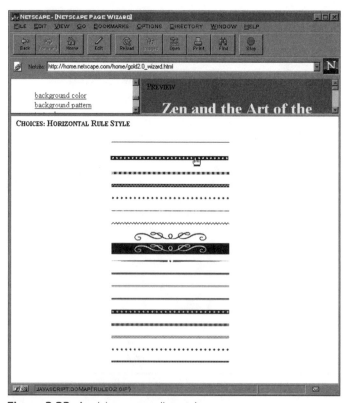

Figure 2-22: Applying a new line style.

Several of the styles available are animations, such as the second from the top in Figure 2-22. These are cute, but they are also very distracting. Be sure your readers will tolerate this level of stimulation! If you click and apply a line style, and don't like its appearance, just click on a different line style to change to that style. I selected the squiggly line style, shown in Figure 2-23.

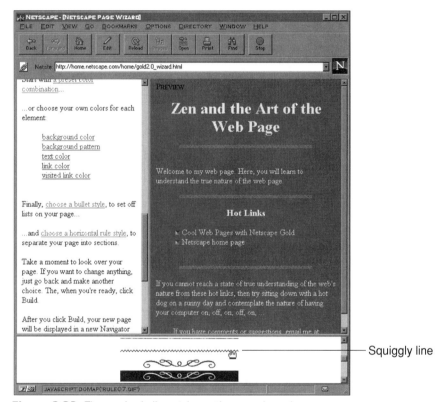

Figure 2-23: The squiggly line style on the sample web page.

9. Finishing your web page

To complete your Wizard web page, scroll to the end of the left frame, and click on the Build button (see Figure 2-24). After a brief delay, you'll see your newly designed web page full-size in Netscape Gold (see Figure 2-25). Note that the "location" of this web page has an odd-looking name:

```
http://cgi.netscape.com/cgi-bin/yourpage.html
```

This name indicates that the page is actually a temporary entity, sitting on the web server at Netscape.

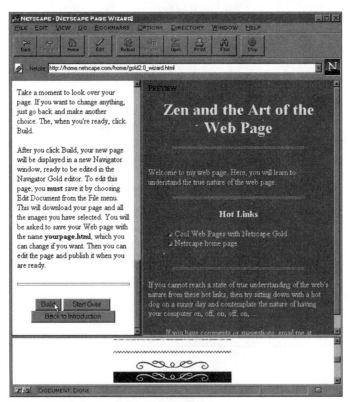

Figure 2-24: Building your web page.

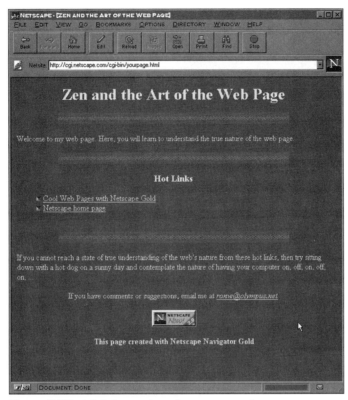

Figure 2-25: A full-size version of your new web page.

10. Saving your web page

Before you can use the web page, you need to save it locally, on your hard disk. To save the page you created, click the File I Edit Document menu selection. You'll see the dialog box shown in Figure 2-26. This dialog box appears whenever you try to save a remote document to your local hard disk.

Make sure that both check boxes are checked. The top check box (Links) determines whether the hyperlinks in the document will work properly. The bottom check box (Save images with document) determines whether images associated with the document will be downloaded to your local hard disk when the HTML file for the web page is saved locally. Make sure that both check boxes are checked (see Figure 2-27), and click the Save button to continue. This displays yet another dialog box which tells you to be careful of copyright when downloading remote files. If you don't want to see this warning again, click the check box in the dialog box. Click OK to close the warning dialog box.

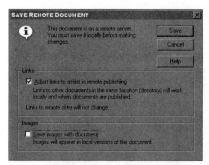

Figure 2-26: Saving a remote document to your hard disk.

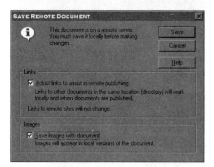

Figure 2-27: Saving images with a document.

At long last you will see the dialog box show in Figure 2-28: a Save As dialog box. The default filename is `yourpage.html`. I suggest saving the new file in a folder specifically meant to hold the web pages you create for this book. That would be `C:\Gold Pages`, which you created earlier, while working in Chapter 1. If you haven't already created this folder, please do so before saving `yourpage.html`.

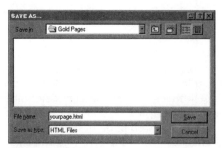

Figure 2-28: Saving your web page.

Once you save the page locally, you can edit it to add/remove/change elements on the page. See the section *Editing an existing page* at the end of Chapter 3 for details.

Creating Pages from a Template

The Netscape Gold Wizard is the easiest way to create web pages, but if you want to create pages for specific applications, templates offer a better solution. The Wizard guides you through the page creation process like a close friend, but the options are limited. Templates offer a much wider range of possibilities.

When you install Netscape Gold for the first time, you gain access to an online set of templates on Netscape's web server. There are templates for several different web pages, from resumes to small business pages, from job listings to an online calculator featuring JavaScript (a simple web page programming language, if any programming language can fairly be called "simple"). To use a template, you copy the template to your hard disk, and replace the template's images and text with your own images and text.

You can also tell Netscape Gold to use a different set of templates, such as the templates included on the CD-ROM that comes with this book (See the Appendix). To change the default template location, use the Options|Editor Preferences menu selection (General tab). The New document template location is set by entering a filename or URL in the text box shown in Figure 2-29. Note that you can also change the default programs used to edit HTML source files (Notepad is a good choice, and a "source file" is just a web page where you can see all the HTML tags) and images (I use Photoshop). You can also enter your name as author in the top text box.

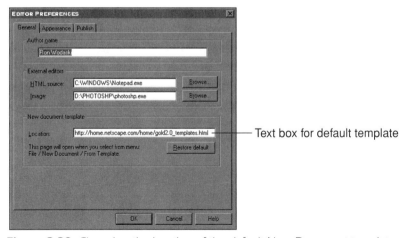

———— Text box for default template

Figure 2-29: Changing the location of the default New Document template.

To create a new web page using Netscape's templates, use the File | New Document | From Template menu selection (see Figure 2-30). Make sure that you are online when you create a new document from a template — the templates are located on Netscape's server. If you accidentally try to create from a template when you are not online, I recommend closing Netscape Gold and running it again. This time, click on the Connect button at the bottom left of the connection dialog box when it appears.

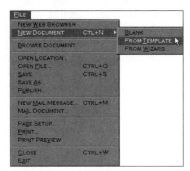

Figure 2-30: Creating a new web page with a template.

Although you are creating a new document, Netscape Gold stays in Browse mode. You will change to Edit mode later, after you pick the template to use for your new web page.

Figure 2-31 shows the page you see when you begin the process of creating a new document from a template. It contains instructions under the heading *How to Use a Template*. In this section, I'm going to expand on those instructions and provide some hints that will help you get the most out of both Netscape's templates, and the templates on the CD-ROM.

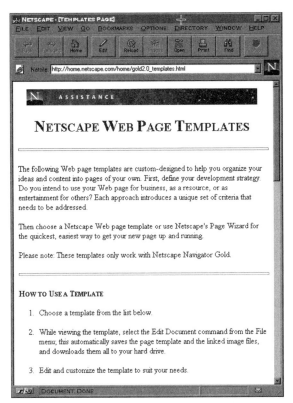

Figure 2-31: Getting started with the template process.

Figure 2-31a shows the available templates on the Netscape web server. The list may change by the time you read this. The list offers a variety of different kinds of templates, each with its own layout, images, text blocks, tables, forms, JavaScript, and so on.

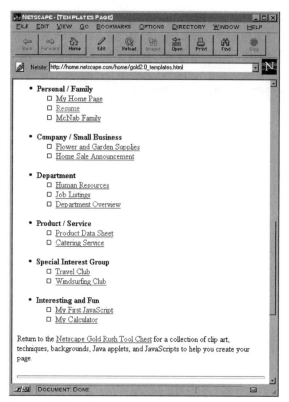

Figure 2-31a: The Netscape templates section.

Unfortunately, there is no thumbnail image to show what each template looks like. To see each template, click on the text hyperlink for the template (Resume, My Home Page, Travel Club, and others). If the template won't meet your needs, click the Back button in the Netscape Gold toolbar to return to the list. For example, if you click on the Travel Club hyperlink, you'll see a template like the one in Figure 2-32.

Figure 2-32: A sample template.

Using templates

Templates are easy to use. In fact, Netscape's programmers have gone out of their way to remind you of the basic steps in using a template. You'll find a list of steps on the web page for templates, and you get a summary at the top of every template. The overall process is simple:

1. Find the template that fits your needs.

2. Save the template to your hard disk.

3. Replace template images and text with your own images and text.

4. Revise the template as needed to meet your needs.

5. Save the result.

6. Publish to your web site.

The following tutorial covers everything except publishing; see NetKey at the end of this chapter for information about copying files (also called *publishing* or *uploading*) to a web server.

Template tutorial

Before starting this tutorial, copy the following files from the CD-ROM to your hard disk. The files are located in the folder \tutorial\chap02\ on the CD-ROM, and they should be copied to the C:\Gold Pages folder on your hard disk.

```
tophead2.gif
clock.gif
sign.gif
now8.gif
```

The simplest way to copy these files is to open both folders on the desktop, Control-click to select the files in the \tutorial\chap02\ folder, and drag them to the C:\Gold Pages folder.

1. Selecting a template

For this exercise, choose the Home Sale Announcement hyperlink from the list of templates. Figure 2-33 shows the top portion of the template. Note that the text at the top of the template contains a summary of the instructions for working with templates. You will remove this text shortly.

To save the template to your computer, use the File | Edit Document menu selection (see Figure 2-34).

Mouse alternative: You can also simply click the Edit button on the toolbar.

Figure 2-33: Begin by choosing a template.

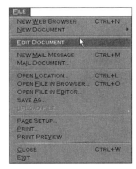

Figure 2-34: Editing the template file.

When you see the Save Remote Document dialog box (see Figure 2-34b), you can leave the lower check box "Save images with document" unchecked. You do not *need* to download the image files from the Netscape server, because you will replace the template images with different images. However, if you do not download the images, you will only be able to see the images when you are connected online. If you want to work offline, then make sure the lower check box is checked so that images get downloaded to your hard disk.

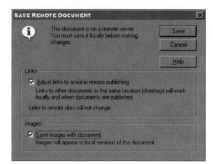

Figure 2-34b: Choose how to save remote images.

Click Save to continue. This opens a Save As dialog box (Figure 2-35). Save the file to the `C:\Gold Pages` folder, using the default filename `realty.html`.

Figure 2-35: Saving the file on a local hard disk.

The template now appears in Edit mode, as shown in Figure 2-36.

Figure 2-36: The template is now available for editing.

To open an edit window first without going through the browser, first right-click and drag the Netscape Gold icon to a new location on your desktop (the original Netscape Gold icon should be sitting on your desktop) to create a new shortcut for Netscape Gold. Right-click on the new shortcut icon and choose Properties. Click the Shortcut tab, and add " -edit" at the end of the text in the Target text box. The exact contents will vary depending on where you installed Netscape Gold; my Target looks like this:

```
D:\NavGold\Program\netscape.exe -edit
```

2. Cleaning up the template

The first step in editing the template is to remove the instructions at the top of the template. Click and drag to select the "How to use this template" text at the top of the page and the horizontal lines immediately above and below the text (see Figure 2-37).

Figure 2-37: Removing the instructions from the top of the template page.

3. Replacing images

Begin by clicking on the company logo at the top of the page. A border appears around the image, but it is hard to see because this image uses so many different colors near the edge.

Click the Image button on the toolbar (see margin) to open the Properties dialog box (Figure 2-38). You can also right-click on the image, and choose the Image properties menu selection (see Figure 2-39).

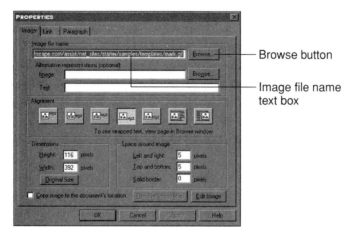

Figure 2-38: Setting image properties.

Figure 2-39: A context menu for accessing image properties.

Note that the image filename points to the original image file on the Netscape web server (`http://home.netscape.com/assist /net_sites/starter/samples/templates/mark.gif`). We did not choose to download the images earlier, so the image reference still points to the original location of the image. Since you will replace this image with another image, this is okay.

Click the Browse button at the right of the "Image file name" text box to locate the replacement image file. This opens the Select Image File dialog. Locate the file `tophead2.gif` in the `C:\Gold Pages` folder. Click the filename to highlight it, and click the Open button to return to the Image Properties dialog box. Note that the new filename appears in the "Image file name" text box. Click OK to accept the changes. Figure 2-40 shows the result.

Figure 2-40: The replacement image at the top of the page.

Alto Clocks is a fictitious company I made up for this example. Alto makes creative and unusual clocks.

4. Replacing text

To replace the headline, select the headline text by clicking and dragging (see Figure 2-41). Type

```
Introducing our Route 66 Clock
```

which replaces the selected text. If it appears in normal size (see Figure 2-42), apply a headline style by clicking in the Style drop down box, and clicking on the style Heading 1.

Figure 2-41: Selecting text to be replaced.

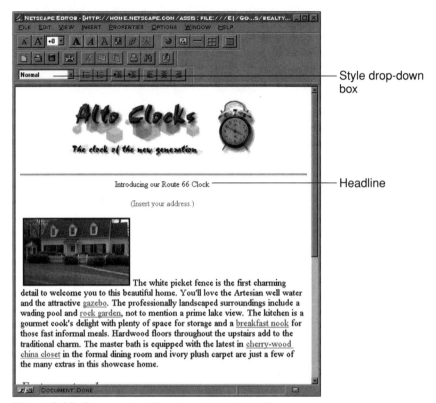

Style drop-down box

Headline

Figure 2-42: The new headline may be a bit small!

 Click on the Center button on the toolbar (see margin) to center the headline (see Figure 2-43). The line break — only the word Clock on the second line — is awkward. Your headline may look different (it may not even have a break at all), depending on the width of your Netscape Gold window. To guarantee pleasing results for various window widths, click to place the cursor just before the "R" in "Route." Hold down the Shift key while pressing Enter to add a line break at this location. Click and drag to select the lower line ("Route 66 Clock"), as shown in Figure 2-44.

Figure 2-43: Centering the headline.

Holding down Shift while pressing Enter creates a new line with very little vertical space between it and the previous line. This is called a line break. Normally, when you simply press Enter, you will get a significant amount of white space between lines. This is called a paragraph break. A line break works better than a paragraph break because it makes the headline look like a single block of text.

Figure 2-44: Selecting a portion of the headline.

To change the color of the selected text, click on the Text Color tool on the toolbar (see margin). This opens the color selection dialog box (see Figure 2-45); choose a nice bright red by clicking on a color square. Click OK to continue.

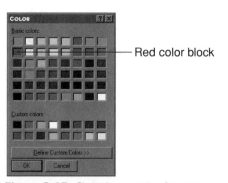

— Red color block

Figure 2-45: Choosing a color for text.

Figure 2-45b shows the result. Editing of the template file continues in this fashion until you have replaced all of the text and images from the template with your own text and images.

Figure 2-45b: Results of your color choice.

To view the changes made so far, as well as some additional changes, open the file \tutorial\chap02\alto.htm on the CD-ROM disc. To open this file in Browse mode, even while you are looking at a file in Edit mode, start by clicking the File | New Web Browser menu selection. This opens a new Browser mode window. In the new window, use the File | Open File in Browser menu selection to locate the file \tutorial\chap02\alto.htm on the CD-ROM disc. This file contains numerous other changes that I made to the template to create a file appropriate for the Alto Clock company. Note that I replaced the image of a house with (I'm sure you are shocked and surprised to learn this!) an image of a clock. Right-click on any page element to learn what settings it uses.

5. Adding hyperlinks

To edit the file you just opened (`alto.htm`), click the Edit button. The document appears in a new Edit window. Close the previous Edit window before continuing.

 Remember that the file `alto.htm` comes from a CD-ROM disc, which is read-only. Before continuing, save this file to the `C:\Gold Pages` folder using the File I Save As menu selection.

 Find the second paragraph of text, and locate the words "road sign" in the third sentence (refer to Figure 2-46). Select this text by clicking and dragging. Then click the Hyperlink button on the toolbar (see margin) to open the Properties dialog box to the Link tab (see Figure 2-47).

Figure 2-46: Selecting text for a hyperlink.

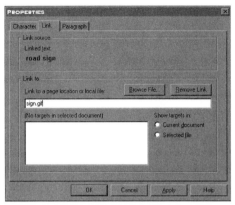

Figure 2-47: Adding a hyperlink to an image file.

The top portion of the dialog box shows the text for the hyperlink, "road sign." This hyperlink will be to an image of the Route 66 road sign. Type the following filename into the "Link to a page location or local file" text box:

```
sign.gif
```

and click OK to continue.

The text you selected earlier now appears in blue and underlined, indicating it is a hyperlink. Click the Browse button in the toolbar (see margin) to view the result in Browse mode. Click the hyperlink, and the image sign.gif appears in a window of its own (see Figure 2-48).

Figure 2-48: A hyperlink that refers to an image displays the image in a new window.

The file `alto.htm` contains a number of changes that are worth learning about. To find out what properties I set to add various features on this web page, position the mouse pointer over the any object on the page and right-click to display a context menu. Experiment with different context menu selections, especially anything with "properties" in the menu selection name. Figure 2-49 shows the completely revised web page for Alto Clocks.

Using CD-ROM Templates

I have supplied additional templates on the CD-ROM that comes with this book. To access these templates, double-click on the file

```
\Cool Templates\index.htm
```

on the CD-ROM. Then follow the same procedure for working with Netscape's templates:

- ➡ Select the template
- ➡ Click the hyperlink to go to the template
- ➡ Save the template to your hard disk
- ➡ Edit the template to meet your requirements

I have provided thumbnail images to show what each template looks like, as shown in Figure 2-50.

NetKey #2: Publishing with Gold

So far, you have created web pages on your own computer. In order for others to also see your web pages, you must publish them on a web server. There are two common situations that involve publishing:

Company Server: Your company provides the web server, and you can publish simply by copying files to the appropriate network directory.

ISP Server: You pay a monthly fee to an Internet Service Provider (ISP), and you must link to the Web server by modem before moving the files to the Web server.

Figure 2-49: The complete Alto Clock web page.

Figure 2-50: Using thumbnails to select templates.

If you are publishing your files on a company server, contact the webmaster or network administrator to find out the steps involved in publishing to your company's server. You may or may not be able to use the built-in publishing capabilities of Netscape Gold. If your webmaster tells you that you can use FTP (File Transfer Protocol) to copy files to the company server, then you can probably use Netscape Gold to publish. If not, your webmaster can give you complete directions for publishing your web pages.

If you are publishing your files on an ISP's server, there is a high probability that you can use Netscape Gold to publish your web pages using the procedures in this NetKey. However, contact your ISP's technical support people, or check out the FAQ (Frequently Asked Questions) files available from your ISP, to see if the ISP supports Netscape Gold publishing.

Using NetKey #2

To begin, double-click on the file

`/tutorial/index.htm`

on the CD-ROM, which will automatically start Netscape Gold in Browse mode. As usual, if you do not want to connect, click the Cancel button when the connection dialog box appears (refer back to Figure 2-1). The appearance of the file `/tutorial/index.htm` is shown in Figure 2-51.

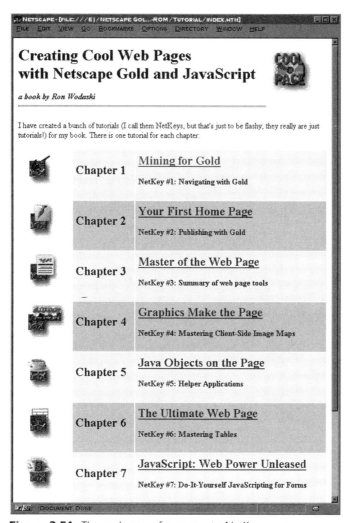

Figure 2-51: The web page for access to NetKey pages.

The file `/tutorial/index.htm` contains hyperlinks to the NetKeys for every chapter in the book. To learn how to publish your web pages with Netscape Gold, click the hyperlink for Chapter 2, *Your First Home Page.* The first NetKey page for this chapter is shown in Figure 2-52. To explore this NetKey, simply click on any and every hyperlink (usually underlined text) that strikes your fancy.

To access the NetKey page for Chapter 2 directly, double-click on the file `/tutorial/chap02/webpage.htm`.

Figure 2-52: The NetKey page for Chapter 2.

Publishing issues

The publishing options built into Netscape Gold will cover many common situations, but they won't cover every possible situation. I have included information on the home page for this book (http://www.olympus. net/biz/mmad/ng/index.html) about a product called WS_FTP, a software program that allows you to use FTP to upload (and download) files from your web server. In some cases, you will need a product like WS_FTP to handle your uploading. In other cases (such as when your web server uses Windows NT as its operating system), you may find that the tools built into the server are more effective than any FTP tools. If all of this sounds too technical, spend some time checking your ISP's web site for FAQ pages that give you information about the ISP's web server. You can also send e-mail to your ISP for clarification. In my experience, if you ask specific questions (even if they are very basic), you will get useful answers.

In still other cases, you may simply want to use the functionality of WS_FTP instead of Netscape Gold to manage your web uploads. WS_FTP has many more features than Netscape Gold when it comes to publishing web pages. If you want reasonable control combined with reasonable ease of use, WS_FTP is a good compromise. When you access the NetKey on the CD-ROM, you will find a hyperlink that allows you to download a free Lite version of WS_FTP to try on your computer.

The methods you use for uploading (publishing) your web pages and the pictures that go with them will vary depending on the abilities of your web server. When in doubt, always contact your webmaster (or at least check out the FAQ files available on the server) to learn how best to handle uploads.

Master of the Web Page

Creating Pages from a Blank Document

The skills you learned while working with templates in Chapter 2 are the same skills you need to create your own custom web pages. The main difference between a template and a custom web page is the added step of designing your own layout for the page. The tutorials in this chapter will also serve up some interesting web page tips and tricks that go beyond the techniques in the first two chapters.

I always follow one cardinal rule when I design my web pages. The first, foremost, and only important rule for designing a web page is:

Start with a plan.

That sounds simple, and it is simple — but it's not necessarily easy to do. A plan results from asking the right questions, such as:

➥ Who is the web page for?

➥ What information should appear on the page?

➥ What kinds of graphics should appear on the page?

➥ What hyperlinks should appear on the page?

As you build the web page, you can modify the plan based on what you learn as you go. For example, the plan might say that the audience for your page is 11-year-old boys. But you might discover that it's important to provide information for their parents, too. A good web page (or *any* good design) changes as you create it because you learn new things as you go.

PageMaster is another hypothetical company that will provide the underpinning for this chapter's tutorial. I will provide a realistic example that shows how web pages are often built. You'll encounter the same opportunities and difficulties that you can expect to find in the real world. PageMaster wants you to build a web page for their hot new web product, HyperZap. Figure 3-1 shows a memo from the Vice President of Inane Details at PageMaster. You are the webmaster (the manager of a web site), and your job is to create a web page that illustrates the virtues of the new product.

PageMaster Design, Inc.

| 9321 Fomulo Drive | Sheboygan, WI 69586 | 800-555-1212 |

Shirley Appleman Webmaster   June 13, 1996
IS Division
Mailstop IS-1

Shirley,

I want to add a web page for the new HyperZap product as soon as possible.

Use the company logo at the top, of course, and I want to see a before and after image of a page showing our product in its best light.

Include the text information attached. It has been approved by the product people, and explains all of the most important features of HyperZap.

If you have any questions, deal directly with the product people, as I will be out of town until they break up the grand jury.

Sincerely,

Vince

Vincent Wannabe

Figure 3-1: The memo with details for the new web page.

You are probably wondering if there are any other rules are for designing web pages. There is only one other rule: There are no rules. To put it another way, if it works, use it. To put it still another way: If it doesn't work, get rid of it. All the fussing in the world won't fix something that has to come out, and if something works, you'll know it in your gut. Creating great web pages is a process of learning to trust your judgments about what works, and what doesn't. Remember the old joke?

"Excuse me, but how do I get to Carnegie Hall?"

"Practice, practice, practice."

A Plan for the Page

The memo from the Vice President mentions an attachment. I have included the text for this example on the CD-ROM. Since the Vice President is out of town, it's up to us to create the best possible page! Begin by locating the file

```
\tutorial\chap03\attached.txt
```

on the CD-ROM. Double-click the file to open it in Notepad. The file contains the raw text you will use to create the web page. This duplicates a common occurrence in the business world. A company has advertising copy or product descriptions or some other text that was used somewhere, sometime to describe a product. Converting such text so it works on the Web is all a part of the process of creating a good web page. Close the file by clicking on the Close icon at top right of the Notepad window (see margin).

Text on the web page isn't just text. The visual appeal of the text is also important. Getting the right size for headlines, leaving enough space around the text to allow readers to orient themselves — all of this makes a web page a better page.

The text is a combination of ideas for the web page and silly filler, so don't be alarmed if it doesn't make a whole lot of sense, and please excuse the inane jokes from the Vice President of Inane Details; he's just doing his job.

Let's begin at the very beginning (with apologies to Rodgers and Hammerstein): It's a very good place to start. Double-click the Netscape Gold icon on your desktop to start the program. Dismiss the connection dialog box by clicking the Cancel button; we won't need to go online for this exercise. You should have either a blank Netscape Gold window, or one that contains the version of your home page from the last time you went online.

Click the File | New Document | Blank menu selection (see Figure 3-2). This opens an Edit mode window for Netscape Gold. You are now faced with a blank slate upon which you will create a custom web page.

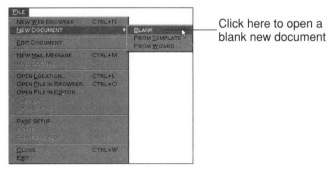

Click here to open a
blank new document

Figure 3-2: Opening a blank new document.

Save before you create

Before you even put the first page element on the web page, you should save your document. Web pages use something called a relative reference to specify where to find page elements. Here's how relative referencing works.

When you save the web page, you tell Netscape Gold where the file lives on your hard disk. This is the base for all future references. It is an absolute reference, consisting of a drive letter, a path specification, and a filename. For example, if you save the blank file you just created in the C:\Gold Pages folder, using the filename FirstPage.htm, then the full absolute reference looks like this:

```
C:\Gold Pages\FirstPage.htm
```

You are already familiar with filenames that look like this; both DOS and Windows 3.x used this same basic technique to locate a file on the hard disk. The only difference is that Windows 95 lets you use long filenames.

In this example, the drive letter is

```
C:
```

and the path specification (path spec for short) is

```
\Gold Pages\
```

and the filename is

```
FirstPage.htm
```

You can also have long path specs, like this:

```
\public\browsers\Netscape Gold\documents\chapter 2\
```

The important point here is that the web page itself is an absolute reference, located at a specific place on your hard drive, in a specific folder, with a specific filename.

Note that I have used backslashes to separate drive letters, folders/directories, and filenames. This is only used for files on a DOS or Windows computer; UNIX machines use a forward slash to separate these items. Since most web servers use the UNIX operating system, you need to be very careful about which kind of slash you use. From now on, we are going to play it safe and use only forward slashes. Netscape Gold can compensate for this, and find files properly on your hard drive. However, it cannot compensate for what happens on a server, and that's why you must always use forward slashes for your relative references. When the files get uploaded to a UNIX web server, the web pages must contain forward slashes!

All elements on the web page (images, hyperlinks,and so on) that refer to files on your hard disk use relative references to locate those files. For example, if you place an image file in the same directory as the web page file (this is the Netscape Gold default), then only the filename is needed to precisely locate the image file:

```
image.gif
```

If you create a subfolder of C:\Gold Pages\ called pictures to hold your images, then a partial path spec is needed to locate the image file relative to the location of the web page:

```
pictures/image.gif
```

If you create a folder at the same level as C:\Gold Pages\, called Gold Pictures, then the partial path spec used by Netscape Gold would look like this:

```
../Gold Pictures/image.gif
```

The double dot at the start of the path spec means "go up one level to the parent folder of the current folder." The good news is that Netscape Gold almost always traverses the relative path for you, and records it properly to the web page file. If you ever run into a problem, and Netscape Gold can't find a file, check the reference to the element, and make sure the relative reference is correct. You can solve a lot of problems just by knowing how Netscape Gold (and all other browsers, for that matter) make use of relative references.

In this case, you will save all of the images in the same folder as the web page document. The images you'll need for your first custom web page are on the CD-ROM, in the folder

```
\tutorial\chap03
```

Click and drag to copy the files

```
monkey1.gif
monkey2.gif
monkey3.gif
monkey4.gif
page01.gid
page02.gif
pm01.gif
pm02.gif
```

from the CD-ROM to the C:\Gold Pages folder on your hard disk. Figure 3-3 shows an example of copying these files by clicking and dragging.

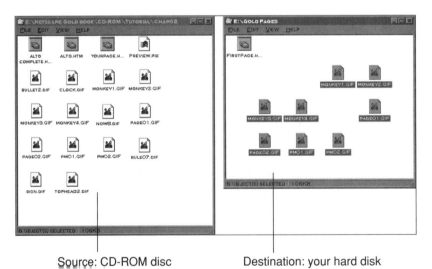

Source: CD-ROM disc   Destination: your hard disk

Figure 3-3: Copying files by clicking and dragging.

You may see slightly different files in the \tutorial\chap03 folder on the CD-ROM, as the final set of tutorial files for this chapter was not complete at the time this section was written. You will, however, see the files listed above, which are used to build the web page that follows.

A quick plan

The best way I have found to create a plan for a web page is to grab a sheet or ordinary paper and a pencil. I sketch out an approximate layout for the page, adding simple blocks for graphics, and I keep that sheet in front of me while I work in Netscape Gold to actually create the page.

If you haven't already opened the text file

```
\tutorial\chap03\attached.txt
```

on the CD-ROM, locate it now and double-click to open it in Notepad (see Figure 3-4).

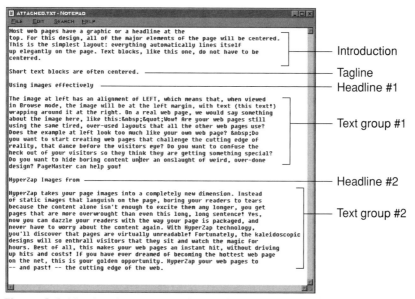

Figure 3-4: Viewing the contents of a text file in Notepad.

There are distinct blocks of information in the text, and it's your job to translate these blocks of text into areas on the web page. There is a medium-sized block at the top, a single line of text, a headline, a large block of text, another headline, and another large block of text. You can think of these blocks like this:

Introduction

Tagline

Headline #1

Text group #1

Headline #2

Text group #2

Any arrangement of these items that preserves their hierarchical relationship to each other is a good arrangement. The details of the arrangement — the size of the characters, whether a headline is left-aligned or centered, and so on — is purely a matter of personal taste. Since we know that

- the Vice President is out of town, and
- he has no taste,

We are free to design this page as we see fit! (So much for mimicking the vicissitudes of the real world!)

Figure 3-5 shows one example of a layout for the web page. It incorporates the text elements from the attachment to the Vice President's memo, as well as a company logo and the two images the VP mentioned. One image shows a typical web page (Figure 3-6) and one shows a web page "enhanced" (I use that word loosely!) with HyperZap (Figure 3-7). The layout shown in Figure 3-5 is our plan for the page. That's how easy it is to create a basic plan: Consider what you have to put on the page, and arrange it on the page so visitors can understand the material.

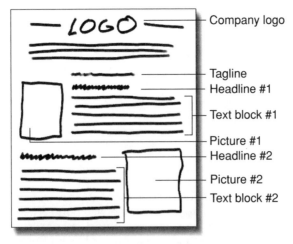

Figure 3-5: An example of a possible page layout.

Figure 3-6: Image showing a typical web page.

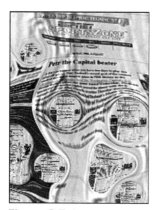

Figure 3-7: Image showing a web page "enhanced" (ugh!) with HyperZap.

There are many other possible arrangements we could use for this page. For example, both images could be on the left or right side of the page. The images could be placed at the center of the page, with each image followed by the text that refers to it. Each image, and the text that goes with it, could be placed on its own page, with hyperlinks to each page from a short, simple page.

You might also want to ask some questions that will help refine the layout of the page:

Who is the web page for? It is intended for customers. We can assume our customers already know how to create a web page (after all, HyperZap is very "advanced" web page technology). All we need to show them is what HyperZap can add to their web pages (Confusion? Chaos?).

What information should appear on the page? All that's needed to get the point across is an example of a standard web page, and a HyperZap web page. There's nothing to change.

What kinds of graphics should appear on the page? That question has been answered by the VP himself, so no changes are needed.

What hyperlinks should appear on the page? At present, there are no hyperlinks in the plan. It would be a good idea to add a hyperlink to the page that will allow the visitor to find out how to purchase HyperZap. Such a link would go near the top of the page, so the interested visitor can quickly make a purchase decision. Exact placement of the hyperlink will have to wait until there is a working version of the page to play with.

There are as many different questions to ask, and as many different ways to lay out this page, as there are grains of sand on the beaches of Southern California. (The interested reader is invited to work out the math to see that this is true.) Just as one must pick one's own little piece of turf on, say, the Santa Monica beach, to spread one's beach towel, one must also settle on a layout and get busy creating it. Like sand castles, web pages are easy to amend if they go awry.

Adding Page Elements

Figure 3-8 shows what Netscape Gold should look like when you begin to create a new document. There are three rows of buttons on the toolbar at the top of the window, and a large blank area where you can create your web page.

Adding images

The plan for the page calls for a company logo at the top of the page. I have thoughtfully supplied a company logo for PageMaster among the files you copied earlier to your hard disk. To add the logo to the page,

 1. Click the Picture button on the toolbar (see margin). The Properties dialog box appears (see Figure 3-9).

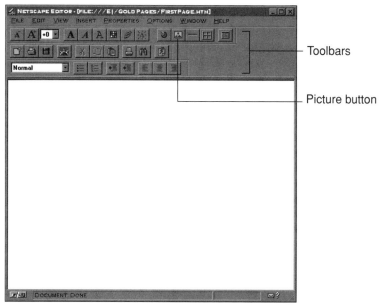

Toolbars

Picture button

Figure 3-8: Starting with a blank document in Netscape Gold.

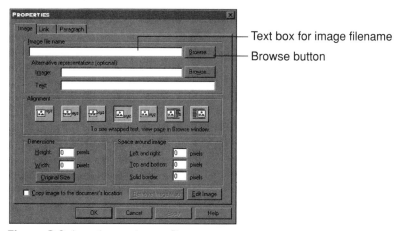

Text box for image filename

Browse button

Figure 3-9: Inserting an image file.

2. Click the Browse button to the right of the text box for the image file name (refer to Figure 3-9). This displays the Select Image File dialog box, shown in Figure 3-10. Highlight the file

```
pm01.gif
```

and click the Open button. The Properties dialog box now contains the image file name (see Figure 3-11).

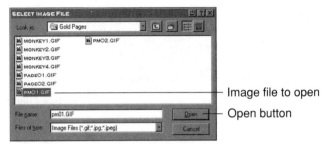

Image file to open
Open button

Figure 3-10: Selecting the image file.

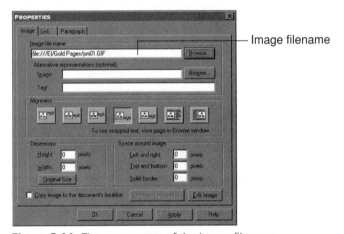

Image filename

Figure 3-11: The appearance of the image filename.

The filename shown in Figure 3-11 may look somewhat strange to you. It's not like a DOS filename, it's not exactly a network filename, and it's not exactly an Internet filename, either. This is the way Netscape keeps track of file locations on your local hard drive. It's a compromise between a DOS filename and an Internet URL, and you need not worry about it. The actual file reference that winds up in your web page will be much shorter (pm01.gif) and much easier to understand. This same method of referring to local files will also appear in the status line of the Netscape Gold window when you pass the cursor over a hyperlink in Browse mode.

3. To add the image to the page, click the OK button (the Apply button will do the job, too, but without closing the Properties dialog box). Figure 3-12 shows the appearance of the web page.

The plan for the page calls for the logo image at center. Click the Center button on the toolbar (see margin). Make sure the cursor is at the far right of the image, then click the Horizontal Rule button on the toolbar (see margin) to add a rule beneath the image. Figure 3-13 shows the image centered and the rule added.

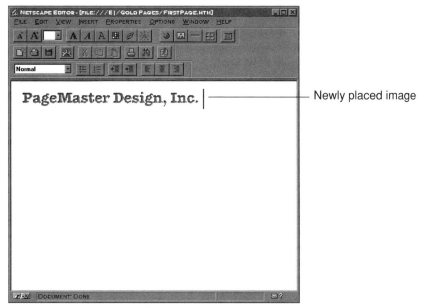

Newly placed image

Figure 3-12: An image added to the web page.

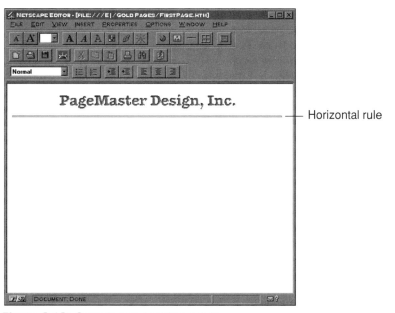

Horizontal rule

Figure 3-13: Centering and adding a rule.

Adding text

The text for the web page is in a file on the CD-ROM. You looked at it earlier in this chapter. It was called the attachment to the Vice President's memo. Double-click on the file

```
\tutorial\chap03\attached.txt
```

to open it in Notepad. Refer back to Figure 3-4, which shows what the contents of the file look like. Click and drag to select the complete first paragraph of the text in Notepad, and copy it to the clipboard using Control + C. Go back to the Netscape Gold window, and click to locate the cursor below the horizontal rule (press Enter to create a line below the rule if necessary). Use Control + V to paste the text into the Netscape Gold window. Figure 3-14 shows the result. The exact appearance may vary, depending on the width of your Netscape Gold window.

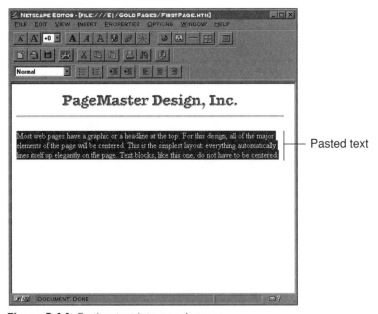

Figure 3-14: Pasting text into a web page.

To fit the text attractively into the page, make the text italic (click the Italic button on the toolbar — see margin) and reduce the font size by one unit (click the Font Smaller button on the toolbar — see margin). If the block of text is not left-aligned, click the Left Alignment button on the toolbar (see margin). The result is shown in Figure 3-15.

Figure 3-15: Changing text characteristics.

TIP

The size of the text on the page has a lot to do with how the visitor perceives the importance of various parts of the page. By reducing the size of this text, we let the visitor know that it isn't the most important text on the page. Note that the text block says nothing about PageMaster (in the real world, it certainly would!). Instead, it offers some suggestions for working with web pages.

Click to place the cursor at the end of the inserted text, and press Enter to create a new line. Copy the tagline from the Notepad window to the Netscape Gold window using the same keystrokes you used earlier (Control+C to copy, Control+V to paste). Taglines are usually limited to a single line, and they can contain many kinds of information — advertising slogans, company mottos, and so on. Figure 3-16 shows the tagline inserted, and centered (click the Center button on the toolbar). I also made the tagline **bold** so it stands out just a bit more than the text above it.

Image alignment

Netscape Gold gives you the option of setting various kinds of image alignment. The next image you add to the web page will use this feature. Before adding the image, position the cursor on a new line following the tagline. Press Enter to create a new line if one does not already exist. If the line does not have a left alignment, click the Left Alignment button on the toolbar (see margin). If the formatting isn't set to Normal (check the style drop-down box, see Figure 3-16), set the style to Normal.

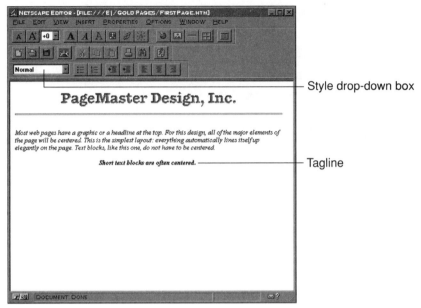

Figure 3-16: Adding a tagline.

 Click the Picture tool (see margin) to open the Properties dialog box. As before, click the Browse button to the right of the text box for the image filename (refer back to Figure 3-9). This opens the Select Image File dialog box. Click on the file C:\Gold Pages\page01.gif, and click the Open button to return to the Properties dialog box.

Notice that row of buttons in the middle of the Properties dialog box. These buttons control how an image is displayed in Browse mode. The functions of these buttons, from left to right, are described in Table 3-1. The first five buttons control vertical alignment, and the last two control horizontal alignment. You cannot have both vertical and horizontal alignment settings for the same image; only one alignment setting is permitted for each image.

 To see examples of image alignment, and to see more information about image alignment, open the file \tutorial\chap03\images.htm on the CD-ROM in Netscape Gold. Figure 3-17 shows a portion of the file's contents. Right-click on any of the images to see the alignment for that image (right-click the image, then click on the Image properties menu selection). The images in the right margin are the buttons to click in the Properties dialog box to set the alignment shown in the left margin. All of the alignment options shown in Figure 3-17 are vertical, relative to any text on the same line as the image. An image placed with text behaves more or less like a single giant text character. Such an image is sometimes called an inline image.

Table 3-1: Image Alignment Buttons

Button	Name	Description
	TEXTTOP	The top of the image aligns with the top of the text.
	CENTER	The center of the image aligns with the center of the text.
	ABSCENTER	The center of the image aligns with the baseline of the text (that is, the bottom of letters such as "s", but not as low as the extender on letters like "y"). DEFAULT The bottom of the image aligns with the baseline of the text.
	DEFAULT	the bottom of the image aligns with the baseline of the text.
	BOTTOM	The bottom of the image aligns with the absolute bottom of the letters (that is, the bottom of extenders such as "y").
	LEFT	The image will appear at the left margin, and text will flow around it. Text flow will continue until there is enough text to create a line that is below the image, and then text will again appear next to the left margin.
	RIGHT	The image will appear at the right margin, and text will flow around it. Wrapping behavior is exactly the same as for LEFT alignment.

Figure 3-18 shows the LEFT and RIGHT alignment settings. These settings control horizontal image placement. The top monkey image has a LEFT alignment. Note that text wraps around the monkey image. The bottom monkey image illustrates RIGHT alignment. In both cases, I also added the image of the button to click in the Properties dialog box to set the desired image alignment.

You cannot set both horizontal and vertical alignment for any one image. You can set an alignment of RIGHT, but you can't then add a setting for BOTTOM. The two kinds of image alignments are mutually exclusive: Setting one option precludes setting any other option

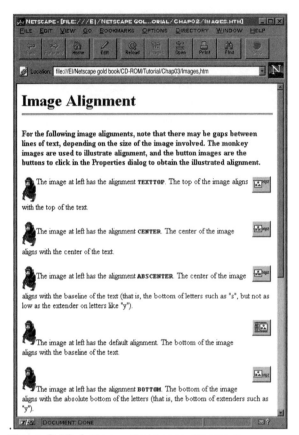

Figure 3-17: Setting vertical image alignment.

Image options

Before all this talk about image alignment, the Properties dialog box was sitting and waiting for a decision. The original plan for this page calls for a left-aligned image. Click the LEFT alignment button (see Figure 3-19). To make sure that the text does not crowd the image, add space around the image, using the lower right portion of the Properties dialog box. Enter a value of 5 for Left and right, and for Top and bottom (see Figure 3-19). Click OK to continue.

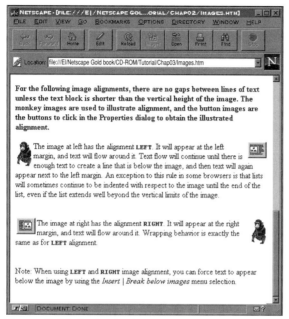

Figure 3-18: Setting horizontal image alignment.

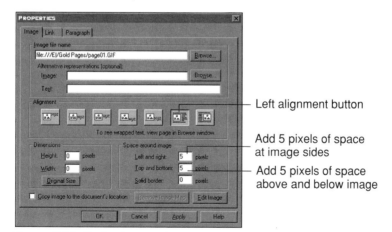

Figure 3-19: Setting image alignment.

The first page image appears at the left of the page (see Figure 3-20), but this isn't because we gave it an alignment of LEFT. In Edit mode, images always appear wherever they are added. You added this image while the cursor was at the left margin, and that's where the image appears. This will be obvious when you add an image with RIGHT alignment, which you will do shortly.

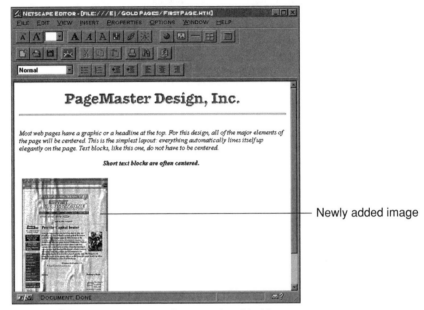

Figure 3-20: The appearance of the newly added image.

The next step is to add the text from the `attached.txt` file to the web page. Click and drag in the Notepad window to select the text for this portion of the web page (see Figure 3-21). The selection consists of a headline, and a block of text. Click to the right of the image in the Netscape Gold window, and use Control+V to paste the text into position. Figure 3-22 shows the result; remember that what you see in Edit mode isn't always the same as what you will see in Browse mode.

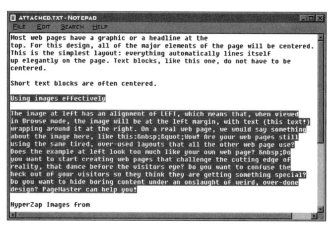

Figure 3-21: Selecting text in Notepad.

Figure 3-22: Pasting text onto the web page.

Select the headline (see Figure 3-23) and use the Style drop-down box to apply the Heading 3 format (see Figure 3-24). Click the Browse button to view your web page in Browse mode.

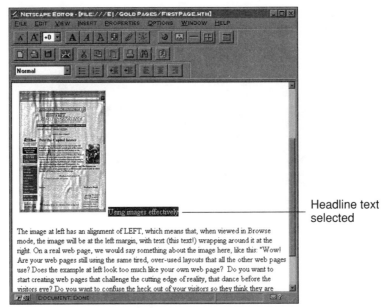

Headline text
selected

Figure 3-23: Selecting the headline.

Figure 3-24: Heading 3 format applied to the headline.

Netscape Gold won't switch to Browse mode. Instead, it will display the dialog box shown in Figure 3-25. I deliberately led you down this path of trickery and deceit to make a point: Before you can view your work in Browse mode, you have to save it. Fortunately, Netscape Gold is a rather pleasant companion, and is offering to let you save your work and continue on to Browse mode. Click Yes to save the file and continue.

 — Click here to save changes

Figure 3-25: *This dialog box appears if you did not save changes prior to selecting Browse mode.*

It's always a good idea to save your work frequently. You never know when a piece of software will crash and take your work with it. You can't predict when the power will fail, sending your work into a black hole of oblivion. You might even make a mistake yourself. Have you ever deleted several paragraphs of the finest text you've composed, intending to move it to a more logical place on the page, only to forget to paste it back in? Well I have, and it's not a pretty sight! Save your work often, and you'll be much more likely to avoid such things as ulcers and nervous tics. The File | Save menu selection should be your closest friend, your confidante, your staunchest ally.

Figure 3-26 shows the current state of your web page in Browse mode. Note that all of the text you added after the image with LEFT alignment wraps neatly around the image.

The next step is to add the second image (page02.gif), the second headline, and the second block of text. The steps are almost exactly the same as the steps for the first group of such items, so I will summarize them for you:

1. Add the image \tutorial\chap03\page02.gif on a new line below the text block you added earlier (refer to Figure 3-26). However, instead of a LEFT alignment, use a RIGHT alignment (last button on the right, in the middle of the Properties dialog box). Note that even with an alignment of RIGHT, the image still appears at the left of the page in Edit mode.

2. Select the second headline/text block in the Notepad window, and copy to the clipboard with Control+C.

3. Click in the Netscape Gold window to the right of the page02.gif image, and paste the new text with Control+V.

4. Apply the Heading 3 style to the heading. The result appears in Figure 3-27.

Figure 3-26: The web page in Browse mode.

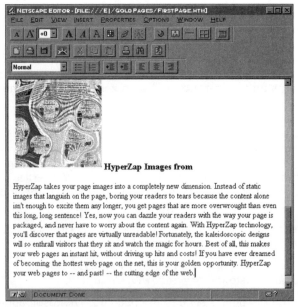

Figure 3-27: Adding the second image, headline, and text.

Note that the company name is missing from the headline. The headline says "HyperZap image from" instead of what you might expect: "HyperZap image from PageMaster." I have included a small version of the PageMaster logo that you can add here. Click to position the cursor at the end of the headline, and click the Picture button in the toolbar (see margin). Click the usual Browse button (top right of the Properties dialog box), and select the image file pm02.gif. Click the third alignment button from the left (ABSCENTER), and set the Space around image, Left and right, to 5 pixels (see Figure 3-28). Click OK to continue. Figure 3-29 shows the bizarre-looking result. Do not be alarmed, Will Robinson! What you see is not what you get.

 If some of the text for the second image appears next to the first image in Browse mode, you should add a "Break below image" after the last character of text for the first image. Position the cursor just after the last character (at the end of the line that ends with "...help you!"), and use the Insert | Break below image menu selection to add the break.

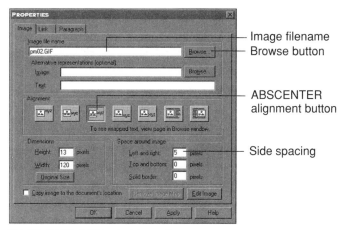

Figure 3-28: Setting image options.

 Although Netscape Gold is, by and large, a What-You-See-Is-What-You-Get web page tool, there are situations where it is not. You saw two of them so far — horizontal image alignment is not shown in Edit mode, and vertical alignment can be quite bizarre in Edit mode. Keep your eyes peeled for other such situations.

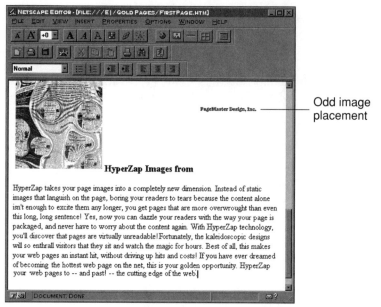

Odd image placement

Figure 3-29: Image alignment can be wacky in Edit mode.

Figure 3-30 shows the appearance of the web page in Browse mode. Note that all images are now exactly where they should be. The page follows the plan set out earlier, but it looks very crowded. There are several ways to deal with this. You could add more space around the images, but that would still leave the large blocks of text. The sad reality is that you cannot always take text from other uses (the Vice President's staff probably dug these text blocks out of a press release, or some wordy internal company document) and plug it straight into a web page. With some judicious editing (translation: after cutting out 90 percent of the text), this web page can yet be saved!

Because a web page must have both visual appeal and text content, lists are a common feature on most web pages. A list is brief and to the point. It does not waste words, nor does it waste web page real estate. Lists are a very efficient way to get the most information on your web page. Last but not least, a list looks much better on a web page than a large block of text. If a web page looks crowded, a list or two might be just the ticket to a clean, open appearance.

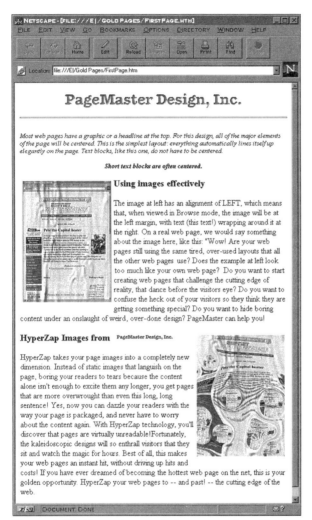

Figure 3-30: The web page in Browse mode, with all images reporting to their proper positions on the page.

Cleaning up a page

Figure 3-31 shows how to change the text. I have reduced the huge block of text to a short introductory paragraph and a list of important points. Delete most of the original material, and add the tongue-in-cheek text shown in the figure before you continue.

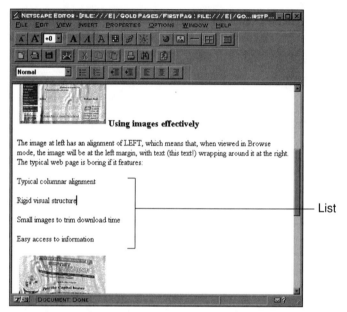

Figure 3-31: *Using a list instead of a large block of text.*

The list as shown in Figure 3-31 is just a group of Normal paragraphs. To convert them to a true list, select the group of lines (see Figure 3-32), and click on the List Item style in the Style drop-down menu (see Figure 3-32). Figure 3-33 shows the result.

By default, the list appears left-aligned. Right-align the list by clicking on the Align Right button on the toolbar (see margin). You can change the appearance of the list in several different ways. To access list options, select the entire list by clicking and dragging, and right-click on the selection. This displays the context menu shown in Figure 3-34. Select Paragraph/List Properties. This displays the Properties dialog box with the Paragraph tab preselected (see Figure 3-35).

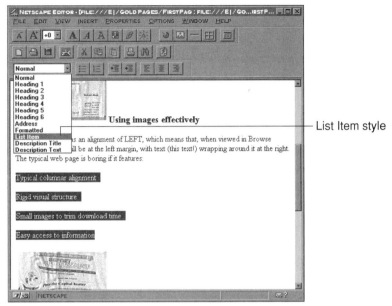

Figure 3-32: Converting to a List Item style.

List Item style

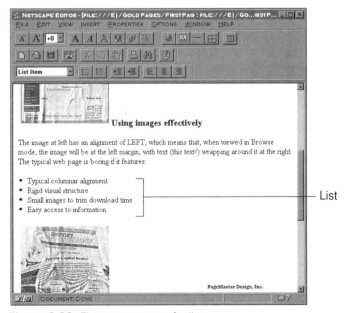

Figure 3-33: The appearance of a list.

List

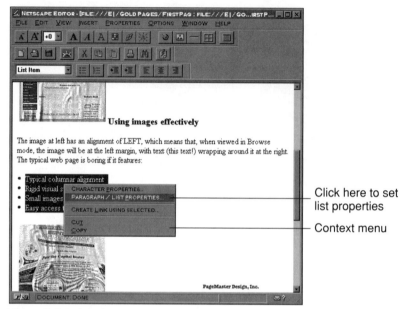

Figure 3-34: A right-click displays this context menu.

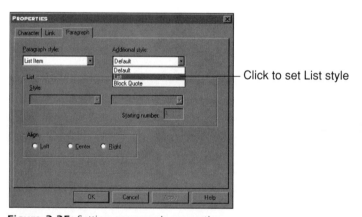

Figure 3-35: Setting paragraph properties.

The Paragraph style is set to List Item. The Additional Style drop-down, top right, is set to Default. Change it to List, as shown in Figure 3-35. Click on the List Style drop-down (left center) to see a list of the list styles available. For this list, the choice Unnumbered list (this is actually a bulleted list) is most appropriate (see Figure 3-36).

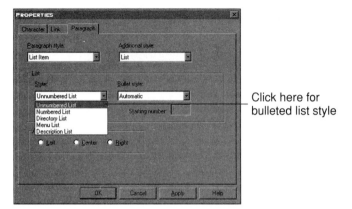

Figure 3-36: Choosing a List style.

You also have the option of setting one of four different Bullet styles for a list (see Figure 3-37). For this example, select Solid square. Click OK to continue. Figure 3-38 shows the appearance of the right-aligned, square-bulleted list.

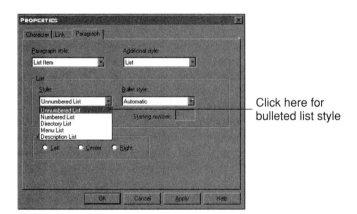

Figure 3-37: Choosing a Bullet style.

 Save your work, and then view it in Browse mode by clicking the Browse button on the toolbar (see margin). Figure 3-39 shows how the page looks.

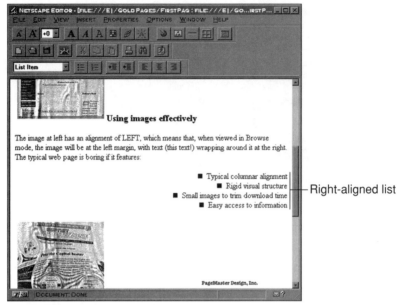

Right-aligned list

Figure 3-38: The appearance of the revised list in Edit mode.

Figure 3-39: The page in Browse mode.

Note that the headline for the second page image appears to the right of the first page image instead of where it belongs (to the left of the second page image). Because we removed some text that applies to the first image, the headline moved up next to the first image. This problem occurs frequently, and there is a very simple solution. Return to Edit mode, and click to place the cursor at the end of the last line of text you want to appear next to the first image (that is, at the end of the last line of the list). Use the Insert | Break below image(s) menu selection to add a break. All text that follows this break will appear below the first image. Figure 3-40 shows the result in Browse mode.

Figure 3-40: The page with a break inserted below the first page image.

I also edited the text for the second page image. Figure 3-41 shows the changes; duplicate these changes before you continue.

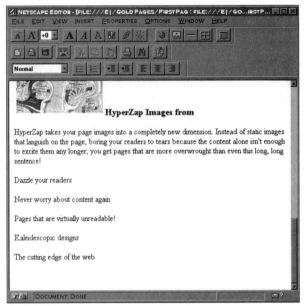

Figure 3-41: Changes to the second text block.

To format this list, use almost the same steps as for the first list:

1. Select the list of items.
2. Apply the List Item style.
3. Right-click on the selected list to open the Properties dialog box.
4. Set Additional style to List.
5. Set List Style to Numbered List.
6. Set Number style to A, B, C (see Figure 3-42).
7. Click OK to continue.

In Edit mode, you will see the letter "A" at the beginning of each line in the list. You won't get actual sequential letters until you view the page in Browse mode. Peek ahead to Figure 3-43 to see the result.

Save your work, and view the changes in Browse mode. Figure 3-43 shows the completed web page. The conversion of some of the text to list format opens up the page, and delivers a clean, well-organized appearance.

Later, in Chapter 4, you'll learn how to add a background image to this page. Save the final version before exiting Netscape Gold.

Figure 3-42: Setting list properties.

Click here to use
letter sequence

Figure 3-43: The completed web page.

Adding other page elements

These last steps improved the look of the page, but this is about as far as you can go with the basic tools for text and images. Making more refined pages is easier when you start using Netscape Gold's heavy artillery. Tables, for example, give you much more freedom to lay out page elements attractively. For example, look at Figure 3-44. This page spreads the text and figures over the page, but leaves plenty of white space that allows the visitors eye to flow naturally through the page.

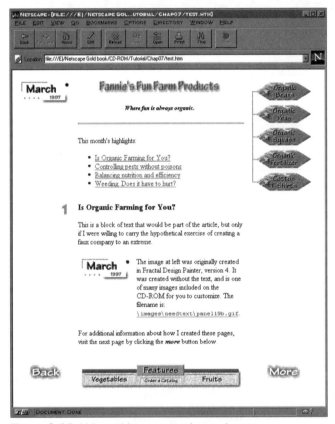

Figure 3-44: Using tables to control page layout.

You can view the web pages shown in Figures 3-44 and 3-45 in full color on the CD-ROM. Double-click on these files:

```
\tutorial\chap07\fanny\noborders.htm
```

```
\tutorial\chap07\borders.htm
```

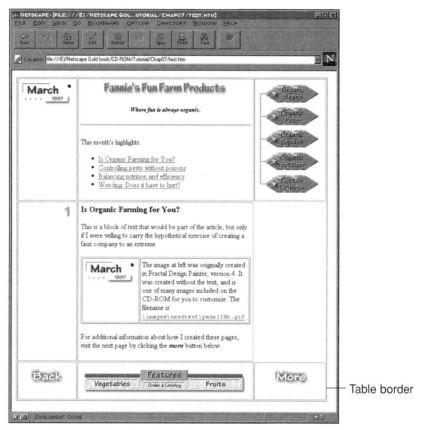

Figure 3-45: Table borders visible.

You can also load these files in Browse mode with the File ➪ Open in Browser menu selection.

The page shown in Figure 3-43, by comparison, is crowded and not nearly as classy. Figure 3-45 shows the table with the borders made visible. You can see that there are really two tables involved. By using tables, and by carefully aligning images and text within the tables cells, you can exercise a much greater degree of control over the appearance of your web pages. If your ambition is to design an exceptional web page, tables are the best choice.

You'll learn more about using fancy graphics in Chapter 4, and you'll learn the secrets of working with tables in Chapter 6.

Editing an Existing Page

You can apply the Netscape Gold editing tools to any existing pages, or to pages you create with the Wizard or the templates. Simply double-click on the icon of the file you want to edit, which will open the file in Browse mode. Click the Edit button in the toolbar (see margin) to switch to Edit mode, and make your changes. Save the file, and examine your changes in Browse mode to verify that they look they way you want them to.

To view your changes in Browse mode, you must save the changes. If you aren't sure about the changes you are making, make a copy of the file first, and apply the changes to the copy. You can save the changes as often as you like without altering the original file. When the edits are satisfactory, you can copy the revised file over the original file.

The most common edit of a web page is adding a hyperlink, or changing an existing hyperlink. Netscape Gold makes this very easy to do. To edit an existing hyperlink, position the cursor anywhere within the link text, then use one of the following methods to open the Hyperlink dialog box:

➡ Click the Hyperlink button on the toolbar (see margin)

➡ Right-click on the link text, and choose Link properties from the context menu.

Edit the hyperlink in the Hyperlink dialog box, and click OK when you are finished. Remember to save your web page to disk before you check the hyperlink in Browse mode.

Chapter 1 includes complete information about creating new hyperlinks. Simply select the text, and type the hyperlink (URL, bookmark, and so on) into the Hyperlink dialog box.

You can also revise the appearance of your web pages at any time. Figure 3-46 shows the Wizard page from Chapter 2. The page isn't quite balanced; two short paragraphs near the bottom are the only material on the page that isn't centered. Centering this text would improve the appearance of the page. Click and drag to select the text in those two paragraphs, as shown in Figure 3-46. Click the Center Text icon on the toolbar (see margin) and the text appears centered (see Figure 3-47).

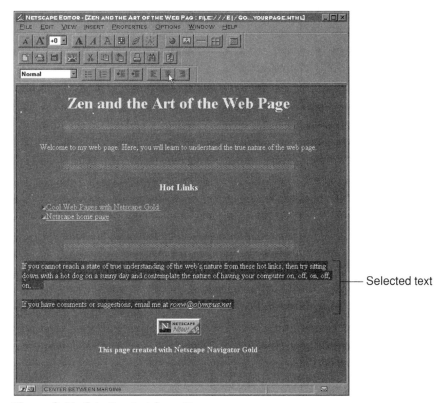

— Selected text

Figure 3-46: Selecting text for editing page appearance.

Remember that the people who visit your web page will view it under different conditions, and with different browsers. For example, the page width might be smaller for some visitors, as shown in Figure 3-48. Make sure that your web page looks good at various page widths — you can't control how visitors arrange their browser windows!

After you make any changes, remember to upload the revised web page to the web server. If you didn't change any images or add new images, you can click the Select none button in the Publish File dialog box before uploading. See the NetKey for Chapter 2 for details on publishing/uploading your web pages.

Editing a page you are browsing

You can edit a page that you are browsing. The process is almost exactly like the process in Chapter 2 for creating a page from a template. In effect, the page you are browsing becomes your template. The easiest way to edit the page in the Browse window is to click the Edit button. Netscape Gold will prompt you through the steps for copying the web page and any images to your hard disk.

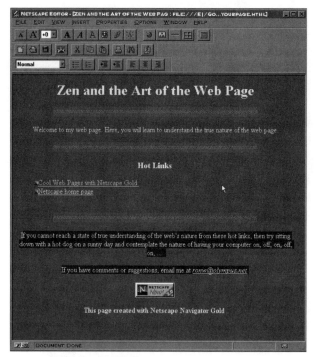

Figure 3-47: Centering text.

 You'll see a dialog box whenever you attempt to edit a page you are browsing. The dialog box uses some pretty stern language to warn you about copyright laws. I can't explain everything about copyright law — even highly paid lawyers disagree about some aspects of the law. I can tell you that if you don't own the rights to some part of a web page, such as text, images, video, or music, then you probably shouldn't be using it on your web page. Some web pages explicitly give you permission to use material from the page, and that's the only time you should feel free to make use of someone else's materials.

For example, the web page at

```
http://www.access.digex.net/~tmartin/noetic.html
```

includes some nifty images (see Figure 3-48). The artist provides clear instructions on whether and how you can make use of those images, right on the web page. There are many other pages around the World Wide Web that provide similar access to backgrounds, icons, and images. They are a good source of free artwork for your web pages. I have also included some art on the CD-ROM; see the file viewme.htm in the root directory of the CD for information about graphics included on the CD.

Figure 3-48: A sample of clip art available on the Web.

Images are the heart and soul of a great web page. To really earn your MWP (Master of the Web Page) degree, you'll need to move on to Chapter 4, where the deepest and darkest secrets of web images are revealed.

NetKey #3: Summary of Web Page Tools

In this chapter, you have learned how to use some of Netscape Gold's tools to create a web page from scratch. There are many more tools available than I can describe in a single chapter, so I have included a handy reference on the CD-ROM. It contains detailed information about all of the key tools at your disposal — toolbars, context menus, drag and drop, and so on.

Using NetKey #3

To begin, double-click on the file

```
/tutorial/index.htm
```

on the CD-ROM, which will automatically start Netscape Gold in Browse mode. As usual, if you do not want to connect, click the Cancel button when the connection dialog box appears. The appearance of the file /tutorial/index.htm is shown in Figure 3-49.

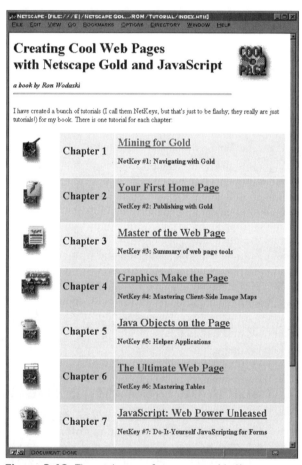

Figure 3-49: The web page for access to NetKey pages.

The file `/tutorial/index.htm` contains hyperlinks to the NetKeys for every chapter in the book. To learn how to publish your web pages with Netscape Gold, click the hyperlink for Chapter 3, Summary of Web Page Tools. The first NetKey page for this chapter is shown in Figure 3-50. To explore this NetKey, simply click on any and every hyperlink (usually underlined text) that strikes your fancy.

To access the NetKey page for Chapter 3 directly, double-click on the file `/tutorial/chap03/webpage.htm`.

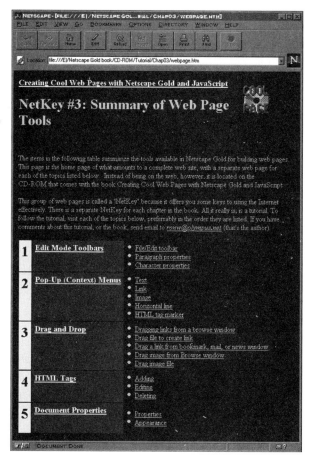

Figure 3-50: The NetKey page for Chapter 3.

Graphics Make the Page

Netscape Gold and Graphics

Netscape Gold makes it easy to add graphics to your web pages. However, the actual management of graphic images can be confusing at times. Before we dive headlong into the subject of graphics, I'll mention some of the rough spots you may encounter, and offer suggestions for dealing with them.

The most important point I can make about web graphics is that you can't ignore them. Don't expect to just roam around your hard disk, adding images as the whim strikes you. Your best strategy is to start out by managing your web graphics — group them in folders, give them names that relate them to specific web pages, and so on. All such actions can be summed up in a single rule:

Create, organize, and label your web images before you start creating your web page.

In Chapter 3, you learned that you should always develop a plan for your web page. You can create your page with more confidence if you back up that plan with well-organized graphics. The way that you organize your graphics will vary. It depends on how you create your web page. For example, managing graphics for a web page created with the Wizard is a completely different task than managing graphics for a custom web page.

Wizard Graphics

When you create a web page with the Wizard, you select preexisting graphics as you build the web page. You then download the images to your local computer. Netscape automatically puts the graphic images into the same folder/directory as the web page itself. For a web site with one to three pages, this strategy works well. You can put all of your web pages, and all of the graphics that the pages use, in a single folder. If you have more than three pages, however, you can create subfolders to better organize your web site.

Since the Wizard only creates one kind of web page, the single-folder approach is usually the best approach.

Template Graphics

The creation process is quite a bit different when you create a web page from a template. You do have the option of downloading the graphics used in the template, but in almost all cases you will be replacing the template graphics with new graphics of your own. This creates three problems:

- ➦ You don't know how many images you'll need, or what size they should be, until you have downloaded the template.
- ➦ You will need to remove the template's graphics when you are done with them (only if you download the graphics).
- ➦ You will need a method to distinguish the graphics you create from the ones the template uses.

The most efficient way to work with templates is to avoid downloading the template's images in the first place. You can do this by *not* checking the lower check box in the dialog box that appears when you click the Edit button (see Figure 4-1). However, if you do this, you must be connected online in order to see the images in the template. The primary advantage to this approach is that there is no cleanup of template graphics, and no confusion about which images are which. The downside is that you are connected to the Web while you work, which could wind up costing you some money.

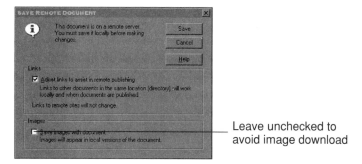

Leave unchecked to
avoid image download

Figure 4-1: How to avoid downloading template images.

If you do download the template's images, make a mental or written note describing which images belong to the template, and which belong to you.

If you are creating multiple web pages from templates, the job of keeping track of graphics rapidly escalates into chaos. A system of keeping track of images becomes essential. At a minimum, I suggest that you create a subfolder of the folder that contains your web page(s). This subfolder contains any and all graphics you use for your web pages. Let Netscape download template graphics into the same folder as the web pages. As long as you put your graphics in their own folder they never get mixed with the template graphics.

If you have many web pages, or many graphics, additional organizing is required. I explain how to do this in the next section.

Custom Page Graphics

When you are creating your own web pages, the process of organizing the various page elements becomes more critical. Folders and subfolders are your primary weapon for managing a web site. The usual method for organizing a web site is shown in Figure 4-2. I call this the *basic layout*. You can vary it as needed to meet the needs of just about any web site.

Using the basic layout for a web site, the highest level folder contains:

➥ The home page, which serves as the entry point for the site.

➥ Other web pages more or less related to the topics on the home page.

➥ Temporary or transient files, such as are used on "Under Construction" pages.

➥ A folder for images (GIF and JPEG graphic files).

➡ Folders for major subdivisions of the main site. For a corporate site, these might be folders for specific parts of the company: Products, Service, Inventory, and others, with related web pages and images grouped in each folder. For a personal site, these folders might be used for video clips, pages relating to hobbies, and so on.

➡ Folders for special files (video clips, sounds, downloads, and so on).

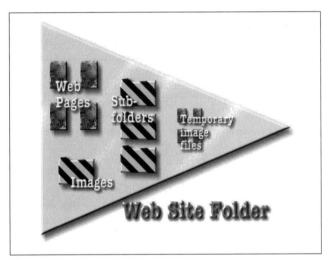

Figure 4-2: One method for organizing web pages and graphics for a web site.

Many or few folders may be in the highest level folder, depending on the amount and kind of information found on the web site. For example, my web site contains several subfolders — one for each book I have written. The various levels of folders for my web site are shown in Figure 4-3.

The highest level is arranged according to the basic web site layout from Figure 4-1. The lower levels are arranged in ways that suit the requirements of each sublevel. I can easily add new features to my web site, either by adding a web page at the top level, or by adding a new subfolder for a major new feature (that is, a feature with multiple web pages and many images). Figure 4-4 shows several folders for my web site and their contents.

The basic layout won't solve every web site's organizational problems. However, for 99 percent of the web sites out there, the basic layout (or some variation of it) will keep you sufficiently organized. If the basic layout won't solve your problems, look to more sophisticated web site management tools such as Microsoft FrontPage.

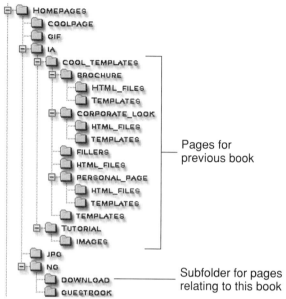

Pages for previous book

Subfolder for pages relating to this book

Figure 4-3: The layout of the author's web site.

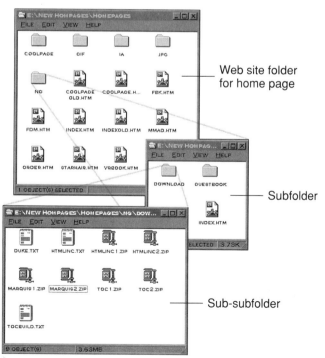

Web site folder for home page

Subfolder

Sub-subfolder

Figure 4-4: Contents of folders for my web site.

Graphic Rules to Live By

You could just throw graphics at a web page in any old order, but there are some simple rules that will give you better-looking web pages. The rules will also make your web pages download to readers' computers faster. A web page that takes forever to download can be downright annoying.

 You will see frequent references to 8-bit images and 24-bit images in this chapter. An 8-bit image uses 8 bits to code color information, and gives you up to 256 colors in an image. A 24-bit image uses 24 bits to code color information, and gives you more than 16 million colors in each pixel of an image. 24-bit color is sometimes called "true color," and now you know why. You'll find a more detailed description of 8- and 24-bit color later in this chapter.

Here are some things to keep in mind when you are working with web page graphics:

Small is beautiful: Large images take a long time to download. Whenever possible, use smaller images. If you use too many images, or too many large images, your visitor may not stay around long enough to see all of your web page. Most visitors are downloading with nothing more speedy than a 28.8 Kbps modem.

Image transparency can be powerful: Image transparency creates interesting image outlines that can add visual punch to a page. You'll see some interesting examples later in this chapter.

Interlace your images: Interlaced images show a rough version of the image quickly, and the image quality improves as the entire image gets downloaded. Visitors are more likely to wait for a long download if they can see an approximation of what they are waiting for. Examples of interlaced images are shown later in this chapter.

White space is essential: Don't crowd images and text together. It's fine to have small groups of images, but put some white space between groups. White space helps the human eye find its way around the page comfortably.

Put your images to work: Don't forget to add hyperlinks to your images when appropriate.

Reuse images as often as possible: Once an image is downloaded, the browser does not need to download it a second time if it is used on another web page at your site. For example, if you create a company logo for your home page, use that same logo for other web pages that need the logo.

Tables make great image organizers: If you want tight control over how images display on the web page, create a table and add the images to the table cells. You'll learn a great deal more about this technique in Chapter 6.

There are plenty of other design rules, but most of those have to do with good image design, and that's different from how you use the images on the page. There are probably thousands of rules for creating beautiful images, but I'll list just the most important for web page graphics.

A busy image isn't an effective image: With rare exceptions, putting too much "stuff" into a single image will only confuse your reader. Of course, if your goal is to create one of those impressively chaotic web pages (think in terms of *Wired* magazine), by all means go for it. For the rest of us, the smaller the size of an image, the simpler it should be.

Use diagonals when arranging details: If you have more than one item in an image, arrange the items using diagonals. For example, if you put small images of a trumpet and a toy in a single graphic, arrange them as shown in Figure 4-5, not as shown in Figure 4-6. The inset images show a line illustrating the linear relationship of the two items in each image.

Figure 4-5: Using a diagonal to arrange images.

If you reduce an image, sharpen it: If you follow the first rule of web page graphics (small is beautiful), you will often find yourself using your image editor to reduce the size of an image. Before reducing the image, make sure you are working in 24-bit mode. If you don't, you will lose an enormous amount of detail in the image. Figure 4-7 shows what happens when you reduce the size of an 8-bit image. After reducing, apply a sharpening filter (Filter menu in Photoshop) to clean up the fuzziness that results from reduction. Don't over-sharpen, or details in the image will get lost. Figure 4-8 shows a reduced image before sharpening, and Figure 4-9 shows the image after sharpening and with too much sharpening.

Figure 4-6: This alignment looks too rigid.

Figure 4-7: An 8-bit (256-color) image after reduction.

Figure 4-8: An image after reduction, without sharpening.

Figure 4-9: An image after reduction, with sharpening (left) and too much sharpening (right).

Use 8-bit tools for transparency: If you create images using 24-bit tools (see Figure 4-10), the edges of the images will blend into the background color (white in Figure 4-10). If you then add transparency, and place the image on a different background color, you will see an unpleasant halo around the image in the original background color (see Figure 4-11). In Photoshop, use the Mode menu to change from 24-bit to 8-bit. Now copy and paste, and you will not see that annoying halo (see Figure 4-12). Most image editing software has some method for switching to 8-bit editing. I still recommend 24 bits for creating images, but 8-bit editing is the only way to go when taking the final step of saving with transparency.

Figure 4-10: A simple image, before transparency is added.

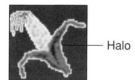

Halo

Figure 4-11: Cutting and pasting in 24-bit color results in a halo.

Figure 4-12: Cutting and pasting in 8-bit color: no halo.

Use appropriate colors: You can use color on your web page in many ways, but only some of them will be right for your web page. For example, if you choose a color set of tans and reds, then make sure that every image you create uses these colors as the dominant colors in the image. If you are forced to use a nonconforming image (let's say that the president of your company wants her picture on the home page), you can add a border to that image using one of your dominant colors. Presto! The image fits right into your color scheme. If the colors in the image are still too strong, reduce the contrast of the image inside the border (or reduce color saturation, whichever looks best to your eye).

If it isn't clear, try again: If you modify an image and the result somehow muddies the colors, or confuses the meaning, then either undo whatever you did, or start over. The penalty for putting unclear images on a web page is visitor confusion. This weakens the impact of the web page, and should be avoided at all costs.

There are many, many different ways to create and edit images, so I cannot provide a comprehensive guide here that will turn you into the World's Greatest Image Creator. It takes time and effort to get good at creating images, and it also takes time and effort to learn the various image creation/editing software available. If you are serious about graphics, and web graphics in particular, here are my recommendations:

Table 4-1: Graphics Tools

Task	Product	More information
Image creation	Fractal Design Painter	http://www.fractal.com
Image editing	Adobe Photoshop	http://www.adobe.com
3D images	Caligari's trueSpace	http://www.caligari.com
Image utility	HyperSnap/32	http://www.kagi.com/authors/gregko
Clip art	PhotoDisc	http://photodisc.connectinc.com/

Graphic Details

The rules I've mentioned so far for working with graphics are fine as far as they go, but what matters in the real world are the steps you take to get the job done. In this section, the focus is on creating and using graphics in lifelike situations. You'll learn how to create graphics and how to organize them on the page, and you'll also learn about some hardware that can make your work with graphics easier.

Graphics and Page Layout

Figure 4-13 shows one of the better-designed Web pages you'll find. It's the ESPN SportsZone home page. Very few web pages can put so much material on one page, and still make it easy to access the information available.

Even though this page is very complicated, the overall design is very simple. The page is divided into three major areas, each of which is subdivided further. The three major areas are:

➡ Banner

➡ Buttons

➡ News

Figure 4-13: A sample web page layout.

The page designer uses a table to divide the web page into these areas. The banner area is a single table cell, with a series of graphic hyperlinks that jump to various web pages. The banner cell uses spanning — a single cell spans three columns. You'll learn how to use cell span later in this section.

The button area also uses a single cell, but this time the cell spans rows, not columns. The buttons could be a stack of individual images, or a single image with hot spots called an image map. You'll learn about creating image maps in the NetKey for this chapter.

The News area comprises several table cells. There is a cell for the major headline of the day, a cell for headlines that serve as hyperlinks to major stories, and a third cell for minor headlines.

You can create a web page similar to the ESPN page using tables in Netscape Gold. Begin by running Netscape Gold. If you created an icon for starting in Edit mode, double-click that icon. If you start in Browse mode, use the File | New Document | Blank menu selection to get to Edit mode.

1. Click the Table button on the toolbar to open the New Table Properties dialog box shown in Figure 4-14. Enter values of **3** for rows, and **3** for columns. Click in the check box to the left of "Table width" to set table width at 100% of the browser window. Do not change any of the other default values in the dialog box. Click the OK button to create the table. This places an empty table on the blank page, as shown in Figure 4-15. The exact width and height of the table and its cells may vary.

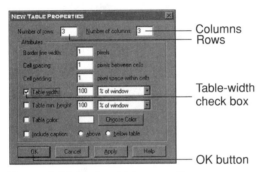

Figure 4-14: Setting table properties.

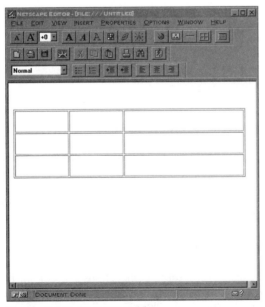

Figure 4-15: An empty table.

2. To get the look of the table from Figure 4-13, you will delete several table cells, and stretch others. To delete the two rightmost cells in the first row, click in the rightmost cell to position the cursor in that cell. Right-click on the rightmost cell to display the context menu shown in Figure 4-16

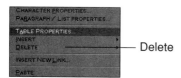 —— Delete

Figure 4-16: A context menu.

3. Click on the Delete menu selection, which displays the delete options in a flyout menu (see Figure 4-17). Click on Cell, which removes the rightmost cell (see Figure 4-18).

 —— Delete cell

Figure 4-17: A flyout menu.

```
+-------+-------+----------+     —— Cell deleted
|       |       |          |
+-------+-------+----------+
|       |       |          |
+-------+-------+----------+
|       |       |          |
+-------+-------+----------+
```

Figure 4-18: The top right cell has been deleted.

4. Repeat the process to delete the middle cell in the top row of the table. Figure 4-19 shows the result: a single cell in the top row.

```
+-------+------------------+     —— Two cells deleted
|       |                  |
+-------+-------+----------+
|       |       |          |
+-------+-------+----------+
|       |       |          |
+-------+-------+----------+
```

Figure 4-19: Only one cell remains in the top row.

5. Right-click in the remaining cell to display the context menu shown in Figure 4-16. Click on Table Properties to display the Table Properties dialog box (see Figure 4-20). If the Cell tab is not

already active, click the Cell tab at the top of the dialog box to switch to Cell properties. At the top of the dialog box, you can set the number or rows and/or columns that a cell should span. In this case, the cell should span three columns. Enter **3** in the text box for column span (see Figure 4-20). Click OK to close the dialog box. Figure 4-21 shows the result.

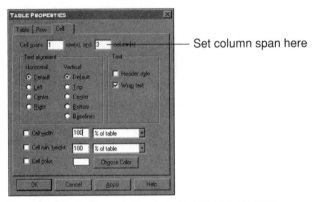
                                                          — Set column span here

Figure 4-20: *Setting a column span of three columns.*

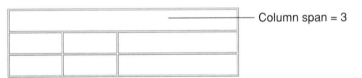
                                                          — Column span = 3

Figure 4-21: *One cell spans three columns.*

6. The next step is to delete the rightmost cell in the second row of the table. Right-click in this cell to display the context menu, and use Delete | Cell menu selection to delete the cell. The result is shown in Figure 4-22.

                                                          — Deleted cell

Figure 4-22: *Another cell deleted.*

7. The middle cell in the middle row should span two columns. Right-click in this cell, then use the Table Properties menu selection to open the Table Properties dialog box. If the Cell tab isn't already active, click it. Enter **2** in the text box for column span. Figure 4-23 shows the result.

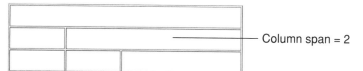

Figure 4-23: *One cell spans two columns.*

8. Delete the leftmost cell in the bottom row of the table (right-click, Delete | Cell). Figure 4-24 shows the result. This may look like you are headed in the wrong direction, but all is well. No matter where in a row you delete a cell, the "empty" space is always at the far right of the row.

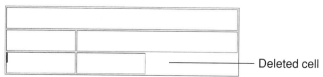

Figure 4-24: *Another deleted cell.*

9. The next step is to make the leftmost cell in the middle row span two rows. Right-click in this cell, select Table Properties, Cell tab, and enter **2** in the textbox for row span. Note that this time, we are setting *row span,* not column span. Figure 4-25 shows the result.

Figure 4-25: *A single cell spans two rows.*

You can view the completed web page for this tutorial on the CD-ROM. Double-click on the file:

```
\tutorial\chap04\Neat table.htm
```

You can click the Cancel button if the connection dialog box appears whenever you are loading a file from the CD-ROM.

You now have an empty table that uses the same overall structure as the ESPN page. You can use similar steps to create almost any kind of complex table. The general process for creating tables that use row and/or column spanning is:

1. Either sketch the table or use a web page as a sample.

2. Determine how many rows and columns you must start with to achieve the final result, and create a table with that number of rows and columns.

3. One row or column at a time, delete cells and change row or column span values until you arrive at the desired result.

 You can also embed tables within tables to make creative page layouts. In fact, you can put a table that uses row and column spans inside another table that also uses row and column spans.

If you want to practice adding text and images to the table you just created, remember to save it to your hard disk. Use the filename `\Gold pages\Sample table.htm`. Figure 4-26 shows an example of what you can do with this kind of table layout.

Figure 4-26: A sample page created from the table.

You can view the completed web page for this tutorial on the CD-ROM. Double-click on the file:

```
\tutorial\chap04\Fancy table.htm
```

There are many, many different ways to lay out a web page. At times, Netscape Gold can seem like such a simple tool. However, if you are willing to spend a little time with it, it will reward you with some very sophisticated web page layouts.

CD-ROM Graphics Collections

One of the biggest problems with graphics is the time and effort it takes to create good ones. To give you some assistance in that direction, I have persuaded several companies that sell collections of graphics to include samples of their wares on the CD-ROM that comes with the book.

Figure 4-27 shows a clip sample from Corel collection of graphics. There are thousands upon thousands of images available from Corel at very modest prices. You'll typically get more than a hundred images on each CD-ROM, and there are hundreds of CD-ROMs to choose from.

Figure 4-27: Sample clip art from Corel.

You can use images as you find them, or you can edit them to suit your needs. One of the most effective edits you can perform is to create a transparent background for the image. Then, no matter what color the page background is, the image will stand out more dramatically. Figure 4-28 shows two examples of transparency with the image from Figure 4-27 — one with a white background, and one with a dark background. You'll learn more about image transparency later in this chapter.

Figure 4-28: Examples of image transparency.

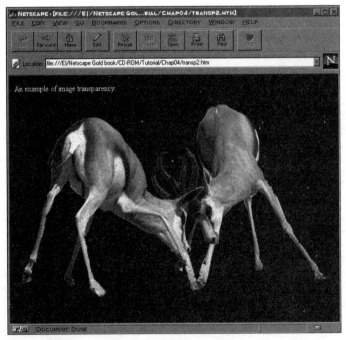

Figure 4-28b: Examples of image transparency.

To view the various images included on the CD-ROM, double-click on the file \graphics\viewme.htm, which allows you to select which graphic vendor's sample images you want to examine. Note that the images you view in this manner are small thumbnails; to see the full-size images, open the folders for the various vendors and double-click on image filenames. For example, to see the full version of the antelope picture, double-click on the file \graphics\corel\antelope.pcd.

Custom Graphics

It's fun and easy to grab graphics from clip art collections, but sometimes a fresh, original graphic is the only solution to your problem. This is particularly true when it comes to such images as company logos, image maps, buttons, and so on. Such images either must match existing images, or must be designed to fit a specific need. Figure 4-26 used several custom images — the logo at the top of the page is a custom image, as is the column of buttons at the left of the page.

I used Fractal Design Painter to create both of these images. Painter, as it is affectionately known, is a tool that allows you to "paint" using your computer. It can create effects that are amazingly similar to natural media tools — from airbrush to oils, from watercolor to chalk, from pencil to charcoal. There are literally thousands of possible variations on the various tools, and you can create artwork that looks just like it was painted by hand. Figure 4-29 shows the start of a painting session.

Figure 4-30 shows an example of the kind of artwork you can create with Painter. As with very few other software packages, your imagination is the only possible limitation. If you can think of it, you can probably do it with Painter.

I use Painter frequently to create original artwork for web pages. Sometimes I just need something quick and easy, such as a bit of text with perhaps a drop shadow (see Figure 4-31). This particular example is a small graphic that I used on the home page for this book, at http://www.olympus.net /biz/mmad/index.htm. Painter will usually allow me to quickly create simple images that still have a certain zing to them.

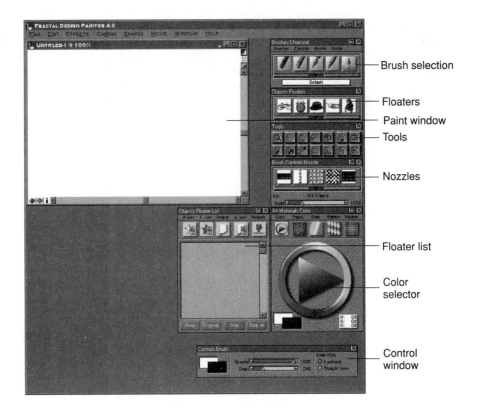

— Brush selection

— Floaters

— Paint window

— Tools

— Nozzles

— Floater list

— Color selector

— Control window

Figure 4-29: Fractal Design Painter interface.

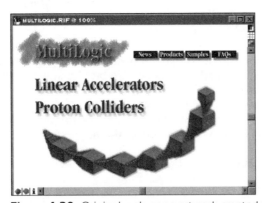

Figure 4-30: Original web page artwork created with Fractal Design Painter.

Netscape Gold News

Figure 4-31: An image I created with Painter.

I don't have nearly enough room to provide a complete tutorial on working with Fractal Design Painter. See the NetKey at the end of this chapter for information about a complete tutorial.

While it's hard to beat the sheer power of Painter for creating original images, I use a different software package for editing images: Adobe Photoshop. For example, I used Photoshop to change the background of the antelope image shown in Figure 4-27 to white. Photoshop contains a wide variety of tools (see Figure 4-32) that give you a great deal of power for editing images. As with Painter, there is also a lot of buried functionality that, once you learn it, gives you an enormous amount of power.

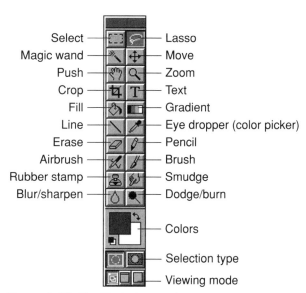

Figure 4-32: The Photoshop tools.

Figure 4-33 shows a typical Photoshop editing session. The current image is the one that I created in Painter. The toolbar is at the left of the window, and several additional palettes are arranged across the bottom of the window. The palettes allow you to set options, change brush size, control how images are pasted from the clipboard, and many other functions.

Photoshop is ideally suited for image editing, although you can also use it create original artwork. Figure 4-34 shows how I modified the original Painter image in Photoshop. I applied a Wind effect, and then used the Smudge tool to drag out wispy tails of color.

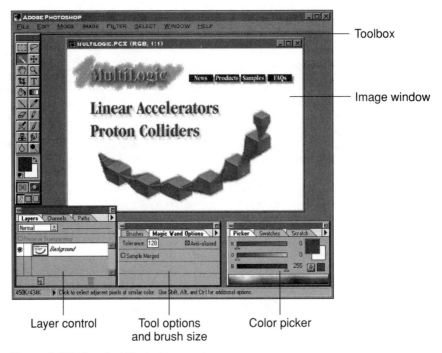

Toolbox

Image window

Layer control

Tool options
and brush size

Color picker

Figure 4-33: A typical Photoshop session.

Figure 4-34: The completed illustration.

There are also many different image editors available, and more and
more of them include specific support for creating images for the Web.
Whichever software package you choose, make sure it has the following
web-specific features:

➡ Supports interlacing of GIF images

➡ Supports transparency for GIF images

➡ Converts readily between 8-bit and 24-bit images

➡ Supports a variety of compression options for JPEG files.

See the section *Graphic Formats* later in this chapter for detailed information about these features.

Scanners

Another way to obtain high-quality images is to scan them into your computer using a color scanner. I use the venerable Hewlett Packard IIIC flatbed scanner, which does a fine job scanning images for both publication and web use. The example of scanning shown here uses my IIIC scanner, but most scanning software has similar features.

Photoshop serves as an excellent front end for scanning. To scan an image, you simply lay the photograph or drawing on the glass bed of the scanner, close the lid, and use the Acquire menu selection in your image editing software. Figure 4-35 shows how to find the correct menu selection in Photoshop.

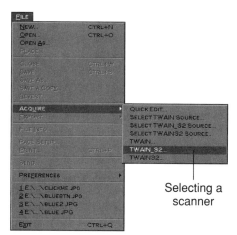

Selecting a scanner

Figure 4-35: *Acquiring an image with a scanner in Photoshop.*

You will see a progress meter of some kind during scanning, either a visual bar or a percentage. Some scanning software automatically runs a preview scan, showing you a low-resolution image of what's on the scanning bed (see Figure 4-36). For this example, I had a photograph handy of some crows in my yard. Most of the scanning bed was empty, because the scanner can scan up to a legal size page (8.5 × 14 inches) at one time. The photograph was only 4 × 6 inches.

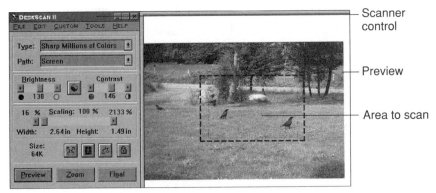

Scanner control

Preview

Area to scan

Figure 4-36: A preview scan.

Many times, you will only want to scan a portion of the image. You can click and drag to mark a rectangle for scanning. If necessary, you can zoom scan to show just that portion of the image. This allows you to mark exactly the part of the image you want to scan. Figure 4-37 shows a zoom scan, where I carefully adjusted the rectangle marking the limit of the scan. I then set for a 300 dpi (dots per inch) scan, and clicked the Final button. The scanner lit up, and in a few seconds I was back in Photoshop with the scanned image in the active document (see Figure 4-38).

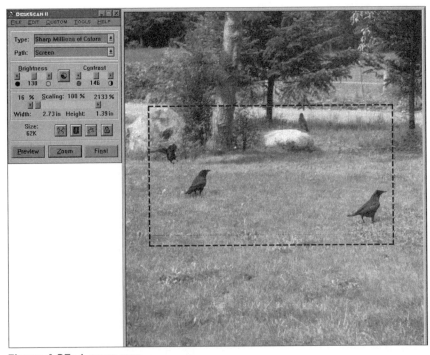

Figure 4-37: A zoom scan.

Figure 4-38: The scanned image in Photoshop.

I then used Photoshop's lasso tool to select one of the crows, copied it to the clipboard, and pasted it into an image with a white background (see Figure 4-39).

Figure 4-39: Pasting a crow into a new image.

I converted the image to 8-bit color, and saved it as a GIF file. I set the background as transparent (see Figure 4-40). Now I have a crow image I can add to any web page. It would make an excellent bullet figure, or you could add a line (like an electric transmission wire) and use it as a section divider for your web pages. Check out the image files

```
\tutorial\chap04\crow1.gif

\tutorial\chap04\crow2.gif (and variations: crow2b.gif,
crow2c.gif, etc.)

\tutorial\chap04\crow3.gif (and variation: crow2b.gif)
```

to see examples of the scan results (see Figure 4-41).

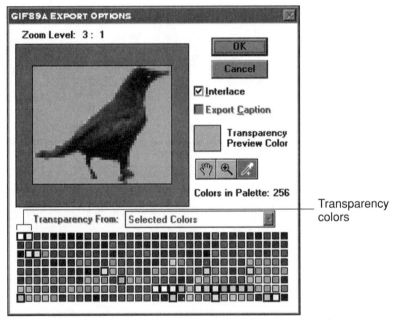

Figure 4-40: Setting a transparent background.

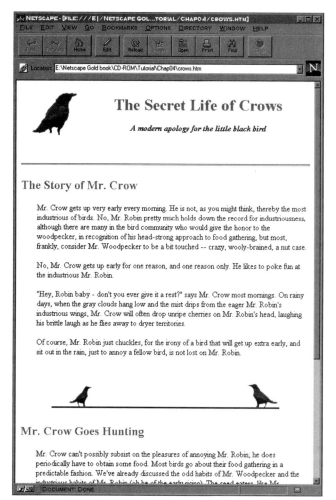

Figure 4-41: Some crow images at work on a web page.

Digitizers

If you are serious about creating original graphics, I also highly recommend switching to a stylus and digitizer (see Figure 4-42). This puts a penlike stylus in your hand, and the pen is much easier to draw with than a mouse. You can choose from a wide variety of tablet sizes, from 4" × 6" to 18" × 18" and larger. I used a CalComp DrawingSlate II to create images for this book and for my web pages, and it has been a flawless performer. For example, the little corn plant in Figure 4-10 was created with the DrawingSlate II and a cordless stylus.

Figure 4-42: A Calcomp drawing tablet can make creating images much easier.

Graphic Formats

I have referred to two kinds of image files in this book: GIF (pronounced *jiff*) and JPEG (pronounced *jay-peg*). These are two common image file formats found on the Web. Another common file format you will encounter in the Windows environment is BMP (pronounced *bump,* but usually called a *bitmap)*. Each of these image formats has certain advantages and disadvantages. This section will help you choose which format to use on your web pages. In most situations, you will find that a combination of GIF and JPEG images works best. BMP files, while common under Windows, are often not supported on the Web.

A file format is simply a method for storing the image data on a disk. However, different file formats store that information in different ways. There are many more image file formats than the three described here — PCX, CGM, EPS, and others. However, the primary image formats for the Web are GIF and JPEG, and thus they are the only file formats covered here in detail.

In order to understand the difference between GIF and JPEG image formats, it's important to know about bit depth and colors. Bit depth is the number of bits that are used to define the colors in an image. Individual bits can have a value of 1 or 0. This is the binary counting system, the number system used by computers.

If an image has a bit depth of 1 (that is, one bit is used for each color), there are only two possible colors (usually, black and white). Each pixel in the image will have a value of 1 or 0.

If an image has a bit depth of 2, there are four possible colors, represented by the following binary numbers:

00

01

10

11

The more bits used (that is, the greater the bit depth), the more colors an image can contain. Table 4-2 shows the number of colors possible for commonly encountered bit depths.

Table 4-2: Bit Depth Chart

Bits	Number of possible colors
1	2
2	4
3	8
4	16
5	32
6	64
7	128
8	256
15	32,768
16	65,536
24	16,777,216

If you are familiar with mathematics, you may have noticed that the formula for the number of colors is 2 raised to the power of the bit depth, or 2^b where b = bit depth.

By far the most common bit depth used for Web images is 8, giving 256 colors. The GIF format uses this bit depth. However, since more colors usually means a better-looking image, there is also an image format (JPEG) that supports 24-bit images.

BMP

The bitmap is the standard image file format for Windows. If you create an image and want to use it as wallpaper, you convert it to the BMP format. However, this file format isn't supported widely on the Web, so if you encounter an image in this (or any other format besides GIF and JPEG) you will need to convert it to a file format supported on the Web. The primary reason that BMP files are not supported on the Web is that the BMP format is uncompressed — for every pixel in the image, there are one to three bytes in the image file. For a large web image, such as 640 × 480, that can amount to more than 900,000 bytes (900K). Such a large file would take far too long to download. By using compression techniques, the GIF and JPEG formats reduce the size of the image file significantly.

GIF

The GIF format supports 8 bits of color depth. This is usually adequate for most images, but some images will not look their best when only 8 bits of color depth are available. For example, a sunset, which contains many subtly different colors, may show banding when reduced to 8-bit color. Figure 4-43 shows two versions of an image. The left image is in 24-bit color, while the right image is in 8-bit color. Note that the reduction in colors resulted in banding effects.

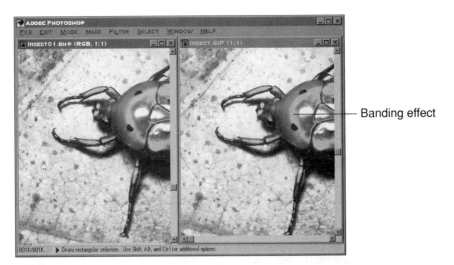

Figure 4-43: A full-color image (left) can look banded when converted to GIF format (right).

However, the GIF format is still extremely useful for many web page images. It uses compression, which results in small file sizes. It is also widely supported by graphic programs. However, the most important feature of the GIF format for web pages is that it supports two key features that are ideal for image on the Web: transparency and interlacing. These features are described in detail in the next section.

JPEG

The JPEG format supports 24 bits of color depth. This allows a rich range of colors in all images. The JPEG format uses compression to reduce the size of an image. As noted earlier, an image that is 640 × 480 pixels has a file size of about 900K. Using JPEG compression, the file size can drop significantly without major harm to the image. Of course, the more you compress the image, the more the image details are lost. Most image software allows you to choose the amount of compression you apply to a JPEG image. For example, Figure 4-44 shows a dialog box from Photoshop, with four different levels of compression available. Figure 4-45 shows an image in two versions, uncompressed on the left and maximally compressed on the right. Note that even with maximum compression, JPEG image quality is still fairly good.

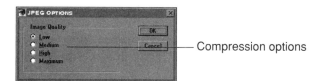

Figure 4-44: The JPEG compression options in Photoshop.

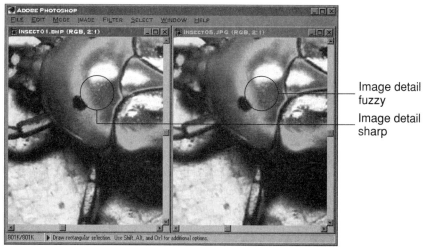

Figure 4-45: An uncompressed image (left) and a maximally compressed JPEG image (right).

Table 4-3 shows how effective JPEG compression can be. The file sizes are for the insect image shown in Figure 4-45. The original file was a 24-bit image.

Table 4-3: Compression and File Sizes

Image format	Compression	File size
BMP	none	900K
GIF	yes	125K
JPEG	low	168K
JPEG	medium	103K
JPEG	high	63K
JPEG	maximum	44K

At maximum compression, the JPEG file size is one-twentieth of the original. This means that a highly compressed JPEG file will take one-twentieth of the time to download, compared to a BMP file. Now you understand why compressed file formats are so desirable for Web pages. The faster an image downloads, the faster the page is useful to the visitor.

When you want transparency, you should automatically use GIF files, as most browsers support transparent GIFs. When you want excellent color, choose JPEG. For other situations, either a GIF or JPEG format will work. When in doubt, create a version of the image in both formats and test to see which yields a smaller file size, and/or a better-looking image.

Transparency and Interlacing

Most image editing software supports adding transparency to GIF files. As shown earlier in this chapter, when you are saving a GIF file in Photoshop, you can select a color in the image to make transparent. Usually, the background color is the transparent color, so that the foreground image is the only part of the image that appears on a page. Figure 4-28 shows an example of transparency.

Interlacing provides a clean way to load images to a web page. Without interlacing, images load from the top down, as shown in Figure 4-46. The figure shows two stages during the download of the image. The top portion shows the image just after it starts to download, the bottom image shows the process about 50 percent complete. While the image downloads, the visitor is left to wonder what the image looks like, and this is not good — the visitor could easily leave without taking the time to find out about your web page! Photoshop, Fractal Design Painter, and many other image editors will save GIF files with interlacing.

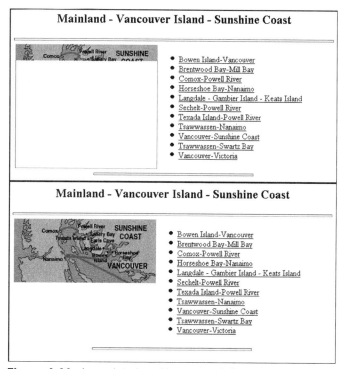

Figure 4-46: A non-interlaced image loads from the top down.

An interlaced image displays nearly all at once, but at a low resolution. This gives the visitor some idea of what the image is, and whether the image is worth waiting for. Figure 4-47 shows a sequence illustrating how an interlaced image reveals a more and more detailed version of itself during the download time.

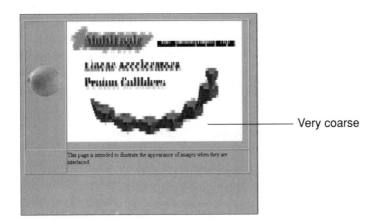

Very coarse

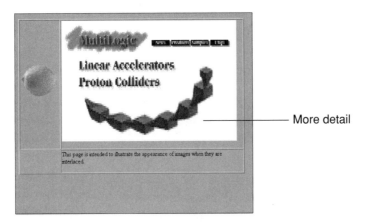

More detail

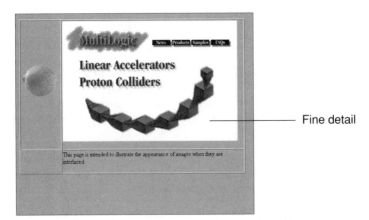

Fine detail

Figure 4-47: Stages in the download of an interlaced image.

The lemon in Figure 4-47 is another example of a transparent image. I used HyperSnap, a shareware utility, to make the otherwise white background of the lemon image transparent.

You can use HyperSnap to add transparency and/or interlacing to existing GIF images. I use HyperSnap routinely, and it does an excellent job. You can download the latest version of HyperSnap from the author's home page at

```
http://www.kagi.com/authors/gregko
```

I have also included a version of HyperSnap on the CD-ROM, in the directory

```
\shareware\HyperSnap
```

To install HyperSnap for the following tutorial:

1. Create a folder on your hard disk called `HyperSnap`.

2. Copy the files from the CD-ROM folder `\shareware\HyperSnap` to the folder you just created on your hard disk. You can simply click and drag to select the files in the CD-ROM folder, and drag them to the hard disk folder (see Figure 4-48).

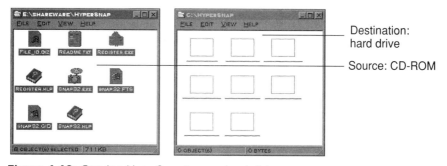

Figure 4-48: Copying HyperSnap to your hard disk.

SNAP32.EXE

To run HyperSnap, double-click on the Snap32.exe icon (see margin). You'll see a blank window. To load a file, use the File | Open menu selection. In the File Open dialog box, locate the CD-ROM file

```
\tutorial\chap04\66.gif
```

Highlight the file and click the Open button to load the file into HyperSnap. You can also simply drag and drop the file from the `\tutorial\chap04\` folder into HyperSnap. Figure 4-49 shows the image loaded into HyperSnap.

Figure 4-49: Loading an image into HyperSnap.

HyperSnap isn't an image editor, so there is nothing to do but save the image, adding transparency and interlacing along the way. Use the File | Save As menu selection to open the Save As dialog box (see Figure 4-50).

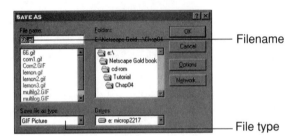

Figure 4-50: Saving a file.

You can't save the file back to the CD-ROM (CDs are read only), so change to drive C:, and the \Gold Pages folder. Make sure the file type at lower left in the Save As dialog box is GIF Picture; if it isn't, click the drop-down and select GIF Picture. Now click the Options button, which displays the dialog box shown in Figure 4-51.

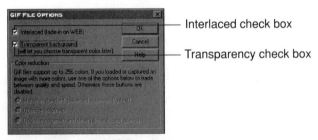

Figure 4-51: Setting GIF options.

There are two check boxes at the top of the dialog box. The first one sets interlacing, and the second one sets image transparency. For this example, both check boxes should be checked. If they are not, check them now. Click OK to continue.

The lower portion of the dialog box is active only when you are saving a 24-bit image (which supports more than 16 million colors) in the GIF format (which only supports 256 colors). You can choose from three different methods for reducing the colors in the image. From top to bottom, the radio buttons direct HyperSnap to use progressively more sophisticated (and slower) methods for converting colors. For best results, use the bottom radio button, which says "Optimize colormap and dither (slowest, best quality)."

If the file already exists, you will be warned about overwriting the existing file. Otherwise, you will return to the HyperSnap main window. Note that the top of the main window is now blinking, and asking you to please click and select the color that is to be the transparent color. The cursor changes to a cross-hair. For this example, the transparent color is the background color (white), so click anywhere on the white background. This displays a dialog box (see Figure 4-52) that asks you to confirm that you have picked the correct color. If the color is correct, click the Accept button. If not, click the Change button and click to select the correct color.

 —— Transparent color

Figure 4-52: Confirming transparency color.

If you forget to click and select a color, the file will not be saved. When this happens, you will probably find yourself hunting around for the missing image file. HyperSnap is very patient. When you remember that you forgot to pick the color, just go back and click on the background color, and HyperSnap will save the file for you.

Figure 4-53 shows a sample file I created that illustrates one of the pitfalls of image transparency. The background of the image at top left is white (yes, this is the same image you just worked with). Since some of the pixels in the image proper are also white, when you make white the transparent color, all of the white pixels become transparent — not just the background.

To correct this problem, I used Photoshop to convert the background color to a color that is not otherwise used in the image (in this example, a light blue). Since the image was already a 256-color (8-bit) image, and most likely using all 256 colors, I first converted the image to 24 bits of color. I then selected the background using the Photoshop Magic Wand tool, and changed the color using Edit | Fill. I chose light blue because, after looking carefully at an enlargement of the image (Control + Plus key), it was clear that there are no blue pixels in the image. Now, when the image is saved with transparency, only the background will be transparent. The images at lower right in Figure 4-53 shows the result of changing the background color.

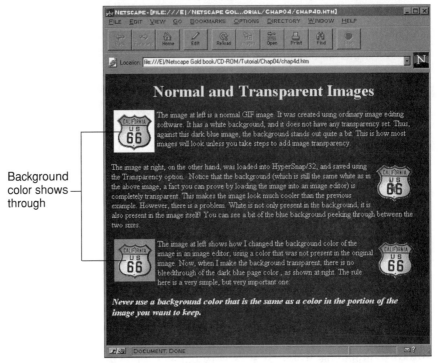

Background color shows through

Figure 4-53: The pitfalls of image transparency.

If an image does not contain a solid background, you can use an image editor to select just the background, and fill it with a solid color. For best results, use a software package that allows you to zoom in while you work; selecting irregular areas for filling requires a very steady hand!

Graphic Hotspots: Image Maps

Graphics on a web page are great, but if you can put them to work, they are even better. You learned in earlier chapters how to add a hyperlink to an image. Now, you'll learn how to add multiple hyperlinks to a single image. This is called an image map, and you'll use a freeware utility called MapTHIS! to create one.

MapTHIS!

You can download a copy of MapTHIS from

```
http://www.incontext.ca/demo/mapthis.html
```

or you can install the version I included on the CD-ROM. To install the CD-ROM version, use the same process you used for HyperSnap. MapTHIS is located in the folder

```
\shareware\HyperSnap
```

To install MapTHIS for the following tutorial:

1. Create a folder on your hard disk called MapTHIS.

2. Copy the files from the CD-ROM folder \shareware\MapTHIS to the folder you just created on your hard disk. You can simply click and drag to select the files in the CD-ROM folder, and drag them to the hard disk folder (see Figure 4-54).

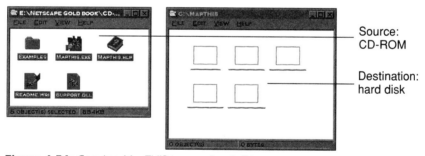

Figure 4-54: Copying MapTHIS to your hard disk.

To complete the following tutorial, also copy a file from the CD-ROM to your hard disk. Open the folders \tutorial\chap04 and \Gold Pages on your desktop, and then drag the files imap.htm and multilg2.gif from the CD-ROM folder to \Gold Pages. Now you are ready to start the tutorial.

Double-click the MapTHIS icon to run the program (mapthis.exe). Figure 4-55 shows what you will see: A blank window. To learn what the various buttons on the toolbar are for, pass your mouse cursor over each button.

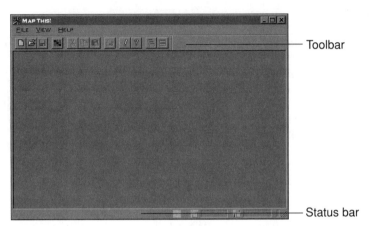

Toolbar

Status bar

Figure 4-55: The MapTHIS window.

Use the File | New menu selection to start a new image map file. MapTHIS will display the dialog box shown in Figure 4-56, proving that it does have a sense of humor. Click the Let's go find one! button. This displays the Open Existing Image dialog box. Locate one of the files you recently copied, \Gold Pages\multilg2.gif, and click it to highlight it. Click the Open button to continue.

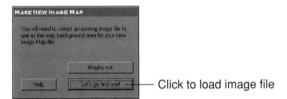

Click to load image file

Figure 4-56: Starting a new image map.

MapTHIS loads the image file, and displays it as shown in Figure 4-57. Click the maximize button on the image's window (not on the main MapTHIS window!), and stretch the size of the MapTHIS main window to roughly match the size of the image. You'll know you have it the correct size when both the horizontal and vertical scroll bars disappear (see Figure 4-58).

Before adding hot spots to the image, it's a good idea to specify basic information about the map. Use the Edit | Edit Map Info menu selection to display the dialog box shown in Figure 4-59, and enter the data as shown. Feel free to use your author name. In the text box for Title, enter MultiLogic. Later, when referring to the map on a web page, the title will be the map's name. In the text box for Default URL, enter http://www.multilogic.com.

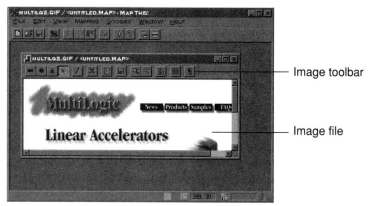

Image toolbar

Image file

Figure 4-57: The image file is visible.

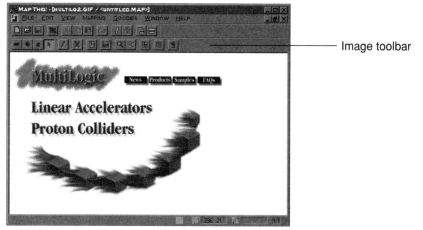

Image toolbar

Figure 4-58: Adjusting window size.

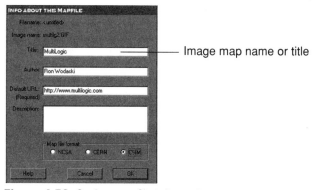

Image map name or title

Figure 4-59: Setting mapfile information.

The default URL is the URL to load whenever the background of the image is clicked (that is, anywhere outside the hot spots). There are three radio buttons at the bottom of the dialog box. These determine what kind of image map file you will create. Click the third radio button, CSIM, to create a Client-Side Image Map. See the section, "Your ISP and image maps," later in this chapter for more information about other kinds of image maps.

Client-side refers to image maps that reside on the client side of the network connection. That's your computer. Server-side image maps put the map information on the server side of the connection. That's a web server. Client-side maps are the easiest, because you don't have to fuss with issues related to the server. Server-side maps can be a hassle, because the exact requirements for server-side maps vary from server to server. In fact, some ISPs (Internet Service Providers) don't even support server-side image maps at all! Client-side image maps are supported by the newer versions of most browsers, but many older browsers don't support them at all.

You are now ready to create the hot spots. Click the rectangle tool at the far left of the lower toolbar (see Figure 4-60). The cursor changes to a small rectangle with an attached arrow (see margin). You will use this tool to drag out rectangles that will become hot spots when linked to specific URLs.

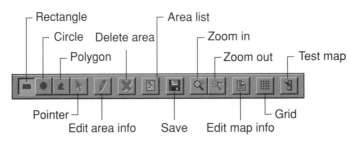

Figure 4-60: Activating the rectangle tool.

The first four hot spots to create are those for the four black buttons at the upper right of the image. The buttons are small, but you can use the Zoom In tool (see margin) to increase the apparent size of the GIF image. Click the Zoom In tool one time to zoom in as shown in Figure 4-61.

To create a hot spot, align the cursor with the top left corner of the first black button, as shown in Figure 4-61. Click and drag until the arrow portion of the cursor lines up with the lower right corner of the button (see Figure 4-62). Release the mouse button to complete the hot spot. If the hot spot isn't exactly right, you can change the size of the area using the handles at the corners and sides, as shown in Figure 4-62.

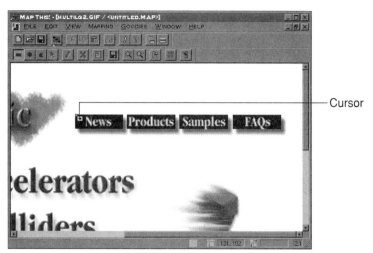

Figure 4-61: Zooming in.

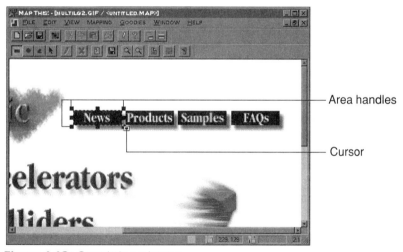

Figure 4-62: Completing a button.

Create three more hot spots for the remaining black buttons. Figure 4-63 shows the result. You can zoom back out to see the full image by clicking the Zoom Out tool (immediately to the right of the Zoom In tool). Create additional hot spots for the two large text blocks ("Linear Accelerators" and "Proton Colliders"). Add one more hot spot for the company name at top left. Figure 4-64 shows all of the hot spots created.

Figure 4-63: Four button hot spots.

Figure 4-64: All hot spots created.

So far, you have defined the position of the hot spots, but you have not linked them to any specific URL. If you tried to save the map file at this point, you would get a warning telling you that you have not defined the links.

To add a link, double-click on the company name hot spot to open the Area Settings dialog box shown in Figure 4-65. Simply type the appropriate URL into the top text box. For this example, pretend that the URL for a company profile for MultiLogic is

```
http://www.multilogic.com/profile.htm
```

and enter that URL into the top text box (refer to Figure 4-65). You are not required to use a complete URL; if the linked document is in the same directory, you could use a relative pathname:

```
profile.htm
```

However, it is safer to use a full URL until you test the shorter version after uploading the completed web page.

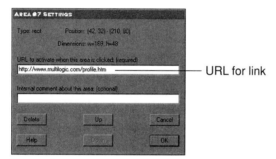

URL for link

Figure 4-65: Adding a link to a hot spot.

You can continue to add links to the various hot spots in this manner, or you can use the View I Area List menu selection to open the Area List window (see Figure 4-66). This lists the hot spots by number, and shows the link (if one exists) for each hot spot. Hot spots that do no yet have a link are shown in red, with an exclamation point. To add links to the various hot spots using the Area list, simply highlight the hot spot listing, and click the Edit button to open the Area Settings dialog box. You can also delete a hot spot using the Area List window.

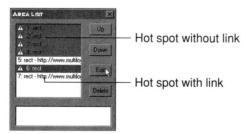

Hot spot without link

Hot spot with link

Figure 4-66: The Area List window.

Add the following links to the various hot spots:

News	`http://www.multilogic.com/news.htm`
Products	`http://www.multilogic.com/products.htm`
Samples	`http://www.multilogic.com/samples.htm`
FAQs	`http://www.multilogic.com/faq.htm`
Linear Accelerators	`http://www.multilogic.com/linear.htm`
Proton Colliders	`http://www.multilogic.com/proton.htm`

This completes the image map. You can, if appropriate, create circular, elliptical, or polygonal hot spots as well as rectangles. Simply select the appropriate tool from the toolbar before drawing the shape.

To save the client-side image map, use the File I Save As menu selection to open the Save As dialog box. Save the file as `mlogic.htm` into the `\Gold Pages` folder. Make sure that the CSIM radio button at the bottom of the Save As dialog box is clicked! Use the File I Exit menu selection to exit MapTHIS.

Adding the map to a web page

Double-click on the `mlogic.htm` file you just saved to open it in Netscape Gold in Browse mode. (Click the Cancel button if you are not online.) Figure 4-67 shows the result: It's not much to look at! The image map codes are hidden, and will only show up in Edit mode. Click the Edit button (see margin) to switch to Edit mode.

Figure 4-67: Viewing a map file in Browse mode.

When you save the map file, you are only saving a text file. The image is not saved in the map file. The image is added to a standard web page, and then the map file's contents are added to the web page. This is a little backward from what you might expect, but it works. The next section provides the details.

Figure 4-68 shows the appearance of the client-side map file in Edit mode. The little yellow tags across the top of the page represent the map codes. Each tag equals one line of map code. If you were to open the map code in a text editor, you would see this:

```
<BODY>
<MAP NAME="MultiLogic">
<!-- #$-:Image Map file created by Map THIS! -->
<!-- #$-:Map THIS! free image map editor by Todd C. Wilson -->
<!-- #$-:Please do not edit lines starting with "#$" -->
<!-- #$VERSION:1.20 -->
<!-- #$AUTHOR:Ron Wodaski -->
<!-- #$DATE:Thu Jul 11 12:06:00 1996 -->
<!-- #$PATH:E:\Netscape Gold book\CD-ROM\Tutorial\Chap04\ -->
<!-- #$GIF:multilg2.GIF -->
<AREA SHAPE=RECT COORDS="249,51,298,65" HREF=news.htm>
<AREA SHAPE=RECT COORDS="302,51,351,65" HREF=products.htm>
<AREA SHAPE=RECT COORDS="355,51,404,65" HREF=samples.htm>
<AREA SHAPE=RECT COORDS="409,51,458,65" HREF=faq.htm>
<AREA SHAPE=RECT COORDS="42,102,316,134"
HREF=http://www.multilogic.com/linear.htm>
<AREA SHAPE=RECT COORDS="40,146,281,186"
HREF=http://www.multilogic.com/proton.htm>
<AREA SHAPE=RECT COORDS="42,32,210,80"
HREF=http://www.multilogic.com/profile.htm>
<AREA SHAPE=default HREF=http://www.multilogic.com>
</MAP></BODY>
```

— Tag

Figure 4-68: Clicking on a tag.

The lines that start with "<!--" are all comments, and are ignored by browsers. However, they contain information that MapTHIS uses, so you shouldn't delete those lines. To check that the little yellow tags indeed contain one line each of map codes, double-click on (for example) tag # 11, counting from left to right. Figure 4-68 shows the exact tag to double-click. Figure 4-69 shows the window that pops up showing you what the tag contains. You can, if necessary, edit the text and save it using this window.

— Tag contents

Figure 4-69: The contents of a tag.

I have created a sample web page (which you earlier copied to your hard disk) to which we will now add the client-side map codes.

1. Click at the left of the line of yellow tags, and then Shift + click at the right end to select all the tags (see Figure 4-70).

Figure 4-70: Selecting tags.

2. Press Control + C to copy the tags to the clipboard.

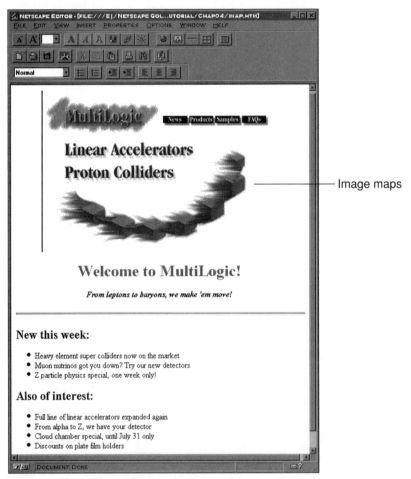

Image maps

Figure 4-71: The `imap.htm` file in Edit mode.

3. Use the File | Open File menu selection to display the Open dialog box. Locate the file `imap.htm`, which you copied from the CD-ROM to the `\Gold Pages` folder earlier, and highlight it by clicking on it. Click the Open button to load the file into a new Netscape Edit mode window (see Figure 4-71).

4. Position the cursor to the left of the large image at the top of the page. Press Control + V to paste the tags into the page. Position the cursor at the right edge of the line of tags, and press Enter to add a line break. You will not see a change when you add the line break, but it will make the next step easier by separating the tags from the image reference in the source file. Figure 4-72 shows the result.

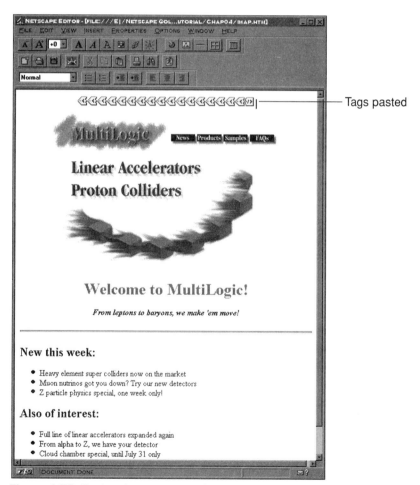

Tags pasted

Figure 4-72: Pasting the tags to a web page.

5. Save your work, and use the View | Edit Document Source menu selection to open the HTML source code in Notepad (see Figure 4-73). Locate the line shown highlighted in Figure 4-73, which is the HTML tag for the large image. The exact text is

```
<IMG SRC="multilg2.GIF" HEIGHT=320 WIDTH=480>
```

However, the position of the text may vary from what you see in Figure 4-73. It may be located further to the right; use the scroll bar at the bottom of the Notepad window to check.

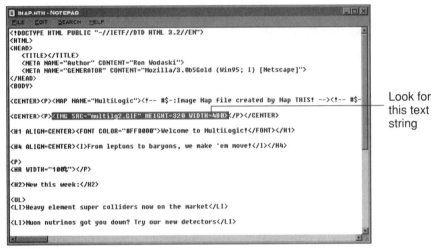

Figure 4-73: Viewing document source in Notepad.

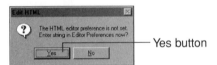

Figure 4-73b: This dialog box appears when no default editor is set.

Revise the text as follows; the new additions are shown in bold type.

```
<IMG ISMAP USEMAP="#MultiLogic" SRC="multilg2.GIF" BORDER=0
HEIGHT=320 WIDTH=480>
```

These additions have the following functions:

ISMAP   Tells the browser that this image is used as
                               an image map.

USEMAP="#MultiLogic" Tells the browser to use the map defined in the codes you pasted in earlier.

BORDER=0 Tells the browser not to display a border around the image. Borders should only be used around images that link to a single URL.

Use the File | Save menu selection in Notepad to save your changes. Close Notepad (File | Exit), and click in the Netscape Edit mode window to activate it. You'll see the dialog box shown in Figure 4-74; click the Yes button to continue.

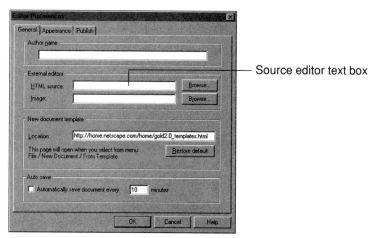

Source editor text box

Figure 4-73c: Viewing document source in Notepad.

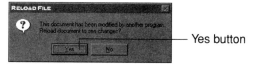

Yes button

Figure 4-74: You'll see this dialog box when you change the document source in Notepad.

When you select the View | Edit Document Source menu selection, you may see the dialog box shown in Figure 4-73b. The dialog box is simply telling you that you have not yet told Netscape Gold what program to use to edit document source. Click the Yes button to continue. This opens the Editor Preferences dialog box (see Figure 4-73c). In the text box to the right of "HTML source," type in notepad.exe, and click OK to continue.

When Netscape Gold is done updating your changes from Notepad, you'll see a thin blue line around the image, indicating it is an image map (see Figure 4-75). To test the client-side image map, click the Browse button (see margin) to switch to Browse mode. When the cursor passes over a hot spot, it should change to a pointing hand, and the URL of the link should show up in the status bar of Netscape Gold (see Figure 4-76).

Blue line

Figure 4-75: The completed image map.

Your ISP and image maps

Client-side image maps aren't the only kind of image maps. There are times and situations where you may want to use a server-side image map. There are two kinds of server-side image maps, called conventions: CERN (Europe), and NCSA (North America). These are simply two different ways of defining an image map, created by two different worldwide standards bodies. Even though one standard is for Europe and one for North America, you may find either standard in use on any given web server. The only way to find out which standard is used on a server is to ask the webmaster for that server. MapTHIS can save an image map using either convention. Use the Edit | Edit Map Info menu selection to choose which convention to use.

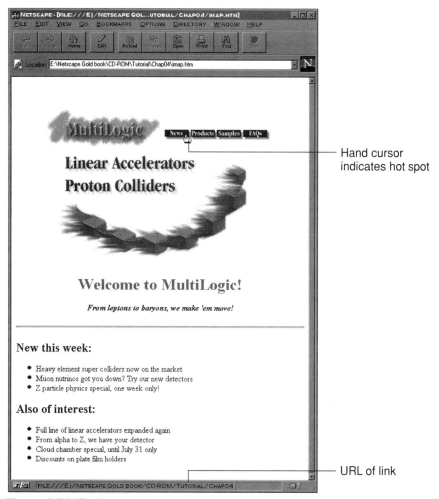

Figure 4-76: The image map in Browse mode.

Server-side image maps are a completely different kettle of fish from client-side image maps. The rules for implementing them vary from one ISP to the next. Thus, I cannot give you specific information about how to get server-side image maps up and running. That's why I provided the detailed tutorial on client-side image maps: They are much easier to create.

In fact, some ISPs don't support server-side image maps at all. Contact your ISP, or visit your ISP's FAQ (Frequently Asked Questions) pages to find out if server-side image maps are used, and, if so, how you can use them.

Background Graphics

Netscape Gold allows you to use images as a background, instead of simple colors. I have included two sample web pages in the `\tutorial\chap04` folder that show how to, and how not to, use background images.

Figure 4-77 shows an example of a page that uses a poor choice of background image. In this example, the image map has quite a few off-white pixels that stand out like beach sand on a car seat — very, very annoying. A better solution is to use a lighter background, as shown in Figure 4-78.

The basic rules for using a background image are:

➡ The background image should stay in the background visually. It should not compete with the text or other foreground images for attention. You can achieve this by lightening the image or blurring the image in an image editor.

➡ The background image should not conflict with the edge colors of transparent images.

➡ Adjust the text colors if necessary to accommodate the background image's colors.

➡ The edges of the tiles should match if you want a seamless background.

You can solve background image problems in many ways. You can change text color, you can change the colors in foreground images, and so on. For example, Figure 4-79 shows a revised version of the page in Figure 4-77 that uses a different transparent image (no drop shadows, but the implications of a lemon are perhaps worse!), and a version of the background that is lighter than the dark background of Figure 4-77, and darker than the version shown in Figure 4-78.

To add background images, use the Properties | Document menu selection to open the Document Properties dialog box shown in Figure 4-80. Click the Use Image check box near the bottom of the dialog box, and use the Browse for File button to locate the background image you plan to use. As with all images, I highly recommend that you copy your background image to the working directory for the web page before adding it, so that Netscape Gold uses the correct relative pathname.

Figure 4-77: A poor choice for a background image.

Figure 4-78: A better choice for a background image.

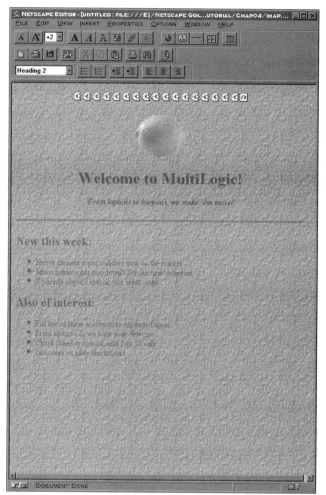

Figure 4-79: A compromise background image, and a new logo.

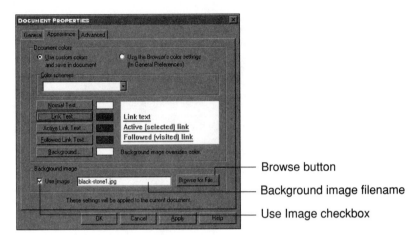

Browse button
Background image filename
Use Image checkbox

Figure 4-80: Adding a background image.

You can view the sample web page with backgrounds on the CD-ROM. Double-click on the files:

```
\tutorial\chap04\backgrnd.htm
\tutorial\chap04\backgrn2.htm
```

The background images for these pages are actually very small. The image gets repeated across the page to create the background. You can use this in different ways. For example, the page in Figure 4-81 uses a long, horizontal image, (1024 pixels wide) shown in Figure 4-82, to create an interesting background. You would use a table to force the text to stay away from the design at the left edge. Put nonbreaking spaces (Insert | Non-breaking space menu selection) in the left column of the table to control the width of the column and thus the spacing between the left margin of the window and the start of the text in column two of the table. You can also use an image in one of the left-column tables to control column width (see Figure 4-83).

You can view several sample web pages with the left margin background on the CD-ROM. Double-click on the following files to see different examples of the background in use.

```
\tutorial\chap04\chap4a.htm
\tutorial\chap04\chap4b.htm
\tutorial\chap04\chap4c.htm
```

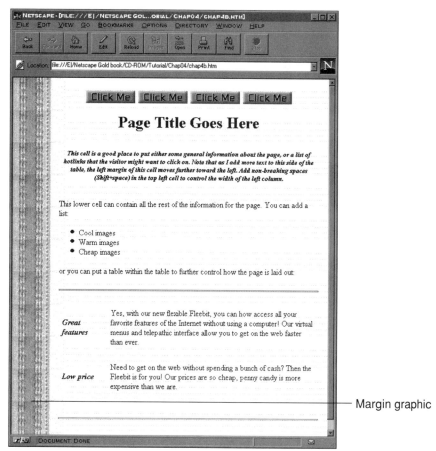

────── Margin graphic

Figure 4-81: A page with a left margin background graphic.

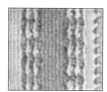

Figure 4-82: The image used in the background of Figure 4-81.

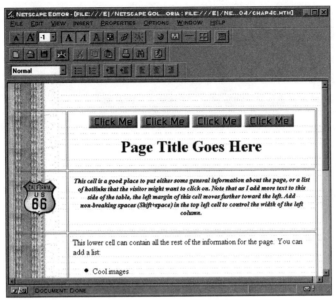

Figure 4-83: Using an image in a left column cell to control column width.

You can experiment with other kinds of background images. Try replacing the background image in any of the preceding examples with these image files:

```
blue.jpg
blue2.jpg
```

Graphics in general, and background images in particular, offer a great many ways to enhance your web pages. The limits are only as close as the furthest reaches of your imagination.

NetKey #4: Fractal Design Painter

In this chapter, you have learned how to use graphics and some graphics tools to create powerful web pages. This chapter is the longest one in the book, and for a good reason: There is an almost infinite variety of possibilities when working with graphics. One of the most powerful programs for creating web images is Fractal Design Painter. NetKey #4 offers a detailed look at how you can use Painter to create awesome graphics.

Using NetKey #4

To begin, double-click on the file

```
/tutorial/index.htm
```

on the CD-ROM, which will automatically start Netscape Gold in Browse mode. As usual, if you do not want to connect, click the Cancel button when the connection dialog box appears. The appearance of the file /tutorial/index.htm is shown in Figure 4-84.

The file /tutorial/index.htm contains hyperlinks to the NetKeys for every chapter in the book. To learn how to create a complex image with Painter, click the hyperlink for Chapter 4, Fractal Design Painter. The first NetKey page for this chapter is shown in Figure 4-85. To explore this NetKey, simply click on any and every hyperlink (usually underlined text) that strikes your fancy.

To access the NetKey page for Chapter 4 directly, double-click on the file /tutorial/chap04/webpage.htm.

Creating Cool Web Pages
with Netscape Gold and JavaScript

a book by Ron Wodaski

I have created a bunch of tutorials (I call them NetKeys, but that's just to be flashy; they really are just tutorials!) for my book. There is one tutorial for each chapter:

	Chapter 1	**Mining for Gold** NetKey #1: Navigating with Gold
	Chapter 2	**Your First Home Page** NetKey #2: Publishing with Gold
	Chapter 3	**Master of the Web Page** NetKey #3: Summary of web page tools
	Chapter 4	**Graphics Make the Page** NetKey #4: Fractal Design Painter
	Chapter 5	**Jump into JavaScript** NetKey #5: Netscape Features and Plug-ins
	Chapter 6	**The Ultimate Web Page** NetKey #6: Mastering Tables
	Chapter 7	**JavaScript: Web Power Unleased** NetKey #7: JavaScript Quick Reference
	Appendix	**CD-ROM Contents**

I have also included a series of templates that you can use to quickly create customized web pages. Just replace the text and images in the templates with your own text and images. You may also want to check out the vast array of graphics I've included on the CD-ROM.

Figure 4-84: The web page for access to NetKey pages.

Creating Cool Navigator Gold Web Pages

NetKey #4: Fractal Design Painter

The items in the following table summarize the steps needed to create a sample web image with Fractal Design Painter. See chapter 4 in the book, which explains how this image is used as an image map on a web page.

This page is the home page of what amounts to a complete web site, with a separate web page for each of the topics listed below. Instead of being on the web, however, it is located on the CD-ROM that comes with the book Creating Cool Web Pages with Netscape Gold and JavaScript.

This group of web pages is called a "NetKey" because it offers you some keys to using the Internet effectively. There is a separate NetKey for each chapter in the book. All it really is, is a tutorial. To follow the tutorial, visit each of the topics below, preferrably in the order they are listed. If you have comments about this tutorial, or the book, send email to *ronw@olympus.net* (that's the author).

1	**Welcome to Painter**	• Selecting brushes • Changing colors
2	**Painting with Painter**	• Scribbling • Image hose • Fonts
3	**Adding Text**	• Placing text • Grouping text • Collapsing text • Surface Texture: 3D • Drop shadow
4	**Adding Buttons**	• Selecting area • Floating • Changing size • Filling with color
5	**Finishing Up**	• Duplicating buttons • Adding text to buttons • Adding hot spot text • Saving as GIF file

Figure 4-85: The NetKey page for Chapter 4.

Jump into JavaScript

In This Chapter

Understanding objects

Having fun with JavaScript

Enhancing forms with JavaScript

NetKey #5: Netscape features and plug-ins

What Is the Object?

The phrase *Object Oriented Programming* is tossed around quite a bit these days, but you are not alone if you wonder what the heck it means. Every year, someone announces that this will be the year of Object Oriented Programming. Can it be mere coincidence that the abbreviation for Object Oriented Programming is OOP?

As in, OOPs, not this year!

The cynics have had their day; OOP is finally here. It arrived in the form of the Java programming language, with JavaScript riding Java's coattails. The best part of Java is that programmers can use it to create **applets**, which are little bitty programs. A full-size, full-featured program is an application; a little program is therefore called an applet. Your word processor is an application; a Java program that makes a button light up when you pass the cursor over it is an applet. Applets and objects are the virtual meat and potatoes of this chapter.

And none of this is to be confused with that old-time candy favorite, Applets and Cotlets™. As for JavaScript, it is a little like the box that the candy comes in. You can use JavaScript to easily and quickly add Java applets (or Java applications, for that matter) to your web pages. You can also use JavaScript to add little goodies to your web pages — from simple buttons to complex things like clocks.

An applet is a kind of object, which after all is the object of Object Oriented Programming. From this point forward, I will quit trying to confuse you with OOP-speak, and start showing you how to do some OOP of your own. In this chapter, you will learn the rudiments of working with Java applets, as well as some useful applications for JavaScript. In-depth coverage of JavaScript is located in Chapter 7.

JavaScript: Fun with Applets

An applet begins as an idea in the mind of a Java programmer, who then creates the applet using the Java programming language. The result is called **source code**, and it lives in a file with the extension .java. That's the hard part; programming with Java is like programming with C++: it's full-steam-ahead, hard-core programming. When the .java file is ready, the programmer compiles it (that is, runs a program that converts it from the Java language to computer language). The applet is then delivered to you, the web page creator, in a tidy little package with the extension .class.

If you aren't familiar with the term C++, you might like to know that it is the programming language used by many (perhaps even most) of the programmers who write personal computer software. It is based on a previous language called C, which was one step up from B (that is, the BASIC programming language). In plain speaking terms, C++ is a complex, powerful language that takes a lot of effort to master.

An Applet tour

Applets can bring a web page to life. A few examples will show you what kind of features you can add to a web page with applets. Figure 5-1 shows an extremely simple Java applet: a button with a rotating animation (see Figure 5-2 for a detail of the animation). If you want to actually see the button rotate, visit the site at http://www.onr.com/user/jeff/pegdelux.htm.

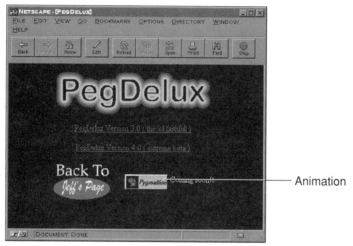

Figure 5-1: A page that uses a simple Java object/applet.

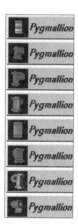

Figure 5-2: Close-up view of the Java animation.

Figure 5-3 shows a more sophisticated use of an applet. The game shown is called Go, an oriental game that has many subtleties; you can play it by visiting

```
http://vanbc.wimsey.com/~igors/java/go.html
```

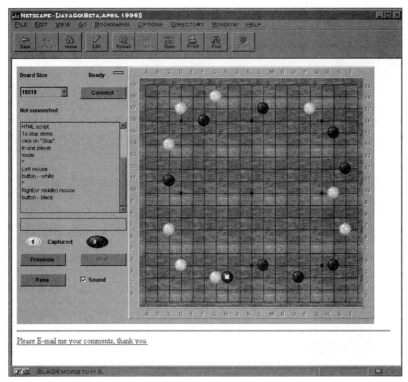

Figure 5-3: A Go game created with Java.

Figure 5-4 shows an applet from the ESPN home page, created specifically to enhance access to coverage of Olympic events. The left portion of the applet displays an advertisement, while the right portion displays a sequence of text descriptions of online services available. As shown in the two-image sequence in Figure 5-4, each description fades into view. There are also two buttons at the bottom. Click the left button, which takes you to ESPN's coverage of the event. Clicking the right button causes the Java applet to appear in a separate window on your desktop.

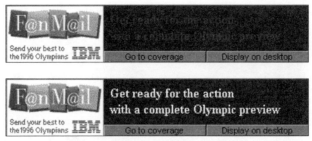

Figure 5-4: A Java applet put to serious use.

Whether you use Java applets for page decoration, such as the flashing text in Figure 5-5, or for serious web page enhancements (Figure 5-6), or for games (Figure 5-7), the hard part is always the Java programming. However, with hundreds of shareware and freeware applets available, it takes just a few minutes to download Java applets that you can use on your own pages.

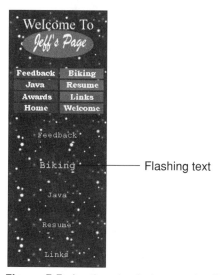

Flashing text

Figure 5-5: Another simple Java applet: flashing text.

Working with Java applets

As you can see from the examples above, a Java applet can be just about anything. Because Java is a bona fide programming language, you can create any kind of program with Java. You could create a Java word processor, for example, or a program to animate a week's worth of weather maps. Spreadsheets, animation, games — the only limitation is the programmer's imagination.

Although it takes a lot of work and effort to create an applet using the Java programming language, it couldn't be easier to add an applet to your web pages. Many, many shareware and freeware Java applets are available on the Web. You can use some simple techniques to add any applet to a web page.

For an overview of the latest and greatest Java applets and applications, visit

```
http://www.jars.com/1.htm
```

where you can find links to the top 1 percent rated Java applets courtesy of JARS, the Java Applet Rating Service. You'll also find links to the top 10 percent of applets and other methods for finding some of the best applets available.

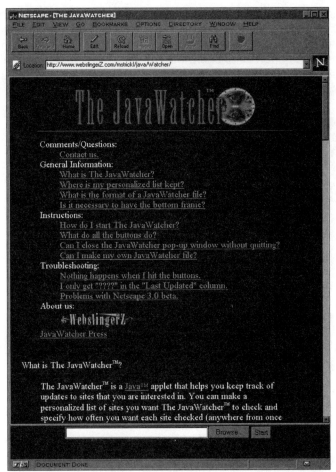

Figure 5-6: Visit http://www.webslingerZ.com/mstrickl/java/Watcher for a Java application to organize your web activities.

Using HTML tags

Newer versions of web browsers, such as Netscape Gold, support Java applets. However, not all of the visitors to your web page will be using such browsers, so not all visitors to your page will be able to see the Java application. If you use a Java applet that includes, for example, hyperlinks, be sure to provide an alternative method for getting to the linked web page, such as a text hyperlink.

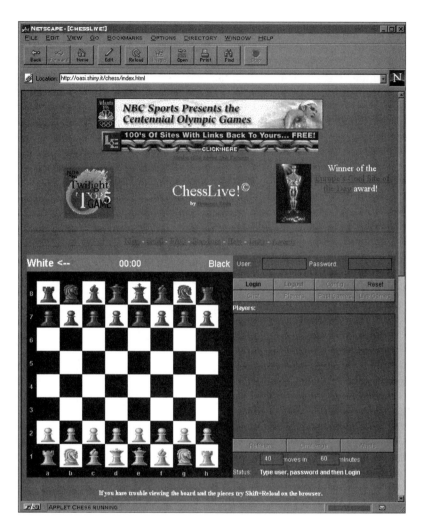

Figure 5-7: Care for a game of Java chess? Visit http://oasi.shiny.it/chess/index.html

To add the applet to the page, you will insert several *tags* on the web page. Normally, HTML tags are hidden when you are working with Netscape Gold. For example, when you add an image, you simply specify the filename and image options using a dialog box. However, when Netscape Gold saves the web page to disk, it uses HTML (HyperText Markup Language) tags to describe the image file and its options. A typical image might have an HTML tag that looks like this:

```
<IMG SRC="boat01.GIF" HEIGHT=120 WIDTH=480>
```

Just about everything you put on a web page has some kind of tag associated with it. A tag starts with this symbol, <, and it ends with this symbol, >. To make text into a Heading 1, for example, Netscape Gold uses two tags. The first tag, in bold in the following example, "turns on" the Heading 1 style. The second tag, also in bold, turns it off. This concept of turning something on, and then turning it off, is common in HTML. In most cases, the tag for turning something on is the same as the tag for turning it off, except for the added slash.

```
<H1>This text will be in the Heading 1 style.</H1>
```

Tags may be upper or lower case. They can be simple, like the Heading 1 tags, or complex, like the image tag in the first example. If you are interested in learning all about HTML, I recommend the book *Creating Cool Web Pages with HTML* by Dave Taylor, published by IDG Books Worldwide.

Adding an applet to a web page

To add an applet, you use the <APPLET> tag to start, and the </APPLET> tag to finish. In between, you will specify parameters that tell the applet exactly how to do its job. Netscape Gold requires that you add tags one at a time. The complete list of tags you will use to add the example applet is shown in Listing 5-1.

Listing 5-1: Adding an applet to a web page

```
<APPLET code=bounce.class width=480 height=240>
<PARAM name=ITEMS value=6>
<PARAM name=PATH value="bird/">
<PARAM name=PREFIX value="bd">
<PARAM name=CAPTION value="Just another gull in the
  forest.">
<PARAM name=BACKGROUND value="forest3.gif">
</APPLET>
```

I will describe the purpose of each tag as you add it to the web page. The applet itself displays an animation made up of six images against a background image. It also displays a text caption at the bottom of the image.

To start, copy the following files from the `\tutorial\chap05\animate` folder to the `\Gold Pages\animate` folder:

```
bird.htm
birdfly.htm
birdx.htm
birdx2.htm
bounce.class
bounceimage.class
cup.gif
html.gif
```

Also, copy the folders `\tutorial\chap05\animate\bird` and `\tutorial\chap05\animate\pics` and the files they contain. The easiest way to copy all of these files and both folders is to open the folder `\tutorial\chap05\`, click and drag to select the `animate` folder, and drag the folder to the `\Gold Pages` folder (see Figure 5-8).

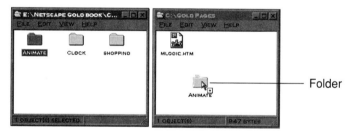

Folder

Figure 5-8: Dragging the `animate` folder.

Open the file `\Gold Pages\animate\bird.htm` in Edit mode (see Figure 5-9). You do not need to connect online when the Connection dialog box appears; click Cancel. Note the red text "Applet goes here" located below the page heading. The applet that you are about to add to the page will replace this text. I have conveniently added the text of the various tags to the page.

If you want to skip ahead and see what the applet looks like when it is working, double-click the file `\Gold Pages\animate\birdfly.htm`. This file also includes extensive additional information about the applet, as well as details about how the various parameters affect the operation of the applet.

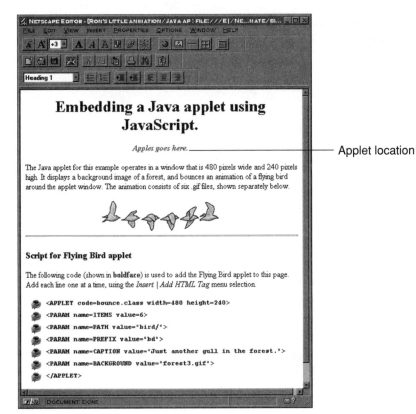

Figure 5-9: The web page for the applet.

1. Use the Insert | HTML Tag menu selection to open the dialog box shown in Figure 5-10. The dialog box will be empty. Type the text shown in Figure 5-10 into the dialog box, exactly as shown below. Click OK to add the tag. A little yellow tag icon appears on the web page in the place where you added the tag (see Figure 5-11). Since this is also the tag that defined the width and height of the applet, you see a rectangle of the size specified in the APPLET tag.

```
<APPLET code=bounce.class width=480 height=240>
```

Figure 5-10: Adding an HTML tag.

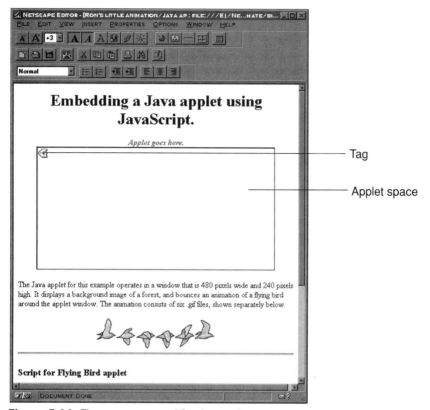

Figure 5-11: The space reserved for the applet.

There are three arguments used in this tag:

code: This points to the applet itself. As I mentioned earlier, Java source code has the extension .java, and the compiled applets have the extension .class.

width: The width, in pixels, that the applet will occupy on the web page.

height: The height, in pixels, that the applet will occupy on the web page.

2. Select the text "Applet goes here." and delete it. Click immediately to the right of the applet rectangle to position the cursor at that location. Use the Insert | HTML Tag menu selection to add the second tag:

```
<PARAM name=ITEMS value=6>
```

Click OK to save the tag; a second yellow tag icon appears on the page, at the location where you added the tag (see Figure 5-12). The new tag is called a parameter tag, and it has two arguments:

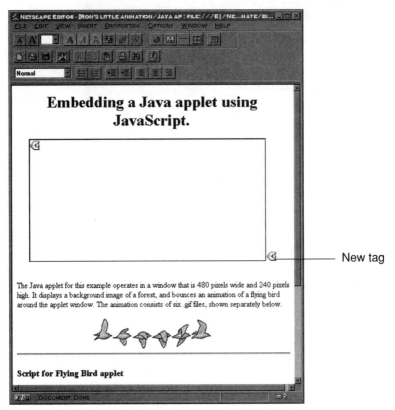

New tag

Figure 5-12: Adding the second tag.

name: The parameter name. Parameter names are case sensitive. In other words, be sure to use exactly the same upper and lower case characters as specified in the documentation for an applet. Be sure to type them in *exactly* as indicated!

value: The value associated with this parameter.

Depending on the width of your Netscape Gold window, the yellow tags may start to wrap a line below the space reserved for the applet (peek ahead to Figure 5-14). Don't worry if this happens; the applet will appear in its proper location no matter how many lines the tags occupy. If an applet had 50 parameters, and the tags wrapped across three lines, the applet would still display correctly.

The ITEMS parameter specifies the number of image files used in the animation. In this example, there are six image files, as shown in Figure 5-13.

Figure 5-13: *The images used in the animation: bd1.gif through bd6.gif.*

3. Add the following tag immediately after the preceding tag:

```
<PARAM name=PATH value="bird/">
```

This is also a parameter tag. Its name is PATH, and it specifies the relative path to the image files used in the animation. In this case, the image files are in a subfolder called "bird." Note that the parameter must end with a forward slash. Remember: when specifying paths for HTML tags, always use a forward slash.

4. Add the following tag immediately after the preceding tag:

```
<PARAM name=PREFIX value="bd">
```

This parameter tag has the name PREFIX, and it specifies the filename prefix used by all size animation images. If you recall, the image files are named `bd1.gif`, `bd2.gif`, and so on. The prefix used for all of the image files is "bd."

5. Add the following tag immediately after the preceding tag:

```
<PARAM name=CAPTION value="Just another gull in the forest.">
```

This parameter is named CAPTION, and it specifies a text caption that is added to the background image. As with all of the value arguments, double quotes enclose the value.

6. Add the following tag immediately after the preceding tag:

```
<PARAM name=BACKGROUND value="forest3.gif">
```

This parameter, BACKGROUND, specifies the filename of the background image.

7. Add the final tag immediately after the preceding tag:

```
</APPLET>
```

This tag is the closing tag for the APPLET tag, and it tells the browser reading the HTML tags that this is the end of any tags associated with this applet. Note that a closing tag gets an icon that is slightly different from the other tags. You might have other applets on the same page. Each applet would have its own <APPLET> and </APPLET> tags, as well as its own <PARAM> tags.

Figure 5-14 shows the appearance of the web page after all the tags are added. The exact number of tags on each line may vary, depending on the width of the Netscape Gold window.

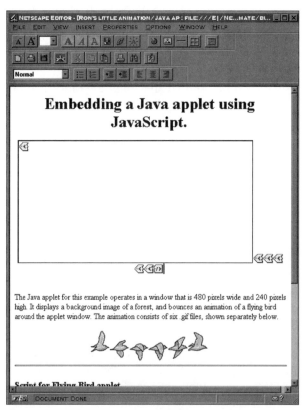

Figure 5-14: The appearance of the page after the tags are added.

NETSCAPE
NAVIGATOR
GOLD

To test the applet, save the file and then click on the Browse button (see margin). You should see the applet in action, as shown in Figure 5-15. Allow eight to twelve seconds for the applet to load and start running. If the applet is not running within 15 seconds, close the Browse window and check your tags carefully in Edit mode. To check the contents of a tag, double-click it to open a dialog showing the tag contents.

When you have corrected the tags, try the page again in Browse mode. If you simply want to see the completed web page in action, open the file \Gold Pages\animate\birdx.htm in Browse mode.

Changing applet parameters

You can easily change the parameters for an applet so that it behaves differently. For example, you could specify a different sequence of animation files, or a different background, for the applet in the previous example. It just so happens that I have included different animation files and a different background that you can use to show that this is true.

Double-click on the file \Gold Pages\animate\birdx.htm. It contains a completed version of the file from the preceding tutorial. You can modify it to use the different animation and background files. Change the tags so they read as shown in Listing 5-2. Double-click each tag to make the parameter changes shown in bold.

Listing 5-2: Revising applet parameters

```
<APPLET code=bounce.class width=480 height=240>
<PARAM name=ITEMS value=6>
<PARAM name=PATH value="pics/">
<PARAM name=PREFIX value="abd">
<PARAM name=CAPTION value="A raven in the city of red
 cubes.">
<PARAM name=BACKGROUND value="city.gif">
</APPLET>
```

Save the changes, and switch to Browse mode. You will see a different animation, as shown in Figure 5-15. The bird is now black, the background is different, and the caption is changed, too. If you simply want to see the changes, open the file \Gold Pages\animate\birdx2.htm in Browse mode.

Working with tags isn't the easiest way to add HTML to a web page, but it does work. You will find that larger projects, such as the form that follows, require careful attention to detail. Adding an applet is small potatoes by comparison!

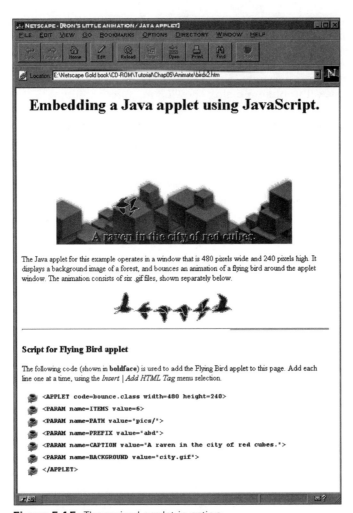

Figure 5-15: The revised applet in action.

Applet magic

The applet used for the preceding examples is a fairly simple Java applet. It is also possible to create very sophisticated applets and applications. Figure 5-16 shows an example. It was written by Eastland Data Systems, a company that specializes in programming for the Web. As a favor to me, they have agreed to include a version of the application on the CD-ROM.

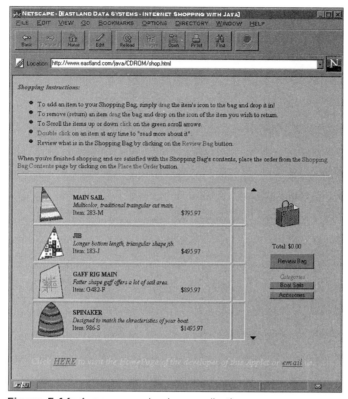

Figure 5-16: A more complex Java application.

To view the applet in action, double-click on the file
`\tutorial\chap05\shopping\shop.htm`. Figure 5-17 shows a complete
web page that includes the shopping application.

The shopping application has no parameter tags, so it only takes two tags
to add this sophisticated application to a web page:

```
<APPLET code="Shop.class" width=600 height=320>
</APPLET>
```

To use the shopping application, just follow the simple instructions on the
web page:

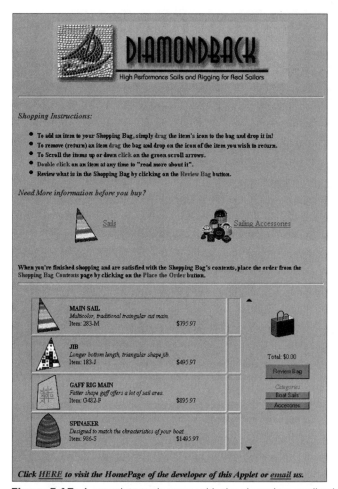

Figure 5-17: A complete web page with the shopping application.

Shopping Instructions:

➡ To add an item to your Shopping Bag, simply drag the item's icon to the bag and drop it in! Refer to Figure 5-18.

➡ To remove (return) an item, drag the bag and drop on the icon of the item you wish to return.

➡ To Scroll the items up or down click on the green scroll arrows.

➡ Double-click on an item at any time to "read more about it."

➡ Review what is in the Shopping Bag by clicking on the Review Bag button. Refer to Figure 5-19.

Figure 5-18: *The shopping bag icon (left), and dragging an icon over the shopping bag (right).*

Resume Shopping				
Place the Order				
Shopping Bag Contents				
Qty	Item	Description	Price	Total
1	283-M	MAIN SAIL	$795.97	$795.97
1	G482-F	GAFF RIG MAIN	$895.97	$895.97
1	986-S	SPINAKER	$1495.97	$1495.97
1	CCJ-21	COMPUTERIZED CHARTS	$3500.78	$3500.78
2	PJJ-9	PROFURL JIB RIG	$899.45	$1798.90
1	FRJ-8	FISH RADAR	$1499.25	$1499.25
				$9986.86

Figure 5-19: *Reviewing shopping bag contents.*

When you're finished shopping and are satisfied with the Shopping Bag's contents, place the order from the Shopping Bag Contents page by clicking on the Place the Order button. This displays the order form, shown in Figure 5-20.

A form is a web page that allows visitors to send you information. You'll learn more about forms in the next section.

JavaScript: Fun with Forms

Before adding JavaScript to a form, you need to know how forms work, and how Netscape Gold works with forms. I'll provide some background on forms, show you how to create forms for Netscape Gold, and then we'll return to JavaScript.

You saw an example of a form in Figure 5-20. The form presents text boxes, and the visitor types information into the text boxes. Every form has a Submit button, which sends the data on the form somewhere. Exactly where the form data goes may vary. There are two common destinations: a CGI (Common Gateway Interface) script, or e-mail.

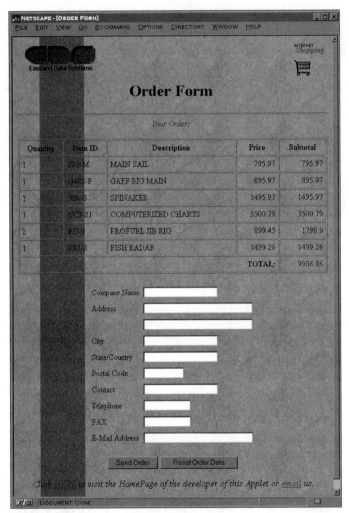

Figure 5-20: The shopping order form.

A CGI script is like a computer program. It receives the form data, processes it in some way, and then sends the result to you. The most common programming language used for CGI scripts (and please don't confuse CGI scripts with JavaScript scripts!) is Perl, although other programming languages are used. If you are curious about Perl and CGI scripts, check out the book *Creating Cool Web Pages with Perl* by Jerry Muelver, published by IDG books Worldwide.

If the form data is sent to a CGI script, the script will process the data in some way, and then send the data to its final destination. This is usually either a disk file or an e-mail address. The processed data is usually well organized, as shown in Figure 5-21.

```
Origin URL:        file:///E|/New Hompages/old stuff/orderx.htm
Remote host:       198.133.237.55
Remote IP address: 198.133.237.55

Hidden Fields
 hide-Form***form
 hide-FeedBkAdrs***ronw@olympus.net

End Of Hidden Fields

Form Fields
 Name***Marvin the Martian
 Address***324 Rue La Marite
 Address2***Olympus Mons, MZ M8374
 Phone***999-555-1111
 Email***mmarvin@olympus.mons
 Brochure***Send
 Comments***I really liked the recipe for Martian Creole.
Please renew my subscription to your cooking
magazine.
 SubmitData***Submit Query

End Of Form Fields
```

Figure 5-21: Processed form data e-mailed from a CGI script.

If the form data is sent via e-mail, with no CGI script to process the data, the e-mail address receives raw form data, which looks like this (except it arrives all on one line):

```
hide-Form=form&hide-FeedBkAdrs=ronw@olympus.net&Name=
Marvin+the+Martian&Address=324+Rue+La+Marite&Address2
=Olympus+Mons%2C+MZ+M8734&Phone=999-555-1111&Email=mm
arvin@olympus.mons&Brochure=Send&Comments=I+really+li
ked+the+recipe+for+Martian+Creole.%0D%0APlease+renew+
my+subscription+to+your+cooking%0D%0Amagazine.&Submit
Data=Submit+Query
```

Parser.EXE

As you can see, it is highly desirable to have a CGI script to process your form data. However, this is not always possible. In such cases, you will need software that will process the raw form data after you receive it as e-mail. I have included on the CD-ROM an application, the Magic Parser, that performs this task. Figure 5-22 shows how the Magic Parser processed the block of data shown above. You can run the Magic Parser directly from the CD-ROM by double-clicking on the program file (see margin) at \parser\parser.exe. You can install it onto your hard disk by double-clicking on the installation file at \parser\setup\setup.exe. Follow the onscreen prompts to complete the installation. Double-click the file \parser\readme.htm for instructions on using the parser.

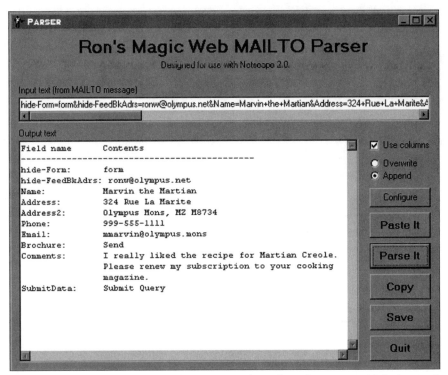

Figure 5-22: The Magic Parser will process raw form data after you receive it via e-mail.

Some web servers do not offer CGI script services. Some ISPs offer CGI scripts, but only the scripts that the ISP writes. Still other ISPs allow you to write custom scripts for your forms. There are good reasons for all three alternatives. Before you create forms, you should know which alternative your ISP provides.

Other major providers, such as CompuServe, do not provide script support at all. Their mission is to provide web servers for home pages, and they provide only the basic level of service needed for a home page. Special services, such as image maps and CGI scripts, are not available.

Most ISPs fall into the middle category: they provide CGI scripts of their own, but they do not allow you to create custom scripts. There are good reasons for this alternative. First, a poorly written or amateur script could easily compromise security on the web server. The most common mistake is for a script to allow form data to be executed by the server — inadvertently giving visitors the ability to access or modify data on the server. This is very dangerous! So do not be surprised if your ISP does not allow you to put custom CGI scripts on the web server.

Some ISPs will allow you to put your own custom CGI scripts on the server. Usually, they will insist on reviewing the scripts and perhaps even testing them before they are placed on the server. In most cases, however, you will be required to have your own web server (a completely separate physical machine) before you will be able to use custom CGI scripts.

If your ISP does provide generic CGI scripts for forms, you will need to contact your provider to find out how to use them. Implementation varies a lot from one ISP to another.

For example, here is how my ISP requires my forms to call the generic forms CGI script:

```
<FORM ACTION="/cgi-bin/formGeneric" METHOD="POST">
<INPUT TYPE="hidden" NAME="hide-Form" VALUE="form">
<INPUT TYPE="hidden" NAME="hide-FeedBkAdrs"
   VALUE="ronw@olympus.net">
```

The FORM ACTION parameter provides the location of the generic forms-processing script. The two hidden form fields tell the generic script what to do. The first hidden field tells the script that the data is form data, and the second hidden field tells the script where to send the processed data. The exact processing that the script performs, and the methods you use to work with the script, will vary.

Netscape Gold and forms

First, some bad news: version 3.0 of Netscape Gold does not support forms directly. You must use tags to add form elements to a web page. As for applets, this works for simple situations, but for complex forms, you may want to explore other options, such as a high-end web page creation tool like Microsoft FrontPage or Adobe PageMill.

The good news is that Netscape Gold is very tolerant of forms that you create by other means. You will see the little yellow tags, and Netscape Gold preserves all of the form's settings as you edit the appearance (but not the layout) of the form. Because you see yellow tags instead of form fields, it's not possible to refine the form's layout in Netscape Gold. You can, however, change text colors, add backgrounds, and perform many other design tasks.

The next section shows you how to use a utility I created, Form Creator, to create forms that you can modify in Netscape Gold. If you already know how to create forms using HTML tags, you can simply add the tags, one by one, using the Insert | HTML Tag menu selection.

Form Creator

If you find the process of creating forms with Netscape Gold's yellow tags tedious and confusing, you are not alone. I created a utility to make it a little easier to create forms for Netscape Gold. It is not a full fledged visual forms generator, but it does allow you to create a basic form, and then make it fancier in Netscape Gold.

FORM CREAT...

You can run the Form Creator directly from the CD-ROM by double-clicking on the program icon (see margin) at \Form Creator\ FormCreate.exe. You can install it to your hard disk by double-clicking on the installation file at \Form Creator\disk1\setup.exe. Follow the on-screen prompts to complete the installation. Double-click the file \Form Creator\readme.htm for instructions on using the Form Creator.

For this example, you will load a file that contains form data, add a new form field, and then use it to generate an HTML file.

To begin, double-click on the CD-ROM file \Form Creator\FormsCreate. exe. This runs the Form Creator (see Figure 5-23). Click the Load Data button to open the dialog box shown in Figure 5-24. Locate the file \Form Creator\output.dat and click it to highlight it. Click the Open button to load the data.

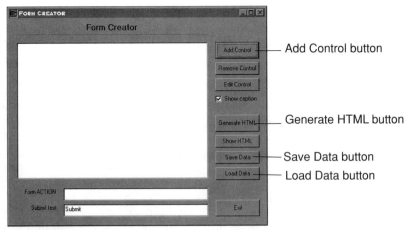

Figure 5-23: The Form Creator.

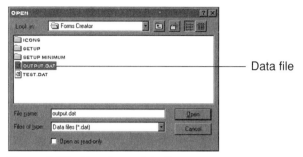

————— Data file

Figure 5-24: Opening a data file.

The data file contains information about a simple form that I created with Form Creator. Form Creator displays the information in a list, with one entry for each form field (see Figure 5-25). There are four fields: three text boxes, and one check box. To see all of the information about these fields, click and drag to widen the Form Creator window (see Figure 5-26).

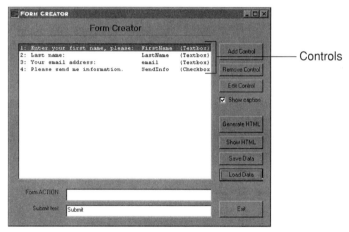

————— Controls

Figure 5-25: Form data loaded.

To add a new form field, click the Add Control button. This displays the dialog box shown in Figure 5-27. The default new field type is Text box. For this exercise, click the field type Radio button group. The dialog box changes to show a different view, as shown in Figure 5-28.

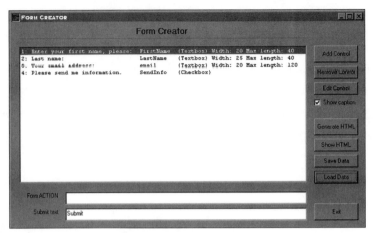

Figure 5-26: Widening the window.

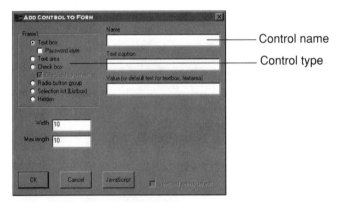

Figure 5-27: Adding a control.

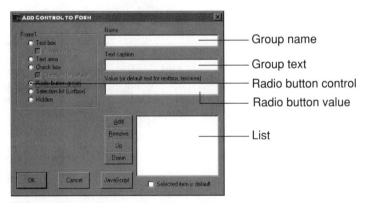

Figure 5-28: Adding a radio button group.

A radio button group contains two or more radio buttons. Each button has its own text string, and clicking one button causes that button to be selected, and the previously selected button to become deselected. In other words, only one button in a radio button group can be selected at one time.

To add choices to the button group, start by giving the entire group a name in the Name text box. Type **Age** into the Name text box. The Text caption also applies to the entire group; type **Please indicate your age:** into the Text caption text box. The first radio button will be for ages under 18; type **Under 18** into the Value text box. Figure 5-29 shows all three text boxes filled in.

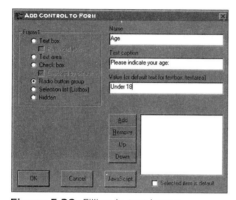

Figure 5-29: Filling in text boxes.

To add the Under 18 radio button, click the Add button. The text caption shows up in the list at bottom right of the dialog (see Figure 5-30). Continue by entering the following text into the Value text box, and clicking the Add button after each item to add it to the list:

18 to 29

30 to 39

40 to 49

50 to 59

60 or more

When you have added all of the radio buttons, the dialog box should look like that in Figure 5-31.

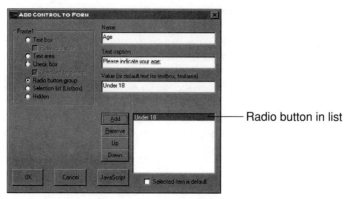

Figure 5-30: The first radio button added.

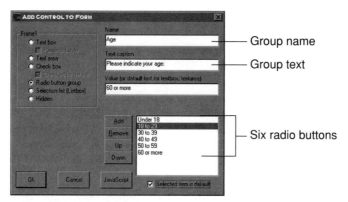

Figure 5-31: All six radio buttons added.

In many cases, you will want to specify a default choice. Simply click the choice in the list (in this example, 18 to 29), and click the check box at bottom right, "Selected item is default." Now click OK to add the radio button group to the form. If you make a mistake, you can highlight the incorrect button's entry in the list, and click the Remove button to remove that item. You can also highlight an item and use the Up and Down buttons to move it up or down in the list.

As you can see in Figure 5-32, the radio button group is added to the list of form fields. Although the group has six buttons, it is still considered one field.

Note in Figure 5-32 that I have filled in the Form ACTION text box to indicate how I want the form to be processed. In this case, the raw form data will be e-mailed to the address me@myaddress.com. You would replace this with your own e-mail address.

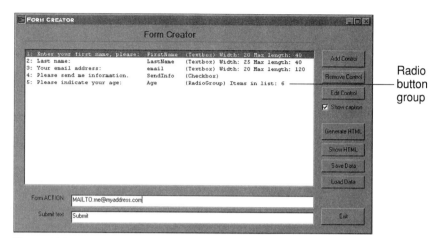

Figure 5-32: The radio button group is added to the form.

If you were creating a form, you would continue to add form fields in this manner until you had all the fields you required.

To create a web page form, click the Generate HTML button. This opens the dialog shown in Figure 5-33. Save the file in the \Gold Pages folder, using the name output.htm, as shown in Figure 5-33. Click the Save button to save the file. When the save is complete, you will see a dialog like the one in Figure 5-34 indicating that the output file is ready.

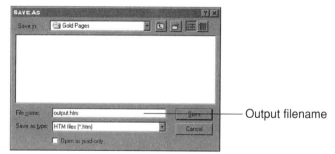

Figure 5-33: Generating a web page.

Figure 5-34: Output is complete.

To save the new form data into a data file, click the Save data button, which opens the dialog shown in Figure 5-35. The output file also should be saved in the \Gold Pages folder, using the filename output.dat. Note that you used the extension .htm for the web page, and .dat for the data file.

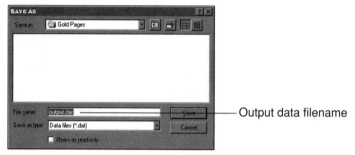

Output data filename

Figure 5-35: Saving form data.

Once you save the form data, you can edit it later. Simply click the Load Data button, and locate the file you saved. The data gets reloaded into Form Creator, where you can add new controls, delete controls, edit controls, and so on. Once you are done making changes, you can once again generate the HTML file for the form, and edit it in Netscape Gold.

To view the generated HTML file, double-click on the file \Gold Pages\output.htm. Figure 5-36 shows what the file should look like. Form Creator has added all of the form fields, and all of the text, as well as a Submit button and a Reset button. If you used your real e-mail address as the form ACTION, you can test the form by filling in the fields (see Figure 5-37) and clicking the Submit button. You should find the raw form data in your e-mail. It will look something like this, depending on exactly how you filled in the form:

```
FirstName=Ron&LastName=Wodaski&email=ronw@olympus.net&
SendInfo=on&Age=40+to+49
```

You can use the Magic Parser to parse the form data:

Field name	Contents
FirstName:	Ron
LastName:	Wodaski
e-mail:	ronw@olympus.net
SendInfo:	on
Age:	40 to 49

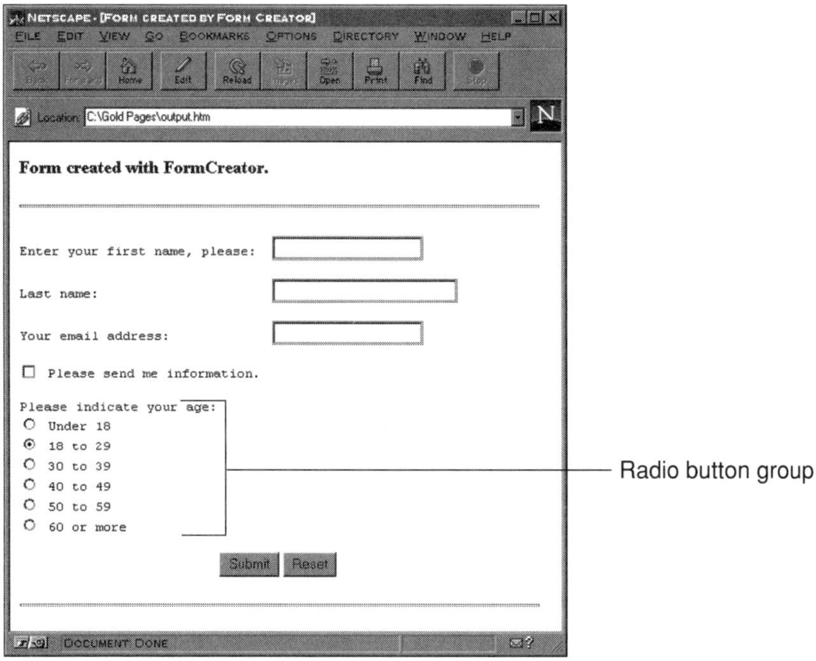

Radio button group

Figure 5-36: The form in Browse mode.

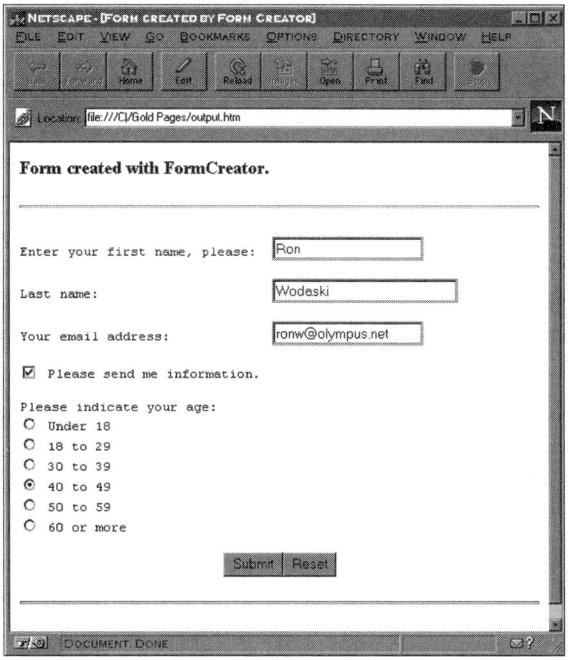

Figure 5-37: Filling out the form.

The SendInfo field is the Submit button. If you are curious about the contents of the form data file, `\Gold Pages\output.dat`, open it using Notepad. You'll see a comma-delimited list of items for each form field. Don't make any changes to the data file, or Form Creator may not be able to open it properly.

You can now edit the form by clicking the Edit button to switch to Edit mode (see Figure 5-38). All of the form tags show up as those little yellow tag icons. You can edit form tags, if necessary. For example, if you change your mind about how wide the text boxes should be, you can double-click the tag and make a change.

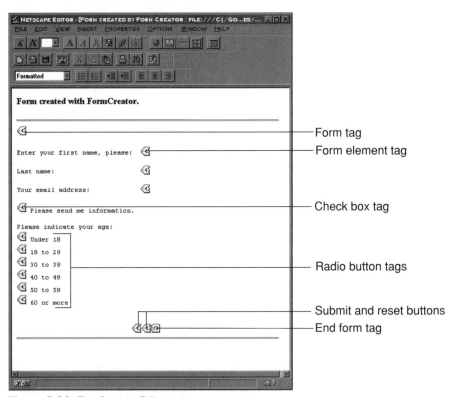

Figure 5-38: The form in Edit mode.

I made a number of changes to the form. I replaced the "Form created with Form Creator" headline with a different headline, and applied some text formatting to various portions of the form. I also shifted the location of some of the form elements (see Figure 5-39). You may want to experiment with some changes of your own. If you do, save the changes to the file `\Gold Pages\NewOutput.htm`. Figure 5-40 shows the changes in Browse mode.

Figure 5-39: The form has been changed.

Figure 5-40: The revised form in Browse mode.

Enhancing Forms with JavaScript

It's been a long road between the first mention of forms and this point, but your patience will now be rewarded. It's time to spice up a form with a little JavaScript. One common use of JavaScript is to update one form field when the visitor makes changes to another form field. This commonly occurs on order forms. Figure 5-41 shows an order form I created in Netscape Gold.

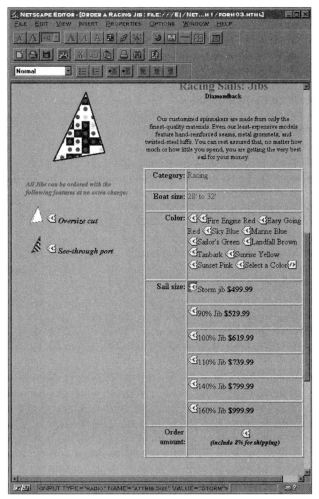

Figure 5-41: A more complex form created in Netscape Gold.

If you want to see how I created the form, open the file \tutorial\chap05\ form1\form01.htm, and then open the file \tutorial\chap05\form1\ form02.htm. View both files in Edit mode. The first file contains just the text for the form, while the second file contains all of the tags, too. I added the tags one by one in Netscape Gold using the Insert I HTML Tag menu selection. To view the tags, switch to Edit mode while viewing the second file. You'll see something like Figure 5-41. You may also want to spend some time exploring how I used tables to arrange items on this web page; there are tables within tables within tables. To view table properties, right-click anywhere in the table and choose the Table properties menu selection in the pop-up menu.

If you double-click on, for example, one of the radio button tags, you'll see something like Figure 5-42.

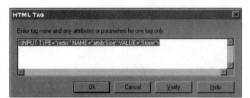

Figure 5-42: Adding a radio button tag manually.

To modify this order form requires two phases. In the first phase, you will add a JavaScript function to the web page. In the second phase, you will add a call to the function in the appropriate form fields. When you are done, clicking a radio button will automatically update the price for that item on the form. Be patient as you step through the process, as it will all come together in a coherent fashion by the end of the tutorial!

To start, copy the following files from the \tutorial\chap05\form1 folder to the \Gold Pages\form1 folder:

boat01.gif

boatlog3.gif

form01.htm

form01x.htm

form02.htm

form03.htm

form04.htm

ijib.gif

ijib2.gif

jib.gif

key02b.gif

script.txt

wrench2.gif

The easiest way to copy all of these files is to open the folder \tutorial\chap05\, click and drag to select the form1 folder, and drag the folder to the \Gold Pages folder.

Phase one: Adding the JavaScript function

Double-click the file \Gold Pages\form1\script.txt to open it in
Notepad (refer to Figure 5-43). The file contains two blocks of text. The
first block, shown in Listing 5-3, is a JavaScript function. The second block
(just a single line, actually, and shown at the bottom of Listing 5-3) is the
JavaScript code to call the function.

Listing 5-3: JavaScript function

```
function getRadioButton (form)
{
        for (i = 0; i < 5; i++)
        {
                if (form.Price[i].checked)
                        break;
        }
    if (i == 0)
        form.OrderTotal.value = ""+(499 + (499*.08));
    if (i == 1)
        form.OrderTotal.value = ""+(529 + (529*.08));
    if (i == 2)
        form.OrderTotal.value = ""+(619 + (619*.08));
    if (i == 3)
        form.OrderTotal.value = ""+(739 + (739*.08));
    if (i == 4)
        form.OrderTotal.value = ""+(799 + (799*.08));
    if (i == 5)
        form.OrderTotal.value = ""+(999 + (999*.08));
}

onClick="getRadioButton(this.form)"
```

The JavaScript function code gives you an idea of how to work with
JavaScript. Let's look at it more closely. The first line declares the function:

```
function getRadioButton (form)
```

The word "function" lets the browser know that this is a function. The
function name is "getRadioButton()". The word "form" is an argument of
the function. Whenever you call this function, you must pass to it a variable
that tells the function which form it is working with.

The JavaScript code for the function is located between curly braces. The
first line after the function name has a curly brace, and the last line of the
function is also a curly brace. Everything between the curly braces belongs
to this function. Note that there are a number of curly braces between the
start and the end of the function's code.

The first statement in the function is

```
for (i = 0; i < 5; i++)
```

This is a for command, and it will be familiar to C and C++ programmers. The for command loops through a series of commands until a specified limit is reached. There are three arguments used by the for command:

i = 0;	Initialization: Sets the variable i equal to zero.
i < 5; as	Limit: Continue processing the commands in the for loop long as i is less than 5.
i++	Increment: Add one to i each time through the loop.

The commands inside the for loop are:

```
{
        if (form.Price[i].checked)
            break;
}
```

Note the use of curly braces to mark the beginning and the end of the JavaScript commands in the loop. The first command is an if command; it tests to see if one of the radio buttons is selected (in JavaScript-speak, "checked"). The if condition is enclosed in parentheses. Here's how the condition breaks down:

form	This is the form referred to by the variable that is passed to the function when the function gets called ("this.form").
.	The period separates the form from the form field (Price). The period indicates a linkage between objects. In this case, the form is the parent object, and is at the left of the period. The radio button group Price is the child object.
Price	This refers to the radio button group used to indicate prices on the form. Because radio buttons are a group, the JavaScript code must loop through all of the individual radio buttons; that's the reason for the for loop.

[i]	This is a counter. Technically speaking, the radio button group is an array, made up of several individual radio buttons. The counter i refers, in turn, to each radio button in the group. The first time through the for loop, the counter is equal to 0; zero refers to the first item in an array. The next time through, the counter is equal to 1, and refers to the second item in the array. Think of it as a sequence number indicating which radio button is selected.
.	Another period, also showing parent/child relationship. The parent is the individual radio button (Price[i]), and the child is the state of that individual button (checked).
checked	A true or false value, depending on whether the individual radio button is selected, or not selected. In this case, the if command is testing to see if the radio button is selected. Since only one radio button can be selected at a time, this is a logical way to find out which radio button is selected. The for loop tests each button in turn until it finds the selected button. When it finds the selected button (that is, when `form.Price[i].checked` is true), the statement following the if command is executed. In this case, the command is a break command, which breaks out of the for loop. The variable i is now set to the sequence number of the radio button that is selected.

In other words, the for loop will iterate through the radio buttons until it finds the one that is selected, incrementing the variable i as it goes. It will then break out of the loop, leaving i set.

After the break, there is a series of six if commands. Only one of the commands will be executed, depending on the value of i. For example, if i = 3, then the following statement will get executed:

```
form.OrderTotal.value = ""+(619 + (619*.08));
```

This statement again strings together words using periods. Working from right to left, we see that the value of the form field OrderTotal for this form will be set to the price of that item, plus 8 percent for shipping. All of the six if commands do the same thing, but using different prices for different items.

To add the JavaScript function to the form, double-click the file \GoldPages\ form1\form03.htm to open it in Browse mode, and follow these steps:

1. Select only the function text in the Notepad window (see Figure 5-43). Copy the text to the clipboard using the Edit | Copy menu selection.

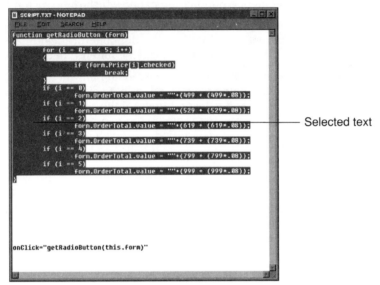

Figure 5-43: *Selecting the function text in Notepad.*

2. Create a new line at the top of the form by pressing Enter. Position the cursor above the first tag on the web page form (see Figure 5-44) on the new line. Use the Edit | Paste menu selection to paste the function onto the page. It gets pasted as a single paragraph. Don't try to break it up into separate paragraphs; Netscape Gold will make a mess of things if you do!

    Figure 5-45 shows what you should see: a big block of function text. Don't worry if it is difficult to read; Netscape Gold can still read it, and that is all that matters.

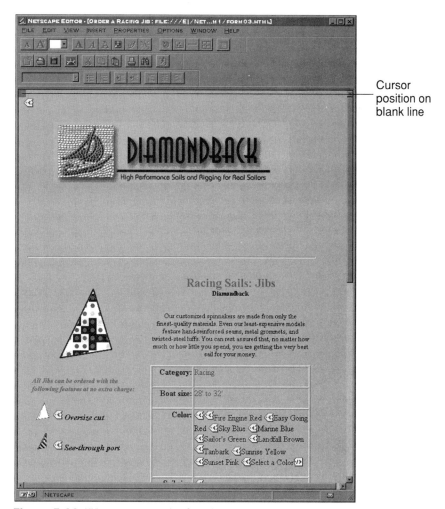

Cursor
position on
blank line

Figure 5-44: Where to paste the function code.

If the little yellow tag is on the same line as the text you inserted, you need to move it before you continue. Position the cursor just to the left of the little yellow tag, and press Enter to move the tag to a new line; it should now look like Figure 5-45.

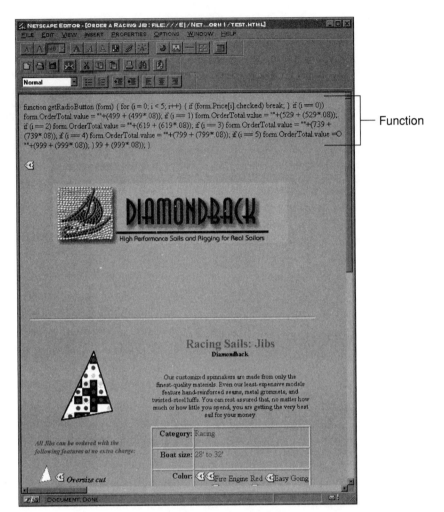

Figure 5-45: The function pasted into Netscape Gold.

3. Right now, the function is just another block of text. To tell Netscape Gold that this is a JavaScript function, carefully select just the function text and click the menu selection Properties | Character | JavaScript (Client). The JavaScript code turns red, and is now all on one line (see Figure 5-46). Save your work to the hard disk.

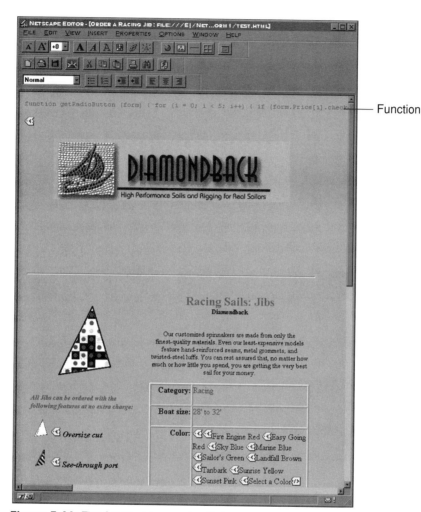

Function

Figure 5-46: The function is now JavaScript.

This is a very long line of JavaScript. Beta versions of Netscape Gold had some trouble coping with such long lines when you try to edit them. The final version of Netscape Gold may fix this problem, or it may not. If you have trouble moving the cursor along the line, or if you see garbage on screen, you'll know that the problem persists. However, if you simply save your work at this point, there is no problem. The problem isn't with the long line itself, but with the display of the line on the screen.

This completes the first phase; that's all it takes to add one or more functions to a web page.

Phase two: adding the function calls

Before you can add the function calls, use the vertical scroll bar to make all of the radio button tags visible (see Figure 5-47). Double-click on the first radio button tag to open the dialog shown in Figure 5-48.

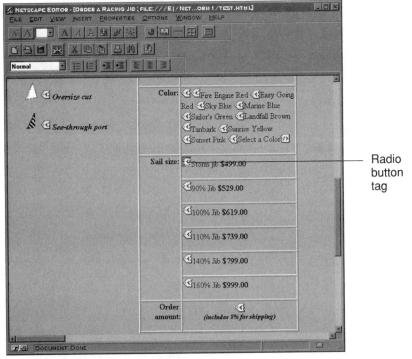

Figure 5-47: Working on the radio button tags.

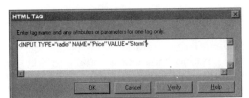

Figure 5-48: The contents of the radio button tag.

The task here is to add the function call to the tag. Go back to the `script.txt` file, which should still be open in Notepad. If it is not, double-click on the file `\Gold Pages\script.txt` to open it. Select just the text for the function call (see Figure 5-49) and copy it to the clipboard (Edit | Copy).

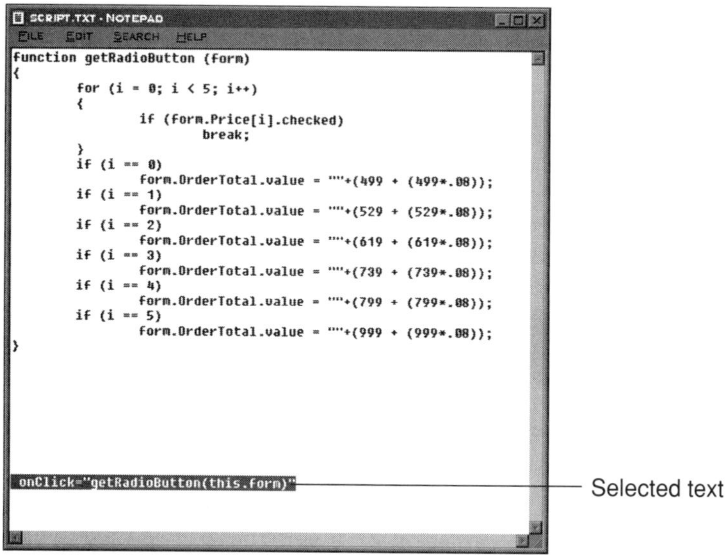

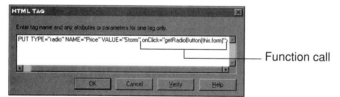

Figure 5-49: Selecting the function call text.

Go back to the radio button tag dialog, and position the cursor exactly after the quote mark following the word Storm and before the final angle bracket (>). Add a space, and then paste in the function call text (Control+V). The result should look exactly like Figure 5-50.

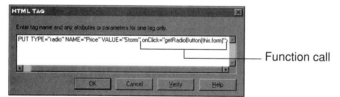

Figure 5-50: Adding the function call.

The function call has two parts, separated by an equal sign. The left portion, onClick, tells the browser when to call the function (the right portion is the function call). If you click on this radio button, the function will be called. Whenever the function is called, the text in the OrderTotal text box will reflect the price of the item, plus 8 percent for shipping.

Repeat this process for the other five radio buttons. Keep in mind that each radio button has a unique value; they won't all say "Storm"! However, you will always paste the text just before the ending angle bracket. Don't forget to add the space!

When you have added the function call to all six radio buttons, double-click on the tag for the order total. The tag is currently

```
<INPUT TYPE="text" NAME="OrderTotal" SIZE=20 MAXLENGTH=20>
```

This time, you are adding an onChange JavaScript command to the form field. If the visitor changes the order total manually, this will make sure that the order total is reset to what it should be. Add the text shown in bold below to the OrderTotal tag. Don't forget to put a space before the added text.

```
<INPUT TYPE="text" NAME="OrderTotal" SIZE=20 MAXLENGTH=20
 onChange="getRadioButton(this.form)">
```

Save your changes. To test your work, view the revised form in Browse mode. Click on the radio buttons, and note how the value that appears in the Order Total text box changes with each click (see Figure 5-51).

If you want to test the form by sending yourself some data, you will need to change the ACTION parameter for the form. Double-click on the very first tag on the form (see Figure 5-52), and change the action to include your own e-mail address. You can then use the Magic Parser to view the form data.

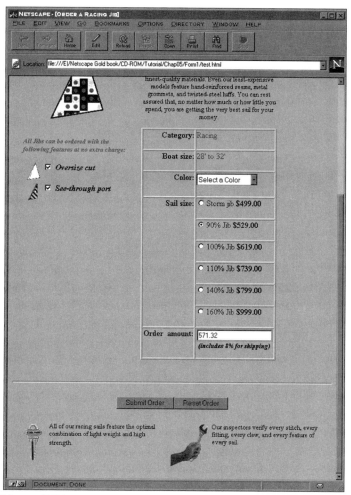

Figure 5-51: The enhanced form in action.

Form ACTION

Figure 5-52: Changing the form ACTION.

JavaScript contains a rich variety of commands that will allow you to make many other useful enhancements to forms. You can also use Java to create complete custom applications for your web page. You'll learn much more about the JavaScript language in Chapter 7. For the most up-to-date listing of JavaScript commands, visit the Netscape page at

```
http://home.netscape.com/eng/mozilla/Gold/handbook/javascript/
```

For a detailed tutorial on building JavaScript applications from scratch, see Chapter 7.

NetKey #5: Netscape Features and Plug-ins

In this chapter, you have learned how to use JavaScript to enhance web pages. You can also add dynamic features to your web pages using new features in version 3.0 of Netscape, or by using Netscape-compatible plug-ins. NetKey #5 offers a detailed look at how you can add a new dimension to your web pages.

Using NetKey #5

To begin, double-click on the file

```
/tutorial/index.htm
```

on the CD-ROM, which will automatically start Netscape Gold in Browse mode. As usual, if you do not want to connect, click the Cancel button when the Connection dialog appears. The appearance of the file /tutorial/index.htm is shown in Figure 5-53.

The file /tutorial/index.htm contains hyperlinks to the NetKeys for every chapter in the book. To learn how to create a complex image with Painter, click the hyperlink for Chapter 5, *Netscape Features and Plug-Ins*. The first NetKey page for this chapter is shown in Figure 5-54. To explore this NetKey, simply click on any and every hyperlink (usually underlined text) that strikes your fancy. Unlike previous NetKeys, this one contains hyperlinks that connect you to pages on the web, not on the CD-ROM.

To access the NetKey page for Chapter 5 directly, double-click on the file /tutorial/chap05/webpage.htm.

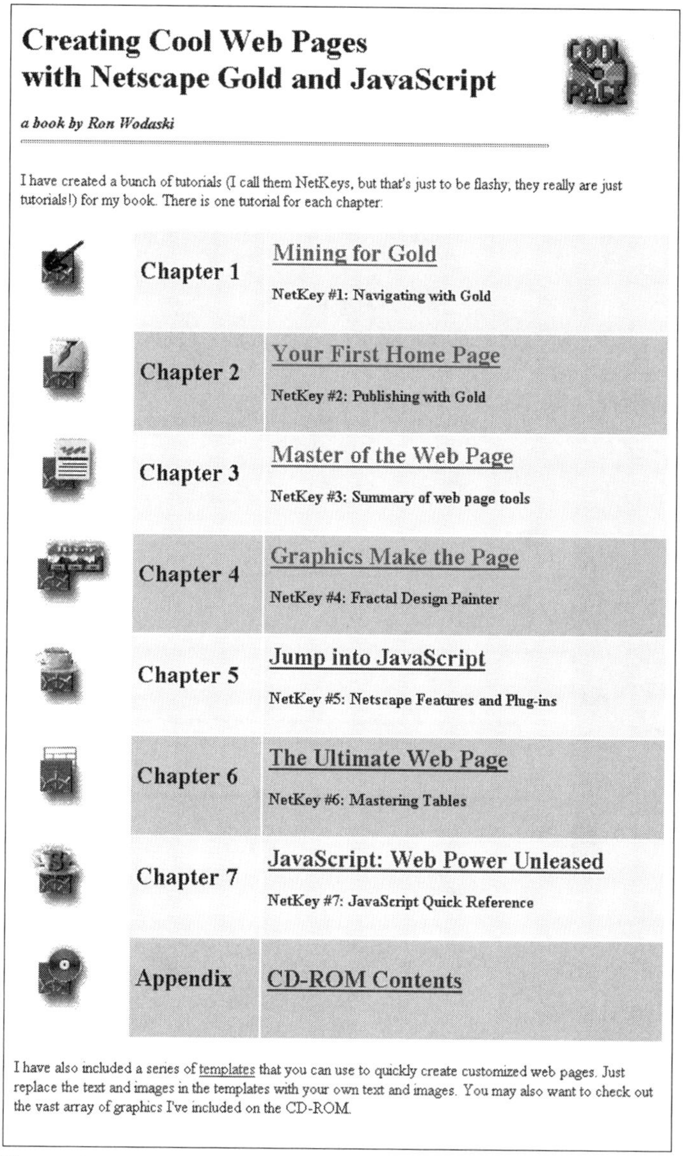

Creating Cool Web Pages with Netscape Gold and JavaScript

a book by Ron Wodaski

I have created a bunch of tutorials (I call them NetKeys, but that's just to be flashy, they really are just tutorials!) for my book. There is one tutorial for each chapter:

	Chapter		
	Chapter 1	**Mining for Gold** NetKey #1: Navigating with Gold
	Chapter 2	**Your First Home Page** NetKey #2: Publishing with Gold
	Chapter 3	**Master of the Web Page** NetKey #3: Summary of web page tools
	Chapter 4	**Graphics Make the Page** NetKey #4: Fractal Design Painter
	Chapter 5	**Jump into JavaScript** NetKey #5: Netscape Features and Plug-ins
	Chapter 6	**The Ultimate Web Page** NetKey #6: Mastering Tables
	Chapter 7	**JavaScript: Web Power Unleased** NetKey #7: JavaScript Quick Reference
	Appendix	**CD-ROM Contents**

I have also included a series of templates that you can use to quickly create customized web pages. Just replace the text and images in the templates with your own text and images. You may also want to check out the vast array of graphics I've included on the CD-ROM.

Figure 5-53: The web page for access to NetKey pages.

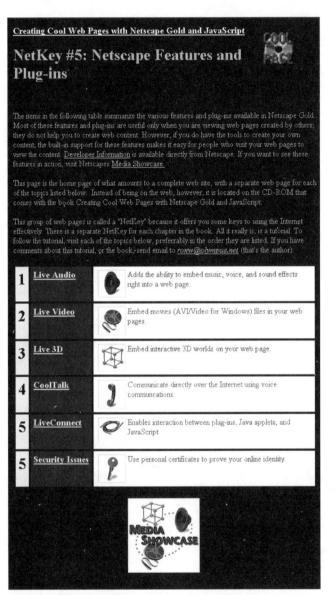

Figure 5-54: The NetKey page for Chapter 5.

The Ultimate Web Page

Fundamentals of Page Design

You learned a lot about page design in Chapter 4, "Graphics Make the Page." That's because graphics do make the page. But good page design requires more than good graphics. A well-designed web page functions as a single entity. Graphics can go a long way toward making that happen. But a web page seldom lives in isolation. Not only can it include hyperlinks, web pages by their nature are almost always small, and a web site will frequently use many pages. Web page design that doesn't take the larger picture into account can leave you with web pages that don't work well together.

In this chapter, you'll learn how to use everything at your disposal to create the best possible web page.

Look before You Leap

I've said it before in this book, and I'll probably say it as long as I can breathe: start with a plan. You might think that a plan ties you down unnecessarily. It doesn't. It gives you freedom. By laying out the rough boundaries of the page, or a collection of pages, you free up your mind to focus on things that fit the overall plan. The human mind loves to have a goal in view. If you set out a plan, you'll be amazed at the things you find that fit into your plan.

This chapter's fictitious company is Fannie's Fun Farm Products. The company sells fruits, vegetables, garden tools, and products featuring the company's logo. Fannie's wants a full-blown web site that covers all aspects of the company's business.

The job is too large for any one web page to handle; this will require a complete collection of web pages. There are a million ways to create a plan for these pages; I'll pick one out of my hat for this demonstration. If you want to have some fun, you can take the collection of graphics I created for this exercise and create your own web site for practice.

Here are the requirements for the web site:

- The home page should provide access to all areas of the web site.
- There are nine areas of the company that qualify as important enough for a web page of their own: fruits, vegetables, catalogs, how to garden, bean planting, pea selection, squash selection, organic fertilizer, and company logo products.
- The nine areas fall into two general kinds of web pages: pages with many products on them (fruits, vegetables, catalogs) and pages that teach the visitor about a specific area (how to garden, bean planting, pea selection, squash selection, and organic fertilizer). The ninth area, logo products, really belongs in the first group, but the company president insists that we group it with the teaching pages ("It just doesn't belong with the other products," she said over and over until we finally gave in).

Given these bare-bones requirements (which aren't quite detailed enough to be called a plan), I tried to find ways to arrange the information on web pages. This is what I came up with:

- The company logo will appear at the top of all pages.
- The company slogan, "Where fun is always organic," will always appear with the logo.
- The three product-intensive areas (fruits, veggies, catalogs) will be accessed through hot spots on a graphic. This graphic will be included on every page, usually at the bottom. It will appear at the top of the home page.

⮕ The teaching areas will be accessed only from the home page.

⮕ The teaching areas will be divided into two types: single page and multiple pages. Multipage areas will have one general subtopic per page. The idea is to mimic a book or magazine article with web pages. The company currently publishes these materials in paper form, but cannot afford first-class layouts or printing. They hope to create clean and very impressive web page layouts from the existing printed materials. The single-page layouts will be based on existing flyers, while the multipage layout will be based on an existing booklet.

This is good enough to qualify as a rough plan for the web site. The next task is to create a more specific plan for the home page. Figure 6-1 shows my original sketch. The company logo and slogan are at the top of the page. A floating image map appears below the slogan, with hyperlinks to the veggie, catalog, and fruit pages. A series of buttons at the left of the page (with headlines and brief text descriptions) provide access to the teaching areas.

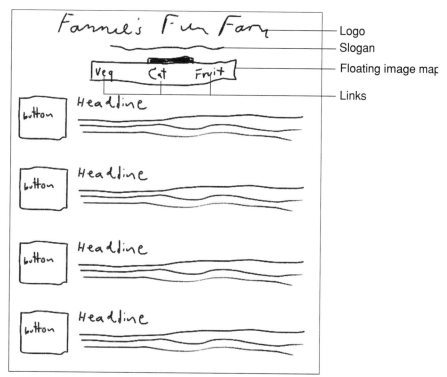

Figure 6-1: A rough plan for the Fannie's Fun Farm home page.

The home page will link to several different kinds of web pages:

➡ Veggie and fruit pages

➡ Catalog page

➡ Single-page teaching pages

➡ Multipage teaching pages

To further simplify web site construction, I arbitrarily decided that the veggie, fruit, and catalog pages would all use the same rough layout. Figure 6-2 shows my sketch for the layout of these pages. Note that I introduced several design elements to these pages: a dark bar at the left of the page, and a column of buttons at top right. The dark bar is an arbitrary design element — I added it because I liked it, and I plan to use it for a page title. The column of buttons duplicates the buttons on the home page. The logo and slogan stay at the top of the page. The floating image map for fruits, veggies, and catalog also remains, but is moved to the bottom of the page. The principal areas of the layout are marked in the figure.

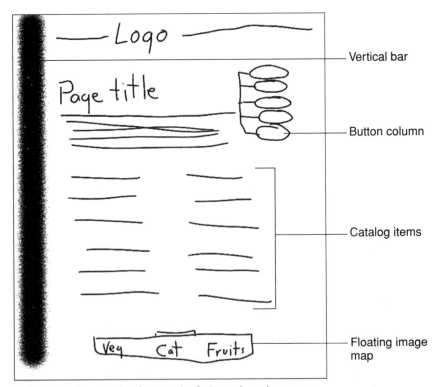

Figure 6-2: Rough plan for veggie, fruit, and catalog pages.

The single-page teaching page design is shown in Figure 6-3. It borrows the vertical bar from the fruit/veggie/catalog page. The top of the page is similar, but instead of a table with many items, there are headlines with brief text contents.

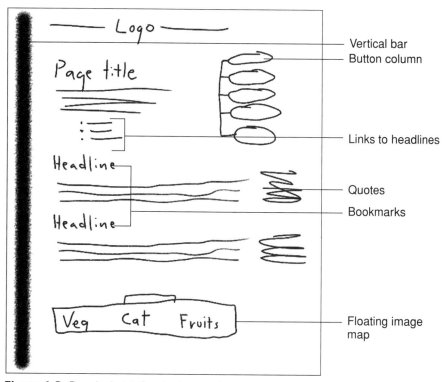

Figure 6-3: *Rough sketch for single-page layout.*

The multipage teaching page design is shown in Figure 6-4. The page top is similar, but a table will be used to provide a lot of white space. There is a page title, no heavy vertical bar, and a section title. Buttons for moving backward and forward between sections are at bottom left and right.

Translating these rough sketches into actual web pages takes some time and effort. However, by starting with a sketch, we make it easier to keep track of the required elements on the page. The final page may vary a bit from the plan, but having a plan enables you to keep track of your progress.

Before we can proceed with creating the web pages, it's a good idea to consider some of the technical issues that might affect the page layout. You'll return to page construction in the section Creating a Web Site later in this chapter.

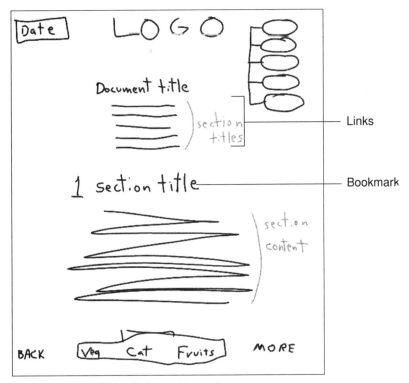

Figure 6-4: Rough sketch for multipage layout.

Technical Issues

Most of the technical issues that affect page layout have to do with the graphics that you place on the web pages. Text is text, and a web page's text contents download quickly and without much fuss. Images are a different story. Large or complex images can have very long download times. Knowing how to minimize download time can help your page display more quickly, and provide a more satisfying experience for visitors.

KISS: Keep it small and simple

When it comes to images, small and simple are the two things to keep in mind. There will definitely be times when a large or complex image is absolutely necessary, but most of the time you will find that small, simple images are best. For example, if a detailed map is a central item on a web page, then by all means provide a large, detailed map — it's necessary to get the information across. However, whenever you feel tempted to add a large image to a web page just because it's a neat image, think twice: Will the time it takes to download the large image detract from its value?

Simplicity is another point to consider when choosing or creating images for a web page. You can increase the size of an image if you keep the design of the image simple. Both the GIF and JPEG image formats use compression to reduce file size. Simple images almost always compress better than complex images. For example, look at the image in Figure 6-5. It uses broad areas of single colors, and has a large, single-color background. This image will compress to a very small file size, and it won't hurt your page to put a large version of this image on the page.

Figure 6-5: An image that uses simple color elements (from http://www.seatimes.com).

Figure 6-6, on the other hand, has areas of complex color, as well as a very complicated background. This image won't compress effectively, and will result in a very large file size, even for small versions of the image. This image could be simplified by giving it a single-color background in a paint program, and by reducing the number of colors used in the image, perhaps by converting from 24-bit color to 256 or even 128 colors.

Figure 6-6: An image that uses complex color elements (from http://www.seatimes.com).

Interlacing

Image interlacing is described in detail in Chapter 4. You add interlacing to an image using any of the various paint programs that support this feature.

Chapter 4 shows examples. Interlacing is important because it allows the visitor to see a rough approximation of your images while waiting for the complete image to download. See Figure 4-64 (in Chapter 4) for an example of interlacing.

Preload a low-resolution image

You can specify a low-resolution image that will load before the high-resolution image loads. This allows your web page to quickly display a rough version of an image that the visitor can see and work with. The low-resolution image will display at the same size as the final image.

One common technique is to create a black-and-white version of the final image, and use that as the low-resolution image. However, unless you are careful about how you create the black-and-white image, it can be three or four times larger than a pure black-and-white image — but it will look much better. To be effective, the black-and-white image must use large areas of black and white, rather than dithering. Figure 6-7 shows a web page image. Figure 6-8 shows the image converted to pure black and white, and Figure 6-9 shows the image converted to black and white with dithering.

Figure 6-7: A full-size color image.

Figure 6-8: A full-size black-and-white image.

Figure 6-9: A full-size dithered black-and-white image.

Another common approach is to use a very small image as the low-resolution image. Typically, making the image one-quarter the size of the original will be adequate. Figure 6-10 shows a one-quarter-size version of the image from Figure 6-7.

Figure 6-10: A quarter-size color image.

If you use a smaller version of an image as the low-resolution image, Netscape Gold may use the dimensions of the smaller image as the dimensions for display. If this happens, the large image will be reduced, instead of the small image enlarged. If this happens, you will have to determine the exact size of the large image, and revise the image height and width in the Image Properties dialog box.

The file sizes of the various images shown here are:

Figure	Filename	Image type	Size
6-7	venus01.gif	Color (GIF)	377k
6-7	venus01.gif	Color (JPEG)	61k
6-8	venus02.gif	Black and white	24k
6-9	venus03.gif	Dithered black and white	67k
6-10	venus01b.jpg	One-quarter-size color (JPEG)	9k

Note that the color JPEG file compresses so well that there is hardly a need for a low-resolution image! You can find the files on the CD-ROM, in the directory \tutorial\chap06. View the images in a paint program, and compare the image quality of the various image types. The file \tutorial\chap06\venus.htm shows how a low-resolution, quarter-size image is displayed before the high-resolution image. The file \tutorial\chap06\venus2.htm shows how a low-resolution, black-and-white image is displayed before the high-resolution image. The file \tutorial\chap06\venus3.htm shows how a low-resolution, dithered black-and-white image is displayed before the high-resolution image.

To specify a low-resolution image using Netscape Gold, right-click an image and select Image Properties from the pop-up menu. This displays the Image Properties dialog box (see Figure 6-11). The low-resolution image filename should be placed below the *Alternative representations (optional):,* in the text box labeled *Image:.* Use the Browse button to the right of this text box to scan the disk for images. In Figure 6-11, the filename is Venus02.GIF. You can also add alternate text for any image, in the *Text* box (below the *Image* box).

 If the low-resolution image is a different size than the original image, Navigator Gold will use the size of the alternate image in the Dimensions area of the Properties dialog box. You can reset the image size by re-browsing for the original image — the last image added controls the *Height* and *Width* settings.

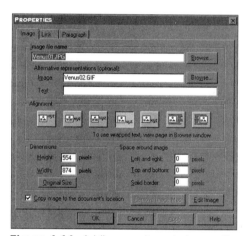

Figure 6-11: Adding an alternate image filename.

 Remember that you should only use images that have already been moved to the proper directory. Adding an image to a web page while it still resides somewhere else on your hard disk could lead to problems when you publish to a web server.

Identical references

You can save download time by reusing an image. For example, if you are using an image for a bulleted list, the image is only downloaded once. If you use the same company logo on four different pages, the image is only downloaded once (provided that caching is turned on in the Browser options).

There is a trick to using the same image over again. You must specify the path to the image exactly the same way every time you use it. In most cases, Netscape Gold should take care of this for you. However, if you are working from templates, or neglect to move a file to the correct directory/folder before you add it to the web page, you may get unexpected results. For example, if one page references the image like this:

```
../images/myimage.gif
```

and another page references the image like this:

```
http://www.me.com/images/myimage.gif
```

then most browsers will play it safe and re-download the image. When I say that the image references must be exactly the same, they must be *exactly* the same!

Tables and Graphics

Unlike desktop publishing, where the person who lays out the page has complete control over the exact placement of every page elements — text, graphics, rules, headers, footers, and so on — web publishing is completely fluid. The browser determines how to lay out the page when it displays the page. There is a very good reason for this: The size of the page varies when the user changes the size of the browser window.

For example, Figure 6-12 shows a web page with one window size, and Figure 6-13 shows the same page when the window size is reduced.

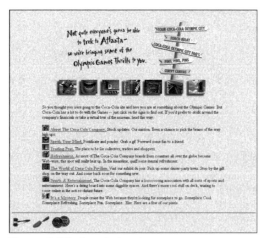

Figure 6-12: A typical web page.

Figure 6-13: A web page with the window size changed.

There is a growing trend to use tables to enforce a specific page size. For example, Figure 6-14 shows a web page at a normal window width. In Figure 6-15, I have widened the window, but the layout of the web page did not change.

The key to using tables to control page layout is the WIDTH parameter of the TABLE tag. In the following example, the table is set to 130 pixels wide:

```
<TABLE WIDTH=130 >
```

The width of a table must be calculated carefully. The above example is from a table that contains a vertical column of button images; the images are 120 pixels wide, so the table is 130 pixels wide.

A multicolumn table would be as wide as the sum of its columns. For most situations, I recommend a three-column table. This usually allows you to have a column of buttons or hypertext links in one narrow column, a wide middle column for the bulk of the text, and a third narrow column for images, highlights, explanations, and other features. You'll see an example of this kind of layout later in this chapter. You can also find many examples on the Web, at such sites as:

```
http://www.newslink.org/menu.html
http://www.denver-rmn.com/
http://espnet.sportszone.com/
```

Column 1   Column 2   Column 3

Figure 6-14: Another typical web page.

Figure 6-15: The page layout did not change.

To set the width of individual columns in a table, right-click in the top cell in the column, and choose the Table Properties menu selection. Click the Cell tab (see Figure 6-16) if it is not already active. You can set a cell's width as a percentage of the table's width, but if you want to lock in the width precisely, use the Pixels setting for cell width. Figure 6-16 shows a cell's width set to 160 pixels. Setting the width to a number automatically causes the Cell width check box to be checked. To turn off cell width, uncheck this box.

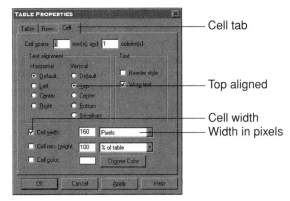

Cell tab

Top aligned

Cell width
Width in pixels

Figure 6-16: Setting cell width.

There is no way to set the width of a column, so you may need to set the width of every cell in the column. If other cells in the column contain material that will not be wider than the column (usually, this means either images or short lines of text), then setting just the first cell in the column will be sufficient. If you have multiline text in other cells in the column, set the width of all cells in the column, one at a time.

TIP

When appropriate, you can set the width of one or two columns, and allow the other columns to adjust their size to the window size.

To set the width of the entire table, right-click in a table cell, and choose the Table Properties menu selection. Click the Table tab (see Figure 6-17) if it is not already active. You can set the width of the table as either a percentage of the window's width, or a set number of pixels. To completely control layout, set a fixed width by setting Table width using the Pixels setting (see Figure 6-17). The number of pixels should be the total width you desire. A typical page, for example, would be about 600 to 650 pixels wide, but this can vary depending on your design.

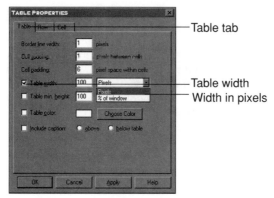

Figure 6-17: Setting table width.

Creating a Web Site

Earlier in this chapter, you saw how to create a plan for a web site. In the rest of the chapter, you'll learn how to move from plan to reality. Figure 6-18 shows the final plan for the web site, showing how pages relate to one another. The dark lines show the primary links between web pages. The home page is the central point for accessing information, but you can also move between pages in a variety of ways. By using buttons and image maps, the web site allows the visitor to quickly jump to almost any page.

The pages you see in Figure 6-18 are miniature versions of the actual pages, which are based on the rough sketches shown at the beginning of the chapter (Figures 6-1 to 6-4). Many of the steps needed to create these pages are based on the tutorials in earlier chapters. Most of the pages are designed using tables, however, and this gives them a more interesting appearance.

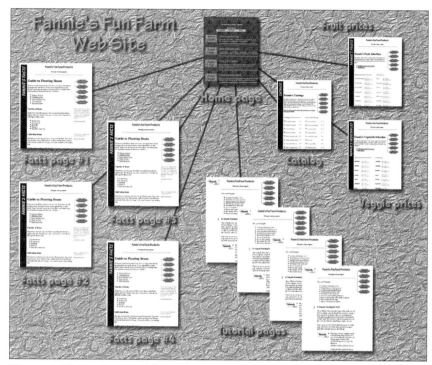

Figure 6-18: The layout of the web site.

Figure 6-18b shows another example of a use for fixed column widths: a drop capital. The large letter D is in a column of its own, as is the vertical blue bar that separates columns of text.

All of the pages for this web site are located on the CD-ROM in the \tutorial\chap06\fanny directory. To access the home page (which provides links to all other pages), double-click on the file \tutorial\ chap06\fanny\index.htm. The file that shows how the drop capital effect was achieved is \tutorial\chap06\drop1s.htm; another version using text instead of graphics is \tutorial\chap06\drop1.htm. Follow the hyperlinks on the drop capital pages to see the details of how the effect is accomplished.

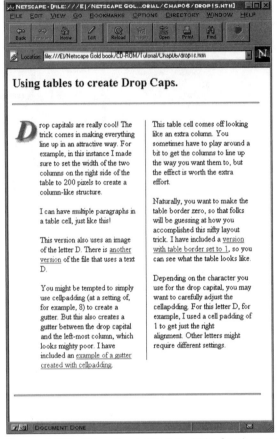

Figure 6-18b: Using fixed column widths for drop capitals.

Creating the Home Page

The final version of the home page is shown in Figure 6-19. I used a background image for this web page. It is a repeating, seamless pattern (see Figure 6-20). The image is the central part of a flower (the aster), and includes the Fannie's logo.

This is the only example of a dark background image anywhere in this book. A dark background can be effective in some situations, but it can also make the web page more difficult to read. Use dark backgrounds with discretion. Make sure that the effect doesn't overwhelm the web page.

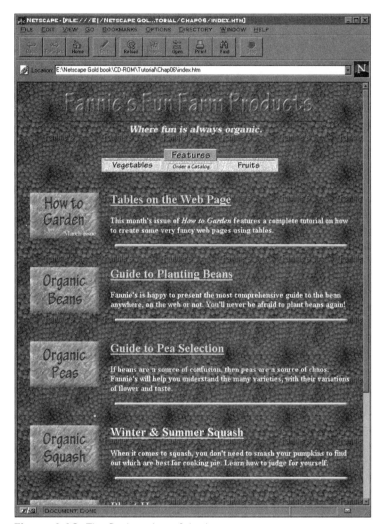

Figure 6-19: The final version of the home page.

Figure 6-20: The background image.

To create this page, I first created a table two columns wide and six rows high (see Figure 6-20b). I added a series of button images to the left column, one for each teaching area. I then added a brief headline and text block explaining each button. I also added a graphic below each block of text to add separation between buttons — otherwise, the buttons tended to crowd each other when the dark background was added. I also added a large version of the company logo, the slogan, and the floating image map. The logo and image map were created in Fractal Design Painter.

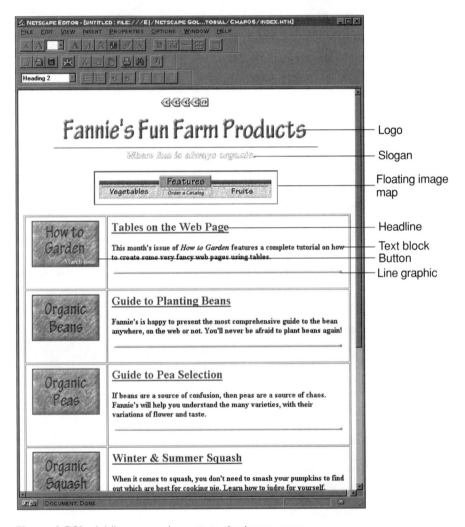

Figure 6-20b: Adding page elements to the home page.

I then added hyperlinks to the buttons and the headlines, and added the image for the background. This completed the home page.

Positive elements: The various web pages that make up the site are easily reached from the home page. The floating image map is attractive, and uses a 3D effect that grabs attention.

Negative elements: The vertical height of the page is too large, leaving some buttons out of sight below the bottom of the window even on a very large desktop such as 1024×768. This could be corrected by using smaller buttons and smaller text for headlines and text blocks. Figure 6-21 shows an alternate version of the page with these corrections.

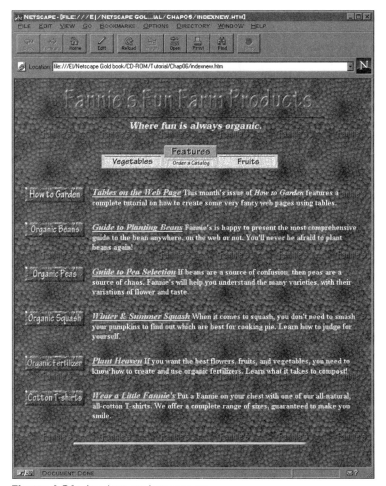

Figure 6-21: An alternate home page.

Creating Teaching Pages #1

There are two kinds of teaching pages: single- and multipage. One of the single-page versions is shown in Figure 6-22. There are three columns, two of which have a fixed width — the left and right columns. The middle column adjusts in width to fit the window width. The left column contains an image with vertical text. The cell's background color is set to black. The right column contains the vertical column of button images at top right, and a series of quotations in light blue text — one for each block of text in the middle column.

To create this page, I started with a table three columns wide and eight rows high. I deleted cells (one cell from the first seven rows; two cells from the bottom row) and adjusted the row span and column span settings of some cells as shown in Figure 6-23.

There are several features of the table in Figure 6-23 that require explanation. Note that the first and third columns are wider than the center column. I set the width of the first column to 50, because I planned to put a 50-pixel-wide image in that column (see Figure 6-24). I set the width of the third column, on the right, to 150 pixels because that's the width of the buttons in the vertical column. I also set the cell color of the left, 8-row-spanning cell to black (see Figure 6-25). To access the dialog box shown in Figure 6-25, right-click on a cell and click the Table Properties menu selection. Click the Cell tab if it is not already active.

Once the table was created and finalized, I simply added the text and images that I had created for the page. The images were created in Fractal Design Painter.

To see this file for yourself, locate the file \tutorial\chap06\fanny\beans.htm and double-click it.

Positive elements: This page works very well. It contains a collection of short text passages, with hyperlinks to each passage available right at the top of the page. The black bar at far left provides a unifying element that binds the separate pieces visually. The third column adds a little spice to the page, providing, in this example, a place for whimsical quotations.

Negative elements: None significant.

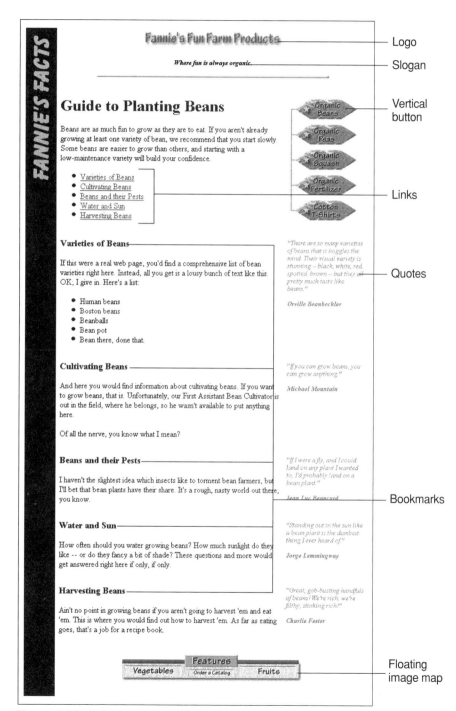

Figure 6-22: A single-page teaching page.

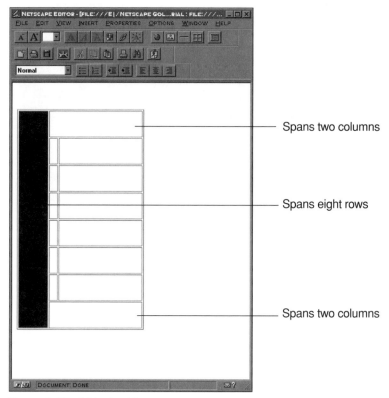

Spans two columns

Spans eight rows

Spans two columns

Figure 6-23: A blank table.

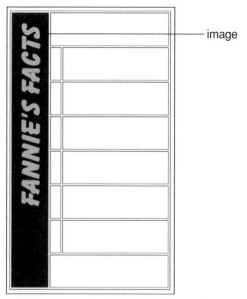

image

Figure 6-24: Adding an image to a cell.

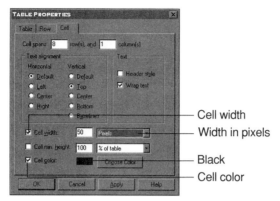

Figure 6-25: *Setting cell color and cell width.*

Creating Teaching Pages #2

The second group of teaching pages, the multipage group, required a different approach. The content of the single-page web pages was more or less static — a simple list of topics, each of which was short. Each of the multipage pages contains a long discourse on a single subject, and will include illustrations as well as text.

I again used a three-column layout, but it is completely different from the previous example. Figure 6-25b shows the realization of the rough sketch. There are several important elements on this page. At upper left, I added a graphic that displays the issue date. This means it will be easy for visitors to know when they are reading an archived issue or the current issue. The logo and vertical column of buttons are carried over from other page designs. Most of the rest of the page is completely different.

It helps to view the layout of this page with table borders visible (see Figure 6-26). You can see that this is a complete 3-by-3 table, with no special changes of any kind. I used alignment to control where in a cell the image or text appears. For example, the page number, in the middle left cell, is aligned TOP and RIGHT. The RIGHT setting can be a text setting, or you can right-click in the cell and set the cell's alignment to RIGHT, or you can right-align the image using the Image Properties dialog box. The TOP setting is set with the cell's Alignment property in the Table Properties dialog box.

I also made use of a table-within-a-table in the central cell. All of the text for each page is added to this one cell. Figure 6-26b shows a complete page, where you can see just how much text and image I tucked into one cell!

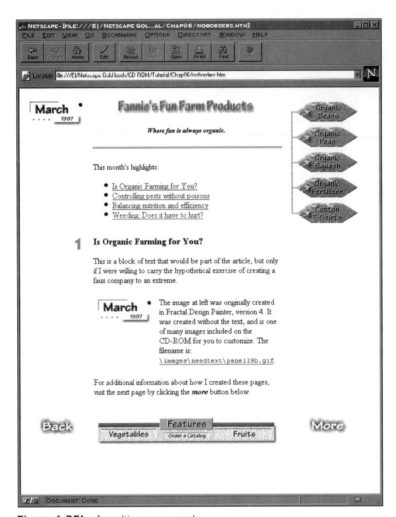

Figure 6-25b: A multipage example.

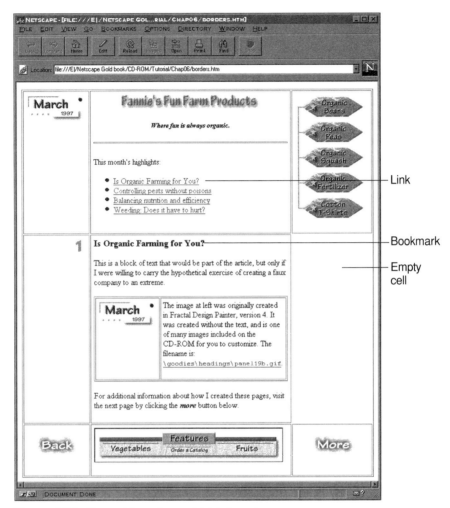

Figure 6-26: The multipage's secret table layout.

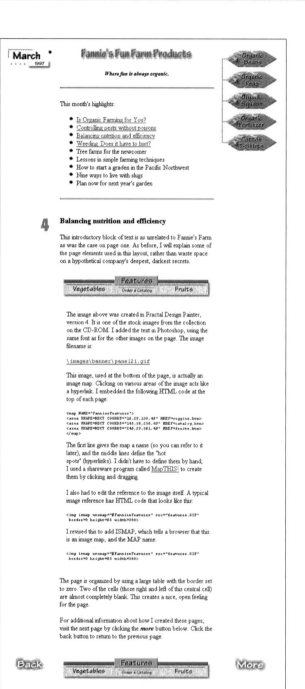

Figure 6-26b: A complete page using the multipage layout.

I added buttons at bottom left and bottom right for moving backward and forward among the multiple pages.

You can find the pages in this section in the folder \tutorial\chap06\fanny. The files borders.htm and noborders.htm show the page layout with and without borders. The files fanny1.htm through fanny4.htm illustrate completed page layouts. The file fanny4.htm contains useful information about how I created the floating image maps found on every page.

Positive elements: This page design is sharp, and has lots of attractive white space. The list of subtopics (one per page) is listed at the top of each page with hyperlinks for easy access. Movement through the pages is fluid, as you can either click hyperlinks or use the Back and More buttons.

Negative elements: The black vertical bar is not used in this layout, which differentiates it from the other layouts. This is a plus if you feel the need to visually distinguish these pages from the other pages, or a minus if you feel that it disrupts the coherence of the site design. I leave the resolution of that argument to you, dear reader!

Creating Product Pages

The product pages are very similar in appearance to the single-page teaching pages (see Figure 6-27). The primary difference is that there is a large, five-column table that takes up the bulk of the page. Figure 6-28 shows the table's borders. Note that I included a fixed-width column at the center of the table. It has one cell with a fixed width (I deleted the other cells, and gave this cell a row span equal to the number of rows in the table).

I used a small font for the text in the table-within-a-table to display as much information as possible at one time.

You can find the pages in this section in the folder \tutorial\chap06\fanny. The files veggies.htm and fruits.htm show the page layouts for the two product pages.

Positive elements: This page is relatively compact. It uses the standard layout (black bar at left, headline and paragraph plus hyperlinks at top, floating image map at bottom). This makes it easy for the user to work with the page.

Negative elements: There is a lot of white space in the table. This could be reduced by using line breaks (Shift + Enter) instead of paragraph breaks (Enter).

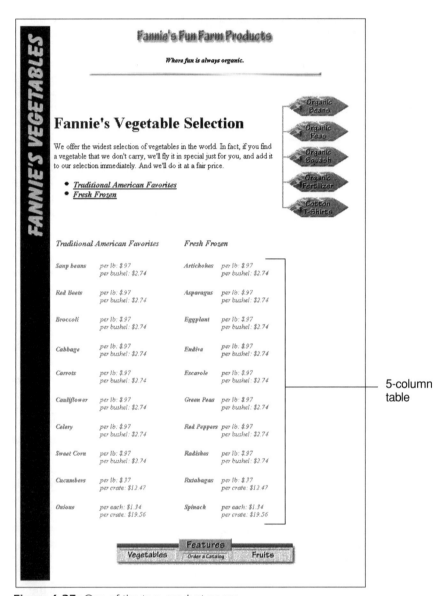

Figure 6-27: One of the two product pages.

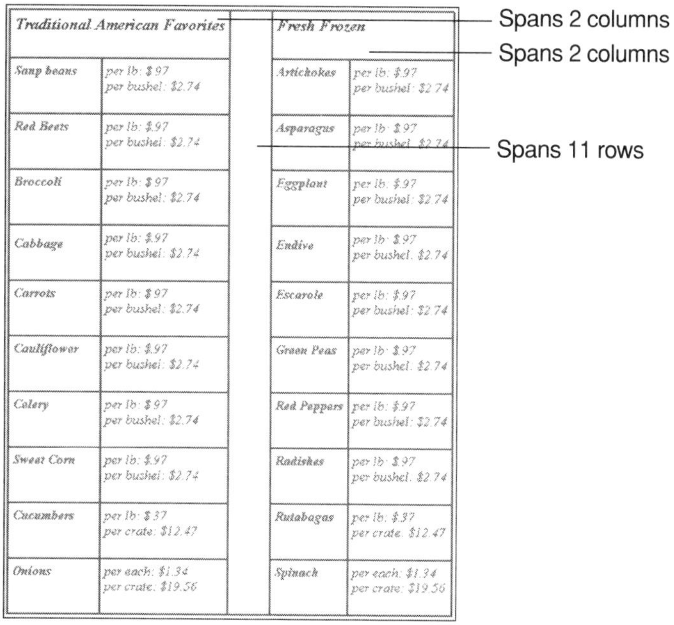

Traditional American Favorites		Fresh Frozen	
Snap beans	per lb: $.97 per bushel: $2.74	Artichokes	per lb: $.97 per bushel: $2.74
Red Beets	per lb: $.97 per bushel: $2.74	Asparagus	per lb: $.97 per bushel: $2.74
Broccoli	per lb: $.97 per bushel: $2.74	Eggplant	per lb: $.97 per bushel: $2.74
Cabbage	per lb: $.97 per bushel: $2.74	Endive	per lb: $.97 per bushel: $2.74
Carrots	per lb: $.97 per bushel: $2.74	Escarole	per lb: $.97 per bushel: $2.74
Cauliflower	per lb: $.97 per bushel: $2.74	Green Peas	per lb: $.97 per bushel: $2.74
Celery	per lb: $.97 per bushel: $2.74	Red Peppers	per lb: $.97 per bushel: $2.74
Sweet Corn	per lb: $.97 per bushel: $2.74	Radishes	per lb: $.97 per bushel: $2.74
Cucumbers	per lb: $.37 per crate: $12.47	Rutabagas	per lb: $.37 per crate: $12.47
Onions	per each: $1.34 per crate: $19.56	Spinach	per each: $1.34 per crate: $19.56

Spans 2 columns
Spans 2 columns
Spans 11 rows

Figure 6-28: The table within the overall table.

Creating Catalog Forms

The catalog form is based on the product pages. Instead of a table listing products as the central element, I use a table with lots and lots of check boxes (see Figure 6-29). This is a two-column table-within-a-table. I created the form in Netscape Gold in three steps, making extensive use of the Insert I HTML Tag menu selection:

1. I added the form start tag at the top of the table cell that contains the table-within-a-table, and the form end tag at the bottom. The start tag uses an ACTION parameter that will e-mail form results.

2. I added the check boxes, one at a time, to each of the cells. I used a different NAME parameter to associate each check box with the catalog listed in that cell.

3. I added the text prompt and text box for the e-mail address, and the Submit *(Order Catalogs Now)* and Reset buttons.

These three steps were completed in Edit mode, as shown in Figure 6-30. Note that there is a little yellow tag (indicating an inserted HTML tag) for every form element you can see in Figure 6-29. Double-click any tag to view the tag's contents.

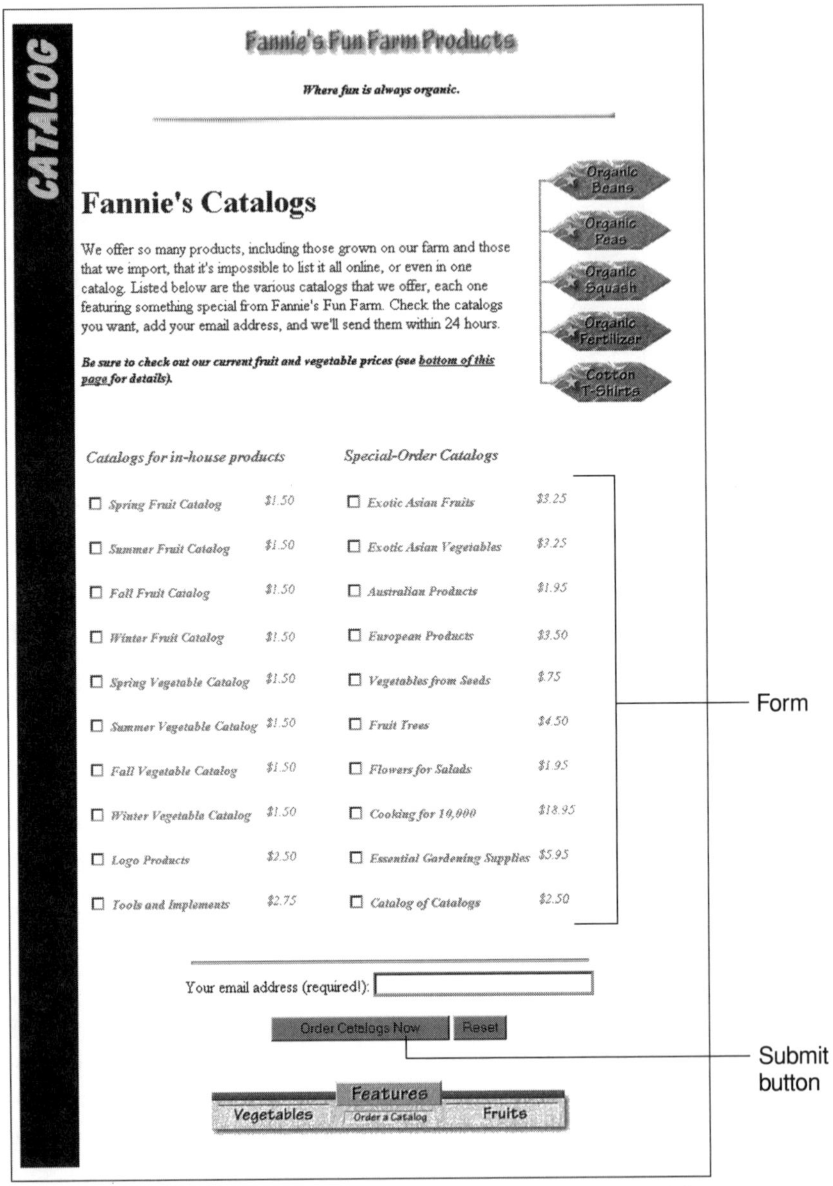

CATALOG

Fannie's Fun Farm Products

Where fun is always organic.

Fannie's Catalogs

We offer so many products, including those grown on our farm and those that we import, that it's impossible to list it all online, or even in one catalog. Listed below are the various catalogs that we offer, each one featuring something special from Fannie's Fun Farm. Check the catalogs you want, add your email address, and we'll send them within 24 hours.

Be sure to check out our current fruit and vegetable prices (see bottom of this page for details).

Organic Beans

Organic Peas

Organic Squash

Organic Fertilizer

Cotton T-Shirts

Catalogs for in-house products

- ☐ *Spring Fruit Catalog* $1.50
- ☐ *Summer Fruit Catalog* $1.50
- ☐ *Fall Fruit Catalog* $1.50
- ☐ *Winter Fruit Catalog* $1.50
- ☐ *Spring Vegetable Catalog* $1.50
- ☐ *Summer Vegetable Catalog* $1.50
- ☐ *Fall Vegetable Catalog* $1.50
- ☐ *Winter Vegetable Catalog* $1.50
- ☐ *Logo Products* $2.50
- ☐ *Tools and Implements* $2.75

Special-Order Catalogs

- ☐ *Exotic Asian Fruits* $3.25
- ☐ *Exotic Asian Vegetables* $3.25
- ☐ *Australian Products* $1.95
- ☐ *European Products* $3.50
- ☐ *Vegetables from Seeds* $.75
- ☐ *Fruit Trees* $4.50
- ☐ *Flowers for Salads* $1.95
- ☐ *Cooking for 10,000* $18.95
- ☐ *Essential Gardening Supplies* $5.95
- ☐ *Catalog of Catalogs* $2.50

— Form

Your email address (required!): [   ]

[Order Catalogs Now] [Reset]

— Submit button

Features

Vegetables   / Order a Catalog   Fruits

Figure 6-29: The catalog page, which includes a form with check boxes.

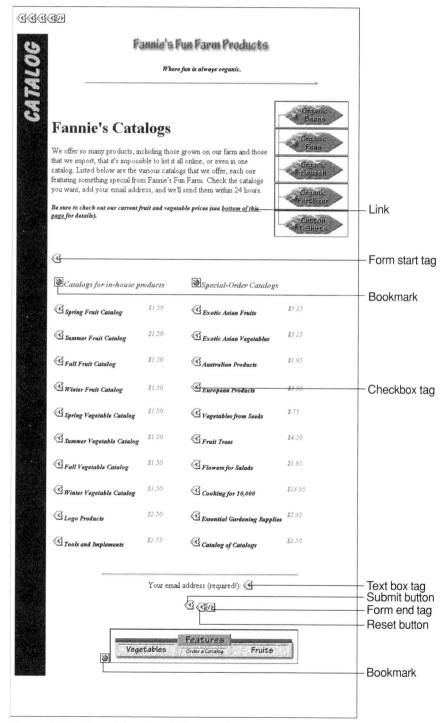

Figure 6-30: The catalog form in Edit mode.

Because the form is set up so that it e-mails results when the Submit button is clicked, you can use the Magic Parser (see Chapter 5) to process the form data. For example, if a user checked off a number of catalogs, and then clicked the Submit button, your e-mail would contain something like this:

```
AsianFruit=on&AussieFruit=on&WinterFruit=on&SeedVeggies=on&
SummerVeggie=on&WinterVeggie=on&Cooking=on&Supplies=on&
CatCat=on&email= ronw@olympus.net
```

The Magic Parser would convert this to readable form, as shown in Figure 6-31.

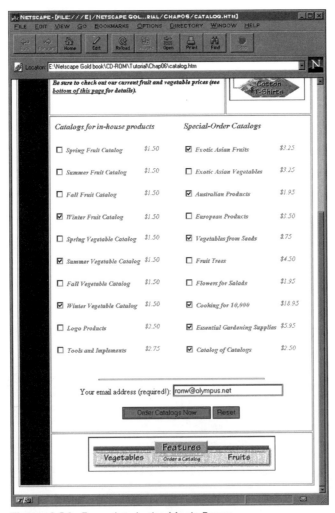

Figure 6-31: Form data in the Magic Parser.

You can find the page in this section in the folder \tutorial\chap06\fanny. The file catalog.htm shows the page layout for the catalog page.

Positive elements: The form packs a lot of information and utility into a small space, and uses the familiar page layout seen elsewhere on this web site.

Negative elements: None significant.

Building on Your Web Site

Once you have a working version of your web site, there is still plenty of work to do. A web site is a complex organism, and can grow and evolve for a variety of reasons. For example, if your company has a new product, if you adopt a new pet, or if you want to add more information to an existing page, you'll have to fit the new stuff into the old web site design.

Sometimes, this is a simple process — just add a page or a paragraph to an existing page. Sometimes, you will have to rethink your entire web site design to accommodate the new material.

As you and your visitors use the pages you build, new ideas will occur to you. For example, the catalog form requires the visitor's e-mail address in order to send the e-mail catalogs. You could write JavaScript code for the form that would execute when the form is submitted. The code would check for the presence of an e-mail address. If there is no address, the form would not get submitted, and an alert box could pop up to alert the visitor to the missing information. The following JavaScript function (see Chapter 7 for JavaScript details) could be called when the Submit button is clicked:

```
function checkForEmailAddress()
{
   if (document.catalogs.email.value == "")
   {
      // There is no email address.
      alert("You did not provide an email address.");
      return false;
   }
   else
   {
      document.catalogs.submit;
      return true;
   }
}
```

You can create your own version of the catalog form that does these things, or you can peek at the file \tutorial\chap06\fanny\catnew.htm to see how I modified the form to check for an e-mail address.

NetKey #6: Mastering Tables

Tables can provide tools for creating cool web pages. There are many ways to enhance the appearance or vary the layout of web pages using tables. The NetKey for this chapter focuses on teaching you how to use tables to control the way a web page displays images and text.

You'll find detailed information about the drop caps mentioned earlier in this chapter, as well as a wealth of other ideas you can put to use quickly and easily on your own web pages. You'll also find links to a huge number of web pages that use tables to enhance their design and functionality

To begin, double-click on the file

/tutorial/index.htm

on the CD-ROM, which will automatically start Netscape Gold in Browse mode. As usual, if you do not want to connect, click the Cancel button when the Connection dialog box appears. The appearance of the file /tutorial/index.htm is shown in Figure 6-32.

The file /tutorial/index.htm contains hyperlinks to the NetKeys for every chapter in the book. To learn how to create a complex image with Painter, click the hyperlink for Chapter 6, *Mastering Tables*. The first NetKey page for this chapter is shown in Figure 6-33. To explore this NetKey, simply click on any and every hyperlink (usually underlined text) that strikes your fancy.

To access the NetKey page for Chapter 6 directly, double-click on the file /tutorial/chap06/webpage.htm.

Using NetKey #6

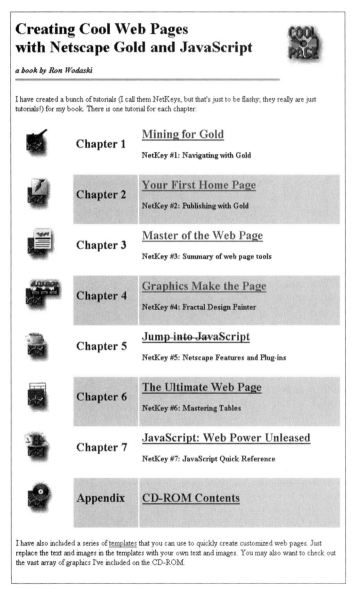

Figure 6-32: The web page for access to NetKey pages.

Figure 6-33: The NetKey page for Chapter 6.

JavaScript: Web Power Unleashed

JavaScript and You

You learned the basics of working with JavaScript in Chapter 5. You saw how easy it is to add Java applets to a web page. You learned about enhancing forms with JavaScript. In this chapter, you'll learn how to do some real programming with JavaScript by creating a JavaScript clock on a web page. The balance of the chapter will focus on the JavaScript language itself, covering the various elements of the language, and how they work together.

I have included a complete JavaScript language reference on the CD-ROM. It contains sample code and full explanations of each element of the JavaScript language. You can access the language reference by double-clicking the file \tutorial\chap07\language.htm.

You can find the complete, exhaustive, and sometimes overly technical Netscape JavaScript reference online at

```
http://home.netscape.com/eng/mozilla/Gold/handbook/javascript/
```

Before we dive head first into JavaScript, however, it's useful to know something about where JavaScript comes from. In the beginning, there was Java. Java is a full-blown programming language that rivals C++ in scope, complexity, and power.

Sample Some Java

For an example of some Java code, consider the animation applet I wrote for Chapter 5. I wrote the Java code in the Notepad editor, one line at a time, borrowing some portions from the sample applets that are included with the Java Developers Kit. I saved the Java applet code in the file `Bounce.java`.

A small portion of that code is shown in Listing 7-1. Unless you have some experience deciphering the C or C++ programming languages, the Java code might not make much sense. If you are intrigued by the idea of Java programming, I would suggest that you look at the book *60 Minute Guide to Java* by Ed Tittel and Mark Gaither.

Listing 7-1: Sample Java code

```
public void oneBounce(long vTime)
{
        boolean collide_horizontal = false;
        boolean collide_vertical   = false;
        float fudgeFactor = (float)Math.random() * .015f --
        .0075f;
        x += Velocity_x * vTime + (Accel_x / 2.0) *
        vTime;
        y += Velocity_y * vTime + (Accel_y / 2.0) *
        vTime;
        if (x <= 0.0f)
        {
                x = 0.0f;
                Velocity_x = -Velocity_x * variation +
        fudgeFactor;
                collide_horizontal = true;
        }
        Dimension d = parent.image_size;
```

```
if (x + width >= d.width)
{
        x = d.width — width;
        Velocity_x = -Velocity_x * variation +
        fudgeFactor;
        collide_horizontal = true;
}
if (y <= 0.01f)
{
        y = 0.0f;
        Velocity_y = -Velocity_y * variation +
        fudgeFactor;
        collide_vertical = true;
}
if (y + height >= d.height-40)
{
        y = d.height — height-45;
        Velocity_x *= variation;

        Velocity_y = -Velocity_y * variation +
        fudgeFactor;
        collide_vertical = true;
}
move(x, y);
if (Velocity_y <= 0)
        Velocity_y = Velocity_y — Accel_y *
        vTime;
else
        Velocity_y = Velocity_y + Accel_y *
        vTime;
if (Velocity_x <= 0)
        Velocity_x = Velocity_x — Accel_x *
        vTime;
else
        Velocity_x = Velocity_x + Accel_x *
        vTime;
findex += Velocity_V * vTime;
if (collide_horizontal)
{
        Velocity_V = 0.006f +
        (float)Math.random() * 0.002f;
         if (Velocity_x < 0)
                Velocity_x = -0.1f;
         else
```

(continued)

Listing 7-1: Sample Java code *(continued)*

```
                        Velocity_x = 0.1f;
        }
        if (collide_vertical)
        {
                Vellocity_V = 0.006f +
        (float)Math.random() * 0.002f;
                if (Velocity_y < 0)
                        Velocity_y = -0.05f;
                else
                        Velocity_y = 0.05f;
        }
        while (findex <= 0.0)
                findex += parent.bounceimages.length;
        index = ((int) findex) %
        parent.bounceimages.length;
}
```

If you are familiar with C or C++ programming, Java code will probably look somewhat familiar. For example, statements like

```
if (x + width >= d.width)
```

look exactly like C/C++ statements. Java is somewhat more purely object-oriented than C and C++, however, and that object orientation applies to JavaScript, too. Java is extremely flexible about objects — you can create new objects, with new properties, from existing objects. JavaScript does not offer this flexibility. JavaScript is used simply to manipulate objects. There are lots of objects to manipulate, however, such as documents, windows, forms, form elements, and so on. You'll find a complete list of objects later in this chapter.

One of the nice thing about *manipulating* objects with JavaScript, as opposed to *programming* them in Java, is that you don't have to work hard at all to add them to your web pages. Figure 7-1 shows the applet from Chapter 5 in action. There is a background image of a forest, a bird that flies above the forest, and a string of text at the bottom of the Java applet.

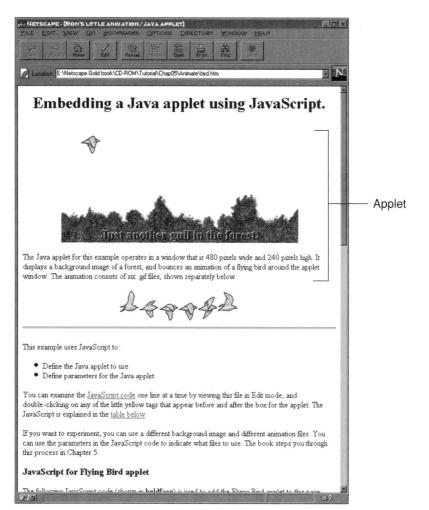

Applet

Figure 7-1: A Java applet on a web page.

Adding applets to web pages is extremely easy. Enhancing a web page with JavaScript is a bit harder, but still within the realm of possiblity for most web page designers. However, JavaScript is a powerful programming language in its own right. It may lack the flexibility of a heavyweight language like Java, but it can do a lot to enhance your web pages.

A JavaScript Primer

JavaScript, as a programming language, is based on objects. Objects have three things associated with them: events, properties, and methods. Events are what happens to objects, such as a mouse click. An object's properties are set with JavaScript, allowing you to change the way the object behaves. An object's methods are available for you to use in JavaScript code, allowing you to make the object perform tricks for you.

The language of object-oriented programming can seem obscure at first. As you get to know the terminology better, you'll find that it stays obscure. Objects and properties are the easiest concepts to understand, and events are reasonably straightforward. However, methods take more than a little bit of getting used to. In order to keep myself straight on the subject, I think of methods as little tricks that objects can perform. If you think of an object as a trained performer of some sort, the whole thing starts to make some sense. This metaphor helps clarify what's what when discussing object-oriented programming. Instead of OOP, we'll use DOG: Deliverance from Object Giddiness.

If you have never programmed before, JavaScript may seem like a foreign language. Fortunately, JavaScript is a lot easier to learn and work with than a foreign language!

Programming Basics

If you have never written a computer program before, you need to know some things about programming before you can get started with JavaScript. Once you understand the basics of programming, you can move on to the practical uses of JavaScript.

Programming languages

A computer program is written in a programming language. Quite a few programming languages are available. Some, like assembly language, are very hard for humans to use, but very easy for computers to understand. These are called low-level languages, and they are extremely technical and challenging. The term-low level is based on the fact that the programs one writes with such languages are very close to the level of the machine. Here's what assembly code looks like:

```
_PROG       SEGMENT   BYTE
            ASSUME    CS:_PROG
```

```
GETPATH     PROC      FAR
            MOV       AX,[BX]
            CMP       AX,0
            JE        Error
            MOV       SI,BX
            MOV       AH,19h
            INT       21h
            ADD       AL,'A'
            MOV       [SI],AL
Error:      RET
GETPATH     ENDP
_PROG       ENDS
            END
```

From a human perspective, that's nearly complete gibberish. You have to know the codes to make any sense of it at all.

Other languages, like C or C++, are a little easier for the average human to work with, still allow the programmer to work at a reasonably low level — but are also several steps up from something like assembly language. Here's what C++ code looks like:

```
CPreviewDC::CPreviewDC()
{
  // Initial scale factor and top-left offset
  m_nScaleNum = m_nScaleDen = 1;
  m_sizeTopLeft.cx = m_sizeTopLeft.cy = 8;
  m_hFont = m_hPrinterFont = NULL;
}
```

This is a little easier to understand (it does use words like "PrinterFont" occasionally!), but portions of it are still very technical, and require serious study to understand completely.

Still other languages, like COBOL or dBASE, make an effort to be somewhat like a human language. This is called a high-level language, because it is well removed from the level at which the machine operates. Such languages look like plain English, but they do require that you learn the special meaning of the English-like words they use. Here's what dBASE code looks like:

```
set alternate to
set format to web
go top
```

(continued)

```
edit
close all
set talk on
set safety on
set display to VGA25
return
```

JavaScript sits somewhere between C and dBASE as a language. It has some elements that are based on languages like C, but it also tries to be fairly readable. Although there is a great deal of hype about JavaScript being accessible and easy to use, the fact is that it really is a programming language, and it really does take a good deal of time and effort to get good at using it. Here's what JavaScript code looks like:

```
function Recalculate()
{
   form = document.form1
   LoanAmount= form.LoanAmount.value
   DownPayment= form.DownPayment.value
   if (DownPayment == "")
{
      DownPayment = "0"
   }
   AnnualInterestRate = form.InterestRate.value/100
   Years= form.NumberOfYears.value
   MonthRate=AnnualInterestRate/12
   NumPayments=Years*12
   Prin=LoanAmount-DownPayment

   MonthPayment=Math.floor((Prin*MonthRate)/(1-Math.pow
   ((1+MonthRate),
                   (-1*NumPayments)))*100)/100
   form.NumberOfPayments.value=NumPayments
   form.MonthlyPayment.value=MonthPayment
}
```

Some plain English is involved, and some obscure elements are involved (all those periods, for example), but by the time you finish this chapter it will all make some sense.

Language elements

Most computer languages share some concepts in common. JavaScript is no exception. To use a computer language, you'll need to know what are such things as variables, statements, and operators. In this section, I'll cover these programming basics. In the next section, I'll cover basic programming elements that are more or less specific to JavaScript.

Literals

Literal values are values that are, well, literal. For example, "7" is a literal: it's literally the number seven. The value of a literal stays constant at all times. Seven, after all, is always seven! The opposite of a literal is a variable. As the name suggest, a variable's value can change.

Variables

You can think of variables as containers. They hold whatever value you put into them. You use the assignment operators (see the next page) to assign a value to a variable. Variables have names; you usually want to give a variable a name that you will understand at a later time, when you come back to your program. For example, a variable name like Monthly Payment is very useful, while the name MP is much less so. You can use letters and numbers in variable names, but it must always start with a letter, and you cannot have any spaces in the name.

To create a variable you can declare it, like this:

```
var MonthlyPayment;
```

You can also supply a value for the variable at the time you declare it:

```
var MonthlyPayment = 120;
```

This is called initializing the variable, and it's usually a good idea to do so. In many cases, you will initialize the variable to zero or null. That way, you can always tell if the variable has been used yet — if it is still zero or null, nothing has been done to the variable.

Variable scope

When you create a variable, you need to decide whether it will have local or global scope. If the variable is global, you can reference it anywhere in your program. If it is local, you can only reference it in the local context, such as a function. Variables declared inside a function with the `var` keyword are always local. Variables declared and initialized without the `var` keyword are always global, such as

```
MonthlyPayment = 120;
```

Variables declared with the `var` keyword, but outside of and before all functions, are also global in scope.

Assignment operators

These operators are used to assign a value. There is always a left-side expression, which receives the value, and the right-side expression, which is the source of the value. If you have never used a language like C or C++, these operators may seem confusing at first. However, they are very useful when you get used to them!

=	Assigns the value of the right-side expression to the left-side expression. For example, x = y takes the value contained in y and puts it in x. The value of y remains the same.
+=	Adds the value of the right-side expression to the left-side expression. For example, x += 7 adds 7 to x.
-=	Subtracts the value of the right-side expression from the left-side expression. For example, x -= 7 subtracts 7 from x.
*=	Multiplies the value of the right-side expression by the left-side expression. For example, x *= y multiplies x by y and stores the result in x.
/=	Divides the value of the right-side expression by the left-side expression. For example, x /= y divides x by y and stores the result in x.

Operators

These "operate" on one or two values to generate a result. The expression combines variables and operators. For example: `totalInventory = totalWarehouse1 + totalWarehouse2`.

+, -, *, /	These are your standard arithmetic operators - add, subtract, multiply and divide with them to your heart's content. Example: `myAge = yourAge + 5;`
+ (string)	Adds one string to another. Example: `lastName="Smith"; fullName = "John" + lastName`.
%	Used for modulo arithmetic. This is the remainder after division. For example, `10 % 3 = 1` (10 divided by three leaves a remainder of 1). Example: `form.balance.value = form.attendance.value % 5`.
++	Increments a value by one. For example, if `myCounter` is 17, then `myCounter++` sets the variable `myCounter` to 18. This is frequently used for counting during a loop. You can use the ++ operator in two ways. If you put it after the variable (postfix), then the variable is incremented after it is used in the line of

code. If you put it before the variable (prefix), the variable is incremented, and then used in code. For example, if you have the statement y = x++, and x is equal to three, then y gets set to three, and then x gets set to 4. If you have the statement y = ++x, then x gets set to 4, and then y gets set to 4.

--	Decrements a value. This works just like the ++ operator, but it lowers a value by one.
-	Changes the sign of a variable.
Bitwise	JavaScript supports numerous bitwise operators, but these are rarely used in nontechnical programming. You can find complete information about bitwise operators in Netscape's online JavaScript documentation.

Comparison operators

These operators are used to compare two values (although some are unary operators that take only one value). The result of the comparison is always a logical (often called Boolean) value: true or false. These are used often with the if statement.

&&	Logical AND. This returns a value of true only if both expressions are true. Example: (timerEnabled && Increase > 5). The first expressions, timerEnabled, is a variable than contains a true or false value. The second expression is Increase > 5. Only if both expressions evaluate to true (that is, if timerEnabled is true, and the variable Increase has a value greater than 5) will the && operator result in a value of true.
||	Logical OR. It returns a value of true only if at least one of two expressions is true. Example: (timerEnabled OR timerRunning). If the timer is enabled, or if the timer is running, this will return true.
!	Logical NOT. If an expression is true, this operator returns false. If an expression is false, this operator returns true. Example: timerEnabled = !timerEnabled. If the timer is already enabled, it is turned off. If it is not enabled, then it is set to enabled. A clean, easy way to toggle logical values.
==	Tests to see if two expressions are equal. If they are equal, returns true. If not equal, returns false.
>	Returns true if the first expression is greater than the second expression. Otherwise, returns false.
>=	Returns true if the first expression is greater than or equal to the second expression. Otherwise, returns false.

<	Returns true if the first expression is less than the second expression. Otherwise, returns false.
<=	Returns true if the first expression is less than or equal to the second expression. Otherwise, returns false.
!=	Tests to see if two expressions are *not* equal. If they are not equal, returns true. If equal, returns false.

Statements

Statements (also often referred to as commands) are language elements that actually do something. Conditional statements, for example, control program flow. One common conditional statement is `if`, which occurs in almost every computer language. Every language has its own statements. Some languages use few statements, and rely on functions to get the job done. C is like that, and so is JavaScript. JavaScript has very few statements, and most are conditional statements that control program flow. Besides `if`, common conditional statements are `while` and `for`, which are used for loops. A `while` loop continues while a condition is true. A `for` loop typically continues for a specified number of iterations.

Some languages rely heavily on statements, and less on functions. The dBASE language uses this approach, as does BASIC. This is mostly a philosophical issue; reliance on statements isn't necessarily better than reliance on functions, and vice versa.

A complete list of JavaScript statements is given later in this chapter.

Functions

Functions are also language elements that do something. Most languages have two kinds of functions: those that are built into the language, and those that the programmer creates (user-defined functions).

For example, the `fopen()` function is a built-in C function that opens a file. It takes two arguments: the filename, and a mode (read or write, for example). A programmer might write a user-defined function to open a file, too. For example, such a function might be called `fileOpenRead`, and take only one argument: the filename. This function would only be called for reading file, and would in turn call the `fopen()` function with the read mode set, and pass along the filename it received. This nesting is common in languages like C, but less common in languages like JavaScript. The lower level a language is, the more likely nesting is to be useful.

Because JavaScript is an object-oriented language, it uses methods instead of functions. However, methods are very, very much like ordinary functions. If you have previous experience with functions, you'll pick up on methods quickly.

JavaScript Basics

As you learned in Chapter 5, you can add JavaScript to a web page easily. Just type in the JavaScript, and then use the Properties I Character I JavaScript (Client) menu selection to tell Netscape Gold that the line is JavaScript. In the version of Netscape Gold on which this book is based, you can only enter one line of JavaScript at a time. Fortunately, you can put more than one JavaScript statement on a single line.

You may have noticed that there is also a menu selection that specifies JavaScript (Server). This is for JavaScript code that is meant to run on the web server, not on the client (local) machine.

When you apply the JavaScript (Client) property to your JavaScript code, Netscape Gold simply places the code between SCRIPT tags. Open a new, blank document in Netscape Gold (File I New Document I Blank). Type the following line into the blank document (see Figure 7-2):

```
document.write("This text was written on the page using
   JavaScript");
```

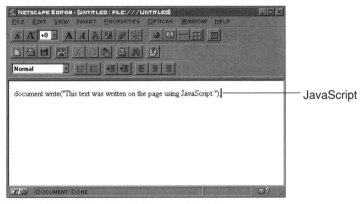

Figure 7-2: Adding JavaScript to a blank document.

Note that the line ends with a semicolon. The semicolon marks the end of a JavaScript statement. You can put more than one JavaScript statement on a single line by putting a semicolon between the statements.

Select the line of text (click and drag from left to right), and then use the Properties I Character I JavaScript (Client) menu selection to tell Netscape Gold you want this to be interpreted as JavaScript code. Save the document on your hard disk as `\Gold Pages\JScript01.htm` (see Figure 7-3). Click the Browse button to view the result in Browse mode. Figure 7-4 shows that the text from the line of JavaScript is all that appears on the page — the

JavaScript code itself is invisible. Note that the JavaScript ran automatically. You didn't have to do anything to make it happen. This is how JavaScript works: The JavaScript code always runs when the web page is loaded into the browser.

 Not all JavaScript will execute automatically. If you use JavaScript to create functions (which are described later in this chapter), the functions are not executed until something on the web page causes the function to execute.

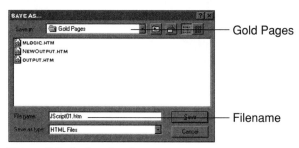

Figure 7-3: Saving the document.

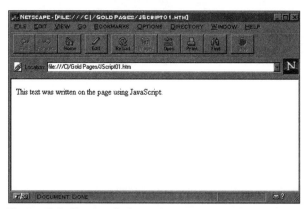

Figure 7-4: The JavaScript code runs automatically, displaying text on the web page.

If you open the file you saved in Notepad (open Notepad, and then click and drag the file's icon into Notepad), you can see how Netscape Gold makes sure that the JavaScript code is correctly interpreted by the browser (see Figure 7-5). The JavaScript code is shown in bold in Listing 7-2 (the line breaks will vary).

Figure 7-5: Some JavaScript code in Notepad.

Listing 7-2: Adding JavaScript to an HTML File

```
<!DOCTYPE HTML PUBLIC "-//IETF//DTD HTML 3.2//EN">
<HTML>
<HEAD>
   <TITLE></TITLE>
   <META NAME="Author" CONTENT="Ron Wodaski">
   <META NAME="GENERATOR" CONTENT="Mozilla/3.0b5Gold
      (Win95; I) [Netscape]">
</HEAD>
<BODY TEXT="#000000" BGCOLOR="#FFFFFF" LINK="#0000EE"
      VLINK="#551A8B" ALINK="#FF0000">
<P><SCRIPT>document.write("This text was written on the
page using
JavaScript.");</SCRIPT></P>
</BODY>
</HTML>
```

Note that Netscape Gold added a <SCRIPT> tag to mark the beginning of the JavaScript code, and a </SCRIPT> tag to mark the end. If you try to enter more than one line of JavaScript code, each line begins and ends with the SCRIPT tags. This is why you must always enter an entire block of JavaScript code as one line, with a semicolon between JavaScript statements. Otherwise, every line of JavaScript becomes a separate script, rather that one large script.

TIP

Until and unless Netscape Gold handles multiple lines of JavaScript appropriately, your best strategy for multiline scripts is to create the script in Notepad, and then paste the entire script into a web page as one line. This technique is explained in detail in Chapter 5. Another strategy is to design and lay out the page in Netscape Gold, and then to open the HTML file itself in Notepad, and put all of your JavaScript code between <SCRIPT> and </SCRIPT> tags that you add yourself.

In this example, the JavaScript code didn't do anything that was really interesting. You could have put the text directly onto the page in Netscape Gold — there was no reason to write a JavaScript script to display the text. In the normal course of events, JavaScript scripts are triggered by various kinds of events. For example, if the visitor to the page clicks on a button, that's an event. If the mouse moves over an object, that's an event. If the visitor types something into a text field on a form, that's an event.

Events

There are different kinds of events, and each event has a name. Table 7-1 summarizes the events that can trigger JavaScript scripts. Note that most of the events have something to do with forms. Several of the events also apply to hyperlinks, and a few apply to the document itself.

Table 7-1: JavaScript Events

Event	Handler	Description
blur	onBlur	A blur event occurs when the user removes input focus from a form element. For example, if a check box currently has the focus (usually, right after it is clicked), and then the user clicks on a different form element, a blur event occurs for the check box object.
click	onClick	A click event occurs whenever the user clicks on a form element or on a hyperlink.
change	onChange	A change event occurs whenever the user changes the content or value of a text box or a text area, or changes the selected item in a selection list.
focus	onFocus	A focus event occurs when the user gives input focus to a form element. For example, if the user clicks in a text box, that's a focus event for that text box.
load	onLoad	A load event occurs when the page is loaded in Netscape Navigator.
mouse over	onMouseOver	A mouse over event occurs when the mouse pointer moves over a link or an anchor (bookmark).
select	onSelect	A select event occurs when the user selects a form element's input field.

Table 7-1: JavaScript events

Event	Handler	Description
submit	onSubmit	A submit event occurs when the form data is submitted by the user. This allows you to preprocess form data before it is sent on, either by e-mail or to a CGI script.
unload	onUnload	An unload event occurs when the user exits a page.

Events fit neatly into the DOG view of object-oriented programming. If you pat the dog on the head, that's an event. If you click a form field, that's an event. If you toss a dog a bone, you've got yourself an event. If you change the contents of a text box, that's an event.

You can find sample JavaScript code for these events on the CD-ROM. Double-click the file\tutorial\chap07\javascript\events.htm, where you will find a list of all of the events. Click on the event name to see sample code that shows you how to work with that event in JavaScript.

The following example of JavaScript shows why events are useful. You will create a simple form that has two text boxes and one button. The user enters a mathematical expression in the first text box, clicks the Calculate button, and the result appears in the second text box. Figure 7-6 shows what the complete web page looks like. To create this page

1. Open a new, blank document in Netscape Gold.

2. Type in a headline for the page: **My Homemade JavaScript Calculator**. Apply the style Heading 1. Add a horizontal line below the headline (see Figure 7-6).

3. Create the form by adding five tags using the Insert | HTML Tag menu selection (see Figure 7-7):

```
<FORM ACTION="mailto:me@myaddress.com "METHOD=POST>
<INPUT TYPE="text" NAME="entry" SIZE=15>
<INPUT TYPE="button" VALUE="Calculate"
onClick="compute(this.form)">
<INPUT TYPE="text" NAME="result" SIZE=15>
</FORM>
```

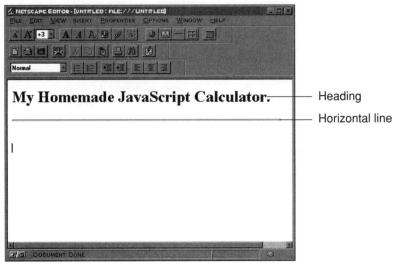

Figure 7-6: Laying out the page.

<FORM ACTION="mailto:me@myaddress.com "METHOD=POST>

    <INPUT TYPE="text" NAME="result" SIZE=15>

      <INPUT TYPE="text" NAME="entry"SIZE=l5>

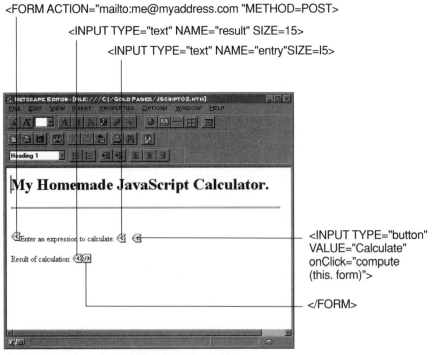

<INPUT TYPE="button"
VALUE="Calculate"
onClick="compute
(this. form)">

</FORM>

Figure 7-7: Adding tags to create a form.

Note that the tag for the Calculate button (tag #3) includes a reference to an event (onClick). When the button is clicked, the event triggers a call to a function (added in step 4) called *compute*.

Add prompts to the page as shown in Figure 7-7. You will need to use three nonbreaking spaces (Shift + space) to put space between the two tags at the end of the first line.

4. Type the following JavaScript code in Notepad. It is a function that takes a value (the current form) and takes data from one form element (the entry text field), evaluates it, and puts the result in another form element (the result text field). If that sounds confusing, all will become clear when you see the page in action following step 5.

```
function compute(form)
{
form.result.value = eval(form.entry.value)
}
```

Copy the code to the clipboard, and then paste it into the web page as the top line (see Figure 7-8). If necessary, make the style Normal.

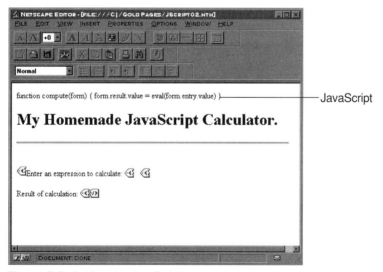

Figure 7-8: Adding the JavaScript.

An alternative way to accomplish step 4 is to type the following text as the first line on the web page (see Figure 7-8). If necessary, make the style Normal.

```
function compute(form) {form.result.value =
eval(form.entry.value)}
```

5. Select the text added in step 4, and use the menu selection Properties I Character I JavaScript (Client) to mark the text as JavaScript code. Figure 7-9 shows the result. Save your work in the file \Gold Pages\JScript02.htm.

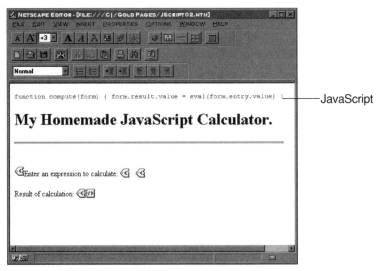

Figure 7-9: The added text is now officially JavaScript.

To test the operation of the form, click the Browse button to switch to Browse mode. The form should look like Figure 7-10. Enter the expression **18 * 2/3** in the first check box. Click the Calculate button. The result, 12, should appear in the lower text box (see Figure 7-11). If it does not, check the JavaScript and form tags carefully for any errors and retry.

Note that this wasn't a "normal" web form. There is no submit button. The form exists purely to use the JavaScript script you added to the web page. This is a whole new use for forms, and one that is specific to JavaScript.

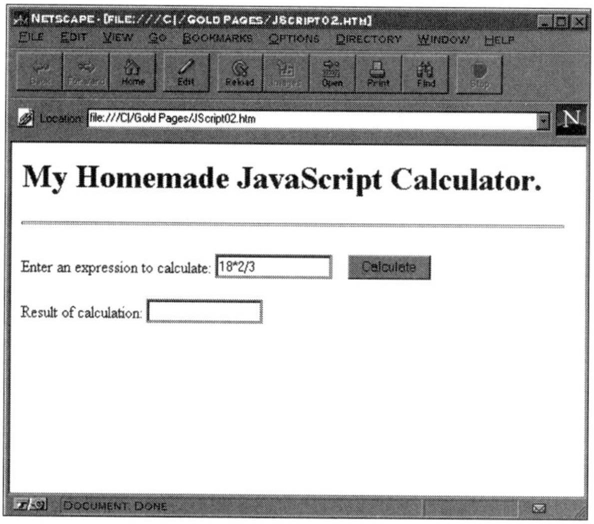

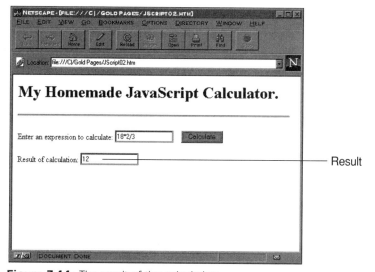

Figure 7-10: The form in Browse mode.

Figure 7-11: The result of the calculation.

Objects

The most important thing to keep in mind when you work with events is that events happen to objects. In the previous example, the event was a click, and the object was a button.

There are many other kinds of objects besides buttons. Table 7-2 summarizes the different kinds of objects that you can refer to in JavaScript code. The first thing you will notice is that there are a lot more objects than there were events (Table 7-1). Note that most objects are a property of another object. (Think of that other object as the parent of the original object, even though object-oriented purists will probably throw up their arms in disgust at such loose terminology. For most of us, a parent is a lot easier to understand than having objects be properties of other objects.)

Table 7-2: JavaScript Objects

Object	Property of	Description
anchor	document	A bookmark on a web page that serves as a target for a hypertext link.
anchors array	document	A list of all of the anchors in the current web page.
button	form	A push button on a form.
check box	form	A toggle switch on a form that can be either checked or unchecked.
Date	none	An object that provides methods (tricks, remember?) for working with dates and times. Note initial upper case "D", which is required.
document	window	An object that contains information about the current document displayed in the browser. It also provides methods/tricks for displaying output in a window.
elements array	form	A list of all the form objects (check boxes, radio buttons, text objects, and so on).
form	document	A collection of form objects, starting with a <FORM> tag and ending with a </FORM> tag.
forms array	document	A list of all the forms in a document.
frame	window	A subpanel of the web page's main window.

Table 7-2: JavaScript Objects

Object	Property of	Description
frames array	window, frame	A list of the frames in the current window.
hidden	form	A nondisplaying form field, usually containing information needed for processing the form.
history	document	An object that contains information about URLs visited within the current window.
link	document	A hyperlink to another file or URL.
links array	document	A list of the links in the document.
location	window	Contains information about the current URL.
Math	none	A built-in object that contains constants (like PI) and functions. Note initial upper case M, which is required.
navigator	none	Contains information about the version of Netscape Navigator in use.
password	form	A special kind of text element on a form (displays asterisks instead of actual text entered).
radio	form	A group of radio buttons on a form.
reset	form	Reset button on a form.
select	form	A selection list or scrolling list on a form.
options array	select	A list of the items in a selection list.
string	none	A collection of text characters.
submit	form	Submit button on a form.
text	form	A text input field on a form.
textarea	form	A multiline text input field on a form.
window	none	The top-level object for a web page.

You can find sample JavaScript code for these objects on the CD-ROM. Double-click the file \tutorial\chap07\javascript\objects.htm, where you will find a list of all of the objects. Click on an object name to see sample code that shows you how to work with that object in JavaScript.

The previous examples of JavaScript in this chapter (and in Chapter 5, for that matter) used objects. In fact, it's difficult to write JavaScript code that doesn't use objects. Objects are the fundamental building blocks of JavaScript.

Objects are arranged in a hierarchy, as shown in Figure 7-12. The window is the topmost object for any web page. The objects shown immediately below the window object in Figure 7-12 are always present for any web page (window, location, history, and document). The other objects may or may not be present on a given web page.

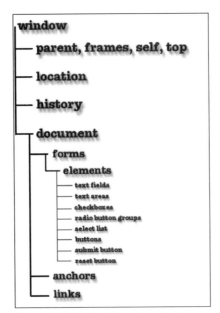

Figure 7-12: The hierarchy of objects on a web page.

When referring to an object, you must specify its entire hierarchy (or, as the JavaScript specification puts it, its entire ancestry). One exception: You do not need to specify the window object, since that is the parent of all objects. For example, to refer to a text box named LastName within a form named MYFORM:

```
document.MYFORM.LastName
```

Note that a period is used to separate the objects in the hierarchy, and that upper and lower case letters in names must match the original. In this example, the FORM tag would have used the name MYFORM:

```
<FORM NAME=MYFORM ACTION="mailto:someone@somewhere"
METHOD=POST>
```

and the INPUT tag for the text box would have used the name LastName:

```
<INPUT TYPE="text" NAME=LastName SIZE=25>
```

To set the value of the text box referred to above, you could use a
JavaScript statement like this one, which sets the text box's value to the
contents of another text box on the form:

```
document.MYFORM.LastName.value =
document.MYFORM.SpouseLastName.value;
```

The word value tacked on at the end of each object hierarchy is a *property*
of the object. You'll learn more about properties in the next section. The
value property provides access to the value of the object. The value of a
text box can be either the default value, when specified, or the text that the
user entered into the text box by typing. In this example, the line of
JavaScript copies the last name from the SpouseLastName text box to the
LastName text box. This would be a useful line of JavaScript on a form that
required both names — you could add a button to the form that copies the
last name, address, phone, and other information from the spouse area of
the form to the main area of the form.

For example, you could write a function like this:

```
<SCRIPT>
function CopyAddress()
{
document.MYFORM.Address1.value =
document.MYFORM.Address1.value;
document.MYFORM.Address2.value =
document.MYFORM.Address2.value;
document.MYFORM.City.value = document.MYFORM.City.value;
document.MYFORM.State.value = document.MYFORM.State.value;
document.MYFORM.ZIP.value = document.MYFORM.ZIP.value;
document.MYFORM.LastName.value =
document.MYFORM.SpouseLastName.value;
}
</SCRIPT>
```

And you could define a button on the form that calls the function when clicked:

```
<INPUT TYPE="button" VALUE="Copy Address Information"
onClick="CopyAddress()">
```

This structure — which is to define a function somewhere on the page between SCRIPT tags, and then call it from a button — is an extremely common use of JavaScript on web pages.

You can also write JavaScript code to report on the objects on a given page. Many of the page's objects are listed in arrays. Using the for statement, you can step through an array one object at a time, and display its properties.

For example, the following JavaScript code "walks" through the array of form elements for a form with the name Form1:

```
<SCRIPT>
document.write("There are "+document.Form1.elements.length+
    " elements in Form1:<P>");
document.write("<UL>");
document.write("<PRE>");
    for (var i = 0; i < document.Form1.elements.length;
i++)
        {
        document.write("<LI>Name:
"+document.Form1.elements[i].name
            + "; Value:
'"+document.Form1.elements[i].value+"'<BR>")
        }
document.write("</UL>");
document.write("</PRE>");
</SCRIPT>
```

I included a web page on the CD-ROM that uses this code to list its form elements. The filename is \tutorial\chap07\Jscript03.htm. Figure 7-13 shows how this web page looks in Browse mode. If you view the page in Edit mode (see Figure 7-14), you'll note that the JavaScript that lists the form elements is located *after* the FORM tags. This reflects something very fundamental about JavaScript: A script can only refer to page objects that appear *before* the script.

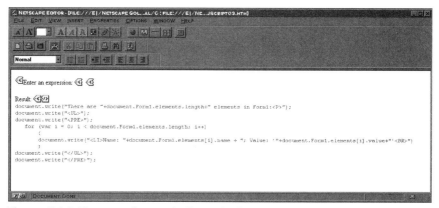

Figure 7-13: A form that uses JavaScript.

Figure 7-14: The same form as in Figure 7-13, but in Edit mode showing the JavaScript.

For more information about the `for` statement used in the preceding example, see the section *Statements* later in this chapter.

Properties

All objects have properties. However, there's a bit of weirdness involved when it comes to properties. I don't like it, but it's a part of JavaScript anyway. This is the weirdness: Objects are considered properties of other objects.

Before you object to this nonsense too loudly, I'll explain what's going on. Consider the way that you refer to the `value` property of a text box, using its entire hierarchy of ancestors:

```
document.MYFORM.LastName.value
```

The form MYFORM is a property of the object document. The text box LastName is a property of the form MYFORM. And the property `value` is a property of the text box LastName.

Got that? Don't worry if you don't; it's weird, remember? And it's only a technicality; the JavaScript police will not show up at your door if you think solely in terms of objects. For example, you could just as easily treat the objects as objects, and reserve the word property for things that really are properties. I think this is the most sensible approach, and I will take it throughout the rest of this chapter. Objects are objects, and properties are properties, and never the twain shall meet. For the sake of clarity, I shall refer to an object that is higher in the hierarchy as a parent, and an object that is lower in the hierarchy as a child. For example, a form has a document object as its parent, and a radio button group as a child object.

Table 7-3 summarizes the properties that you will find when working with JavaScript objects.

TIP

Many of the properties contain Boolean values. If you are not familiar with this term, it means that the value can only have one of two possible states. Usually, these are true and false, but they can also be such things as checked/unchecked, selected/not selected.

Table 7-3: JavaScript Properties

Property	Parent object	Description
action	form	This is the string that specifies how the form data is to be processed.
alinkColor	document	Specifies the color of the active links on the page.
appCodeName	navigator	Specifies the code name of the browser.
appName	navigator	Specifies the name of the browser.
appVersion	navigator	Specifies the version of the browser.
bgColor	document	Specifies the color of the web page background.
checked	check box, radio	Boolean value specifying state of the object.

Table 7-3: JavaScript Properties

Property	Parent object	Description
cookie	document	Contains information about the user. For full information, see `http://home.netscape.com/news ref/std/cookie_spec.html`.
defaultChecked	check box, radio	Boolean value specifying the default state of the object.
defaultSelected	options array	Boolean value specifying the default selection state of an item in a select list.
defaultStatus	window	Default message displayed in the status bar.
defaultValue	text elements[1]	String value specifying the default value of a password, text, or text area object.
E	Math[2]	Euler's constant and the base of natural logarithms. Approximately 2.718.
encoding	form	A string specifying the MIME encoding of a form.
fgColor	document	Specifies the color of text on the web page.
hash	link, location	A string beginning with a hash mark (#) that specifies an anchor name in a URL. This allows you to separate the anchor portion of the URL from the complete URL.
host	link, location	A string that specifies the host portion of a URL. This allows you to separate the host from the complete URL.
hostname	link, location	A string that specifies the hostname portion of a URL. This allows you to separate the host from the complete URL. Host and hostname are often identical.

(continued)

[1] Text elements include text boxes, text areas, and password boxes.

[2] The Math object is a built-in object that contains constants and functions.

Table 7-3: JavaScript Properties *(continued)*

Property	Parent object	Description
href	link, location	A string that specifies the entire URL.
index	options array	An integer representing the index of an option in a select list object.
lastModified	document	Specifies the date when the document was last modified. You can use this to display the last modified date automatically on a web page: `<SCRIPT>document.write (document.lastModified); <SCRIPT>`
length	many[3]	Specifies a length-related feature of the object. For example, it can specify the number of form elements in the elements array, or the length (number of characters) in a string.
linkColor	document	Specifies the color of hyperlinks on the web page.
LN2	Math[2]	Natural logarithm of two, approximately 0.693.
LN10	Math[2]	Natural logarithm of ten, approximately 2.302.
location	document	A string specifying the URL of the document.
LOG2E	Math[2]	The base 2 logarithm of e, approximately 1.442.
LOG10E	Math[2]	The base 10 logarithm of e, approximately 0.434.
method	form	A string specifying how form data is sent to the server (POST or GET).
name	many[3]	A string specifying the name of an object.
parent	frame, window	Synonym for a window or frame containing the current frame.

[3] This property applies to so many different objects that a complete list won't fit. Refer to the Netscape JavaScript documentation at `http://home.netscape.com/eng/mozilla/Gold /handbook/javascript/`for complete details.

Table 7-3: JavaScript Properties

Property	Parent object	Description
pathname	location, link	A string that specifies the URL-path portion of a URL.
PI	Math[2]	Ratio of circumference of a circle to its diameter, approximately 3.14159.
port	location, link	A string that specifies the port portion of a URL.
protocol	location, link	A string that specifies the protocol portion of a URL.
referrer	document	Specifies the URL of the calling document when a user clicks a link. Allows you to return to the caller.
search	location, link	A string beginning with a question mark that specifies any query information in the URL.
selected	options array	Boolean value specifying the current selection state of an option in a select list object.
selectedIndex	select, options	Integer specifying the index number of the selected option in a select list object.
self	frame, window	Synonym for current window or frame object.
SQRT1_2	Math[2]	One over the square root of two, approximately 0.707.
SQRT2	Math[2]	The square root of two, approximately 1.414.
status	window	Specifies the current message in the status bar.
target	form, link	Specifies a window where form responses will be displayed, or a string specifying the name of a window to display the content of a clicked hyperlink. The target property allows you to display form responses and hyperlinks in a window other than the original window.

(continued)

Table 7-3: JavaScript Properties *(continued)*

Property	Parent object	Description
text	options array	A string that specifies the text that follows an OPTION tag in a select list object.
title	document	The title of the document.
top	window	Synonym for the top-most Navigator window.
userAgent	navigator	A string representing the value of the user-agent header sent in the HTTP protocol from client to server.
value	many[3]	A string that specifies the VALUE attribute of an object.
vlinkColor	document	The color of visited links on the web page.

You can find sample JavaScript code for these properties on the CD-ROM. Double-click the file \tutorial\chap07\javasoft\properties.htm, where you will find a list of all of the properties. Click on a property name to see sample code that shows you how to work with that property in JavaScript.

All of the preceding examples in this chapter made some use of properties; it's hard to write JavaScript code without using properties. In fact, the getting and setting of properties makes up the majority of JavaScript.

The following is JavaScript code. To see the code in action, go online with Netscape Gold and visit the URL at \tutorial\chap07\JScript04.htm.

```
<SCRIPT>
var theDest="http://www.netscape.com"
var Dest1="http://www.netscape.com"
var Dest2="http://www.olympus.net/biz/mmad/ng.index.htm"
function setDestination(theDest)
{
    document.links[0].href = theDest;
}
</SCRIPT>
This is a variable <A HREF=""
onClick="this.href=theDest">hyperlink.</A>
<FORM NAME="LinkForm" ACTION="" METHOD=POST>
```

```
<center>
<INPUT TYPE="button" Value="Netscape"
onClick="setDestination(Dest1);">
<INPUT TYPE="button" Value="Author's page"
onClick="setDestination(Dest2);">
</center>
</FORM>
```

Figure 7-15 shows the form in action in Browse mode. To test operation of
the buttons, click one button, then pass the mouse cursor over the hyperlink;
note the link URL in the status bar. Then click the other button, and note the
link URL in the status bar.

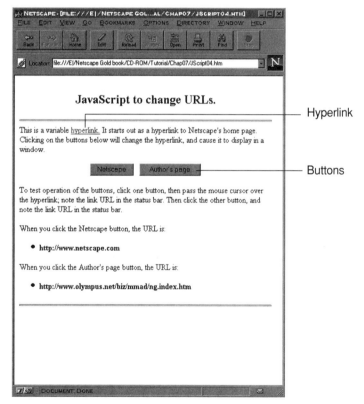

Figure 7-15: The form in Browse mode.

Test the page by clicking buttons, and then passing the mouse over the
hyperlink and checking the status bar:

➡ When you click the Netscape button, the URL is set to:
`http://www.netscape.com`

➡ When you click the Author's page button, the URL is set to:
`http://www.olympus.net/biz/mmad/ng.index.htm`

Let's take a look at how this page operates. When the page gets loaded by the browser, three variables get set: `theDest`, `Dest1`, and `Dest2`. The variable `theDest` contains the default destination, while `Dest1` contains the Netscape home page URL, and `Dest2` contains the URL for this book's home page.

Take a closer look at the hyperlink; it's different from hyperlinks you usually see.

```
<A HREF="" onClick="this.href=theDest">
```

First, there is no HREF at all, just empty quotation marks. There is an onClick handler, just like the handlers you've seen in some of the previous examples. This is the first time I've shown you that links can also have handlers. In this case, the handler causes the following JavaScript to execute:

```
this.href=theDest
```

`This` refers to the current object — in this case, the hyperlink. The property involved is `href`, and it is set to the contents of the variable `theDest` when the hyperlink is clicked. By putting the correct URL in the variable `theDest`, this hyperlink can be changed dynamically. The buttons, when they call the function `setDestination`, do exactly that: They put the desired value into the variable `theDest`.

When you click one of the buttons, the onClick handler calls the function `setDestination`, passing it a variable (`Dest1` or `Dest2`) that contains one of the URLs. The function sets the href property of the first (and only) item in the links array (document.links[0]).

All of the arrays that you can access in JavaScript always start counting at zero, not at one. This is easy to forget! If you ever have trouble accessing an item in an array, your first test should be whether you started counting the items in the array at zero.

You might want to take a look at how this page looks in Edit mode. I created the JavaScript by opening the completed page in Notepad, so the JavaScript is not on a single line. Figure 7-16 shows what this looks like. This is the preferred way for viewing JavaScirpt code, but it's not as convenient as the copy and paste methods outlined earlier.

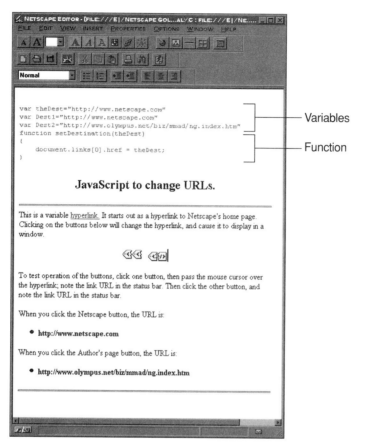

Figure 7-16: Viewing the JavaScript code in Edit mode.

This is just one example of what you can do by setting properties. You can also accomplish a lot simply by reading properties, and writing the results to the document. For example, consider the following JavaScript and HTML code:

```
<HR width="100%">
<B><FONT SIZE=-2>Last modified:
<SCRIPT>document.write(document.lastModified);</SCRIPT>
</FONT></B>
```

By inserting the SCRIPT tags after the "Last modified:" text, the document.write causes the lastModified property of the document object to appear on the web page (see Figure 7-17).

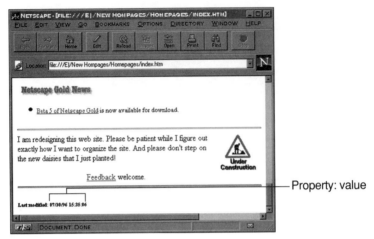

Property: value

Figure 7-17: Writing a property's value to the web page.

Whether you read or write properties, they are a key element of your JavaScript code. It's worth some time and effort to experiment with the various properties in Table 7-3. Try writing these properties to the web page on your own, or try setting some of the properties to see what kind of results you can get. You can get ideas from the files on the CD-ROM (`\tutorial\chap07\javasoft\language.htm`), or from the Netscape language documentation at `http://home.netscape.com/eng/mozilla/Gold/handbook/javascript/`.

Methods and functions

If you have some traditional programming background, you already have some ideas about what a function is. Some, but not all functions, return a value that you can use further in your script. Other functions simply make something happen, and may return nothing more than a true or false value indicating whether they successfully completed the assigned task. But one thing that all functions have in common is that they all do something.

A method looks like a function, and it behaves like a function, too. It's called a method because it belongs to an object. A method is a trick that an object can perform, and in any other programming language, it would probably be called a function.

For example, if you have a string object (that's a string of text characters) called `myString`, you could apply the `bold` method to it and display it on the page like this:

```
myString = "This is some text for a string.";
document.write(myString.bold());
```

This example actually uses two methods: the `write` method of the `document` object, and the `bold` method of the `myString` object.

Some functions — excuse me, I mean methods — take an argument. This is a way of passing information to a method. In the preceding example, `myString.bold()` is an argument that is being passed to the document's `write` method. Yes, you can use one method to pass an argument to another method. The most deeply nested method is the first one evaluated.

If you want to display the third character in `myString`, you would use the `charAt` method:

```
document.write(myString.charAt(3));
```

This would display the single character "i" on the web page.

Table 7-4 summarizes the methods that are available in JavaScript. For detailed information about the syntax of the functions, see the examples on the CD-ROM in the file `\tutorial\chap07\javasoft\methods.htm`.

Table 7-4: JavaScript Methods and Functions

Method	Method of	Description
abs	Math	Returns absolute value of a number.
acos	Math	Returns arc cosine of a number.
alert	window	Displays an alert dialog box with a message and an OK button.
anchor	string	Creates an HTML anchor that can be used as a hyperlink target.
asin	Math	Returns arc sine of a number.
atan	Math	Returns arc tangent of a number.
back	history	Loads the previous URL in the history list into the window.
big	string	Causes a string to be displayed as if it were between <BIG> </BIG> tags.
blink	string	Causes a string to be displayed as if it were between <BLINK> </BLINK> tags.
blur	form elements[1]	Removes focus from the specified object
bold	string	Causes a string to be displayed as if it were between <BOLD> </BOLD> tags.

(continued)

[1] Form elements are password, select, text, and text area.

Table 7-4: JavaScript Methods and Functions *(continued)*

Method	Method of	Description
ceil	Math	Returns the least integer greater than or equal to a number.
charAt	string	Returns the character at the specified index.
clear	document	Clears the document in a window.
clearTime-out	frame, window	Cancels a timeout that was set with the `setTimeout` method.
click	button group[2]	Simulates a mouse click.
close (document)	document	Closes an output stream to a document, and forces the document to display its contents.
close (window)	window	Closes the specified window.
confirm	window	Displays a Confirm dialog box with the specified message and OK and Cancel buttons.
cos	Math	Returns the cosine of a number.
escape	built-in	Returns the ASCII encoding of a character string in the form %xx, where xx is the ASCII equivalent of the character. For example, "!#" returns "%21%23".
eval	Math	Evaluates a string and returns the result.
exp	Math	Returns e^{number}, where number is the argument, and e is Euler's constant, the base of the natural logarithms.
fixed	string	Causes a string to be displayed as if it were between <TT> </TT> tags.
floor	Math	Returns the greatest integer less than or equal to a number.
focus	form elements[1]	Moves focus to the specified object.
fontcolor	string	Applies the specified color to a string.
fontsize	string	Applies the specified font size to a string.

[2] The button group consists of buttons, check boxes, radio button groups, reset buttons, and submit buttons.

Table 7-4: JavaScript Methods and Functions

Method	Method of	Description
forward	history	Loads the next URL in the history list into the window.
getDate	Date[3]	Returns the day of the month for the specified date. Dates are specified in the form "December 25, 1995 23:15:00".
getDay	Date[3]	Returns the day of the week for the specified date.
getHours	Date[3]	Returns the hour for the specified date.
getMinutes	Date[3]	Returns the minutes in the specified date.
getMonth	Date[3]	Returns the month in the specified date.
getSeconds	Date[3]	Returns the seconds in the current time.
getTime	Date[3]	The value returned by the getTime method is the number of milliseconds since 1 January 1970 00:00:00.
getTime-Offset zone	Date[3]	Returns the time zone offset in minutes for the current locale. The time zone offset is the difference between local time and GMT.
getYear	Date[3]	Returns the year in the specified date.
go	history	Loads a URL from the history list. You can specify a relative (plus or minus) position in the history list, or a unique substring of a URL in the history list.
indexOf	string	Returns the location of a string within another string. You supply a search string, and an optional starting offset.
isNaN	built-in	On UNIX platforms, evaluates an argument to determine if it is "NaN" (not a number).
italics	string	Causes a string to be displayed as if it were between <I> </I> tags.
lastIndexOf	string	Returns the location of the last occurrence of a string within another string. You supply a search string, and an optional starting offset.

(continued)

[3] The Date object is a built-in object that contains constants and functions for working with time and dates.

Table 7-4: JavaScript Methods and Functions _(continued)_

Method	Method of	Description
link	string	Creates a hyperlink out of a text string.
log	Math	Returns the natural logarithm (base e) of a number.
max	Math	Returns the greater of two numbers.
min	Math	Returns the smaller of two numbers.
open (document)	document	Opens a stream to collect the output of `write` or `writeln` methods.
open (window)	window	Opens a new web browser window. You can specify many aspects of the new window's appearance.
parse	Date[3]	Returns the number of milliseconds in a date string since January 1, 1970 00:00:00, local time.
parseFloat	built-in	Parses a string argument and returns a floating-point number.
parseInt	built-in	Parses a string argument and returns an integer of the specified radix or base.
pow	Math	Returns base to the exponent power, that is, $base^{exponent}$.
prompt	window	Displays a Prompt dialog box with a message and an input field.
random	Math	Returns a pseudo-random number between zero and one. This method is available on UNIX platforms only.
round	Math	Returns the value of a number rounded to the nearest integer.
select	password, text, text area	Selects the input area of the specified password, text, or text area object.
setDate	Date[3]	Sets the day of the month for a specified date.
setHours	Date[3]	Sets the hours for a specified date.
setMinutes	Date[3]	Sets the minutes for a specified date.
setMonth	Date[3]	Sets the month for a specified date.
setSeconds	Date[3]	Sets the seconds for a specified date.
setTime	Date[3]	Sets the value of a date object.

Table 7-4: JavaScript Methods and Functions

Method	Method of	Description
setTimeout	frame, window	Evaluates an expression after a specified number of milliseconds have elapsed.
setYear	Date[3]	Sets the year for a specified date.
sin	Math	Returns the sine of a number.
small	string	Causes a string to be displayed as if it were between <SMALL> </SMALL> tags (strikethrough).
sqrt	Math	Returns the square root of a number.
strike	string	Causes a string to be displayed as if it were between <STRIKE> </STRIKE> tags
sub	string	Causes a string to be displayed as if it were between <SUB> </SUB> tags (subscript).
submit	form	Submits a form.
substring	string	Returns a portion of a string object.
sup	string	Causes a string to be displayed as if it were between <SUP> </SUP> tags (superscript).
tan	Math	Returns the tangent of a number.
toGMTString	Date[3]	Converts a date to a string, using the Internet GMT conventions. Example: Mon, 18 Dec 1995 17:28:35 GMT
toLocaleString	Date[3]	Converts a date to a string, using the current locale's conventions. The exact format depends on the platform; here's one example: 12/18/95 17:28:35
toLowerCase	string	Converts a string to lower case.
toUpperCase	string	Converts a string to upper case.
unescape	built-in	Returns the ASCII string for the specified value. For example, unescape("%26") returns "&".
UCT	Date[3]	Returns the number of milliseconds in a date object since January 1, 1970 00:00:00, Universal Coordinated Time (GMT).
write	document	Writes one or more HTML expressions to a document in the specified window.
writeln	document	Writes one or more HTML expressions to a document in the specified window and follows them with a newline character.

You can find sample JavaScript code for these methods and functions on the CD-ROM. Double-click the file \tutorial\chap07\javasoft \methods.htm, where you will find a list of all of the methods and functions. Click on the method or function name to see sample code that shows you how to work with that method or function in JavaScript.

The best way to see how methods and functions fit into a JavaScript program is to look at a program that uses them. As I pointed out earlier, almost every single example in the book makes some use of methods, but the following program (Listing 7-3), which displays a JavaScript clock on a web page, makes use of some methods you haven't seen before.

The JavaScript code makes use of a form with a single text box on the form. Because you can write to a form object at any time (as opposed to the web page itself, where you can only write when the page loads), the script uses the setTimeout method to update the form's text box once each second with the current time.

To see the clock in action, double-click the file \tutorial\chap07 \javasoft\JScript05.htm (see Figure 7-18). It's not flashy, but it works. Later in this chapter, you'll see how to use JavaScript to create a clock that uses graphics to show the time.

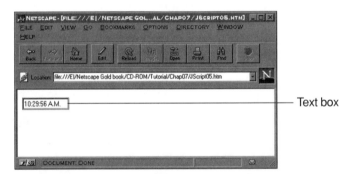

Figure 7-18: A JavaScript clock displayed in a form's text box.

Listing 7-3: A self-updating clock

```
<SCRIPT>
// Initialize variables.
var timerID = null;
var timerRunning = false;
// A function to stop the clock, if it is running.
function stopclock()
```

```
{
    if(timerRunning)
        // Stop the clock.
        clearTimeout(timerID);
    timerRunning = false;
}
function startclock()
{
    // Make sure the clock is stopped
    stopclock();
    // Start the clock.
    showtime();
}
function showtime()
{
    // Put the current time and date in a variable called
    "now"
    var now = new Date()
    // Use some Date methods to extract portions of the
    time.
    var hours = now.getHours()
    var minutes = now.getMinutes()
    var seconds = now.getSeconds()
    // Adjust from 24-hour to 12-hour time, store in
    variable.
    var timeValue = "" + ((hours > 12) ? hours - 12 :
    hours)
    // Add minutes to variable.
    timeValue  += ((minutes < 10) ? ":0" : ":") + minutes
    // Add seconds to variable.
    timeValue  += ((seconds < 10) ? ":0" : ":") + seconds
    // Add am/pm to variable.
    timeValue  += (hours >= 12) ? " P.M." : " A.M."
    // Form is named "clock"; text box is named "face".
    document.clock.face.value = timeValue
    // Wait one second, then run this function again.
    timerID = setTimeout("showtime()",1000)
    timerRunning = true
}
</SCRIPT>
<!-- Start the clock running as soon as the page loads. -->
<BODY onLoad="startclock()">
<!-- Form is named "clock" -->
<FORM NAME="clock" onSubmit="0">
    <!-- A text box named "face" -->
    <INPUT TYPE="text" NAME="face" SIZE=12 VALUE ="">
</FORM>
</BODY>
```

The script uses three user-defined functions. None of the functions uses arguments. The three functions are

stopclock() Uses the variable timerRunning to see if the clock is already "started." If timerRunning = true, then the clock is running, and can be stopped by using the clearTimeout method.

startclock() This function starts the clock. First, it calls the stopclock() function to make sure the clock is stopped before it starts (otherwise, you'd have two timers going at the same time). Then it calls the showtime() function to display the current time.

showtime() This function is the key to the whole operation. Not only does it use various Date methods to construct a string containing the current time, it also sets a timer that runs this function again when the timer goes off. The timer interval is 1,000 milliseconds, or one second.

The JavaScript uses various methods to get the job done. One group of statements uses some Date methods. The first declares a variable called now, and uses the new statement to make it a Date object:

```
var now = new Date()
```

At this point, the variable doesn't contain any data; it's just an empty Date object. The next line of JavaScript declares a variable called hours, and uses the Date object's getHours() method to put the current hour into the variable:

```
var hours = now.getHours()
```

The next line of JavaScript uses the Date object's getMinutes() method to store the current minutes into a variable called (what a surprise!) minutes:

```
var minutes = now.getMinutes()
```

The next line of JavaScript uses the Date object's getSeconds() method to store the current seconds into a variable called seconds:

```
var seconds = now.getSeconds()
```

These three variables now contain the information needed to display the current time. The lines of code that follow the use of the methods use some tricks to create a string that contains a properly formatted version of the time.

This line of JavaScript uses a construction that looks pretty bizarre at first glance:

```
var timeValue = "" + ((hours > 12) ? hours - 12 : hours)
```

Let's break this down into smaller pieces to see what's going on.

To start with, you are creating a variable called `timeValue`. This will be the container for the string you are constructing, and that you will eventually display in the form's text box. To make sure that the contents of this variable actually is a string, the statement uses a nullstring (`""`) just after the equal sign. Anything you add to a null string will be in the form of a string, even if it is a number (as in this case).

Next, there is a plus sign, which will append the rest of the line to the string. This is the very bizarre part of this statement:

```
((hours > 12) ? hours - 12 : hours)
```

This statement has three parts. The first part is to the left of the question mark, the second part is between the question mark and the colon, and the third part is to the right of the colon. The general flow of this statement works like this:

```
(Test an expression) ? (If expression is true, do this.) :
  (If expression is false, do this.)
```

In other words, if the number of hours is greater than 12, subtract 12 from the number of hours before adding it to the string. If the number of hours is less than 12, just add it to the string.

Bizarre-looking, yes, but very, very useful!

The next statement uses the same construction to determine whether to add a zero before the number of minutes, adding a colon to separate hours and minutes:

```
timeValue += ((minutes < 10) ? ":0" : ":") + minutes
```

The next statement in this group does the same with the seconds, also adding a colon to separate minutes and seconds:

```
timeValue += ((seconds < 10) ? ":0" : ":") + seconds
```

At this point, the string contains the current time formatted like this: HH:MM:SS. For example, the time might be 10:46:05. The last statement in this group appends either "P.M." or "A.M." depending on whether the number of hours is greater than or less than 12:

```
timeValue  += (hours >= 12) ? " P.M." : " A.M."
```

The last two lines of the showtime() function have to do with setting the timer. The first line uses the setTimeout method to start the timer:

```
timerID = setTimeout("showtime()",1000)
```

The setTimeout() method takes two arguments. The first is the function to call when the timer goes off, and the second is the timer interval expressed in milliseconds. 1,000 milliseconds is one second, so the timer will go off every second — just perfect for a clock. When the timer does go off, the showtime() function is called, which sets another timer, which will go off in one second and call showtime() again. As long as the web page is displayed, the clock will continue to update.

Note that the variable timerID gets set when setTimeout() is called. setTimeout() returns a unique number each time it is called. the stopclock() function uses this variable to make sure that it stops the correct timer — there may be other timers running at the same time!

The last line of showtime() sets the timerRunning variable to the value true. This variable is only true when the clock is running; if the stopclock() function is called, then the clock is stopped (the timer gets cleared), and the timerRunning variable gets set to false.

```
timerRunning = true
```

We used the new statement in this example. Several other examples used the for statement to create loops. The next two sections provide more detailed information about statements.

Event handlers

All the statements and functions and methods and objects in the world wouldn't do you any good at all if you couldn't find ways to execute the statements. Event handlers are the central mechanism for executing statements in JavaScript. When an event occurs, a function that you write, or one or more JavaScript statements, execute.

For example, one of the frequently used events is the Click event. When you click with the mouse on an object, the browser looks to see whether you have defined a handler for the Click event. You can add a handler using the onClick event handler in the definition of the object. To add an onClick handler to a button, for example, you would use JavaScript code like this:

```
<INPUT TYPE="button" NAME="Total" VALUE="Total"
onClick="dispTotal()">
```

The function dispTotal() must be included on the page somewhere above the form. It might look something like this, assuming that the form has the name OrderForm:

```
function dispTotal()
{
   var orderTotal;
   orderTotal += document.OrderForm.tshirt.value;
   orderTotal += document.OrderForm.keychain.value;
   orderTotal += document.OrderForm.sweats.value;
   orderTotal += document.OrderForm.poster.value;
   document.OrderForm.OrderNet.value = orderTotal;
}
```

The other handlers work in the same way. You can include an event handler in the definition of any object listed in Table 7-5 to the right of the handler in the column labeled *Object*.

Table 7-5: JavaScript Event Handlers

Handler	Object	Description
onBlur	select, text, textarea	Triggered when the input focus shifts away from an object (usually when the user clicks some other object on the form). For example, if text is required in a text box, you could use the onBlur() event (triggered when leaving the text box) to make sure text has been entered.
onChange	select, text, textarea	Triggered when the input focus shifts away from an object, and the object has been changed by the user.
onClick	form group[1]	Triggered when the object is clicked with the mouse.
onFocus	select, text, textarea	Triggered when the object receives input focus.

(continued)

[1] The form group includes button, check box, radio, link, reset, and submit.

Table 7-5: JavaScript Event Handlers *(continued)*

Handler	Object	Description
onLoad	window	Triggered when a document is fully loaded into the window. Use in either the BODY or FRAMESET tags.
onMouseOver	link	Triggered whenever the mouse pointer moves over the link. By default, passing the mouse pointer over a link causes the HREF for the link to be displayed in the status bar; with this event handler, you can write code to do something else.
onSelect	text, textarea	Triggered whenever the user selects text in a text box or text area.
onSubmit	form	Triggered when the form is submitted. You can execute some JavaScript prior to the form being submitted. This is useful for updating form data before it gets sent, for example an order total. To prevent the form from being submitted, return false from the function that handles the event.
onUnload	window	Triggered when exiting a document.

You can find sample JavaScript code for these methods and functions on the CD-ROM. Double-click the file \tutorial\chap07\javasoft\methods.htm, where you will find a list of all of the methods and functions. Click on the method or function name to see sample code that shows you how to work with that method or function in JavaScript.

One of the most common uses for event handlers is enhancing a form. You have already seen examples of this in Chapter 5, where you added event handlers to a form in order to calulcate the amount of an order. If you haven't already looked at the example from Chapter 5, you can find it on the CD-ROM at \tutorial\chap05\form1\form04.htm.

Statements

Statements more or less define the character of most languages. In the case of JavaScript, which has very few statements but plenty of objects, properties, and methods, it is the paucity of statements that defines the language. The language's designers made every effort to minimize the number of statements.

The statements that JavaScript uses are shown in Table 7-6. Although there only a few of them, each is important. Following the table you will find examples of how each of the statements works. Unlike objects, properties, and methods, most of which either have no arguments at all or require very few, statements require very precise usage.

Table 7-6: JavaScript Statements

Statement	Description
break	This statement terminates the current while or for loop. Control is transferred to the statement immediately following the terminated loop.
comment	Comment by the programmer, usually to explain what is going on. There are single-line and multiline comments.
continue	A statement that terminates execution of the block of statements in a while or for loop, and continues execution of the loop with the next iteration. In contrast to the break statement, continue does not terminate the execution of the loop entirely.
for	Creates a loop that executes until a specified condition is met.
for...in	Creates a loop that iterates a variable over all of the properties of an object.
function	Used to declare a JavaScript user-defined function.
if...else	A conditional statement that executes a block of statements if some specified condition is true, or an optional alternate block if not true.
new	Used to create an instance of a user-defined object.
return	Specifies a value to be returned by a user-defined function.
this	A keyword that you can use to refer to the current object. In general, in a method this refers to the calling object.
var	A statement that declares a variable.
while	Creates a loop that evaluates an expression, and continues to execute a block of code as long as the expression evaluates to true.
with object	Specifies an object that is to be treated as the default for a block of statements.

You can find sample JavaScript code for these statements on the CD-ROM. Double-click the file \tutorial\chap07\javasoft\statements.htm, where you will find a list of all of the statements. Click on the statement name to see sample code that shows you how to work with that statement in JavaScript.

The rest of this section describes how to use the various statements. Rather than list them in alphabetical order, they are listed in logical order. Statements that work together are described together.

Comments

It's a very good idea to add comments to your JavaScript code. It may take some time and effort to add comments, but they will be invaluable later, when you come back to make changes to the code. Things that are obvious the first time you write code can be quite obscure a week or a month later.

There are two kinds of comments: single line and multiline. Use two forward slashes to indicate a single-line comment:

```
// This is a comment.
```

Use a slash plus asterisk to start a multiline comment, and an asterisk plus slash to end it:

```
/* This is the first line of comment.
   This is a second line.
   And this is the third and last line. */
```

The key to writing good comments is to write them as if someone else will have to read and understand them. When you come back later, you will then be able to figure out what your code is all about.

var

Use this statement to declare a variable. You do not need to use this statement to declare variables, but it makes your code more readable if you do use it. For example, to declare a variable to hold the total number of students, you might use something like this:

```
var totalStudents;
```

You can declare more than one variable at a time by putting a comma between variables:

```
var totalStudents, mathStudents, writingStudents;
```

You can also set an initial value for a variable when you declare it:

```
var totalStudents = 0, mathStudents = 0,
writingStudents = 0;
```

Syntax:

```
var varname [= value] [..., varname [= value] ]
```

function

```
function funcName([argOne [, argTwo...]])
{
    statement
    statement
    statement
    statement
    [return value]
}
```

Figure 7-19: The syntax of the function statement.

The `function` statement is always the first statement you use when declaring a user-defined function. User-defined functions are a very important part of JavaScript. In most applications, you define one or more functions, and then call those functions using handlers in form elements or links.

Most of the extended JavaScript examples in this chapter make some use of functions. They are easy to create, easy to use, and easy to maintain if adequately commented (see the comment statement above).

The basic format of a function is shown in Figure 7-19. The `function` statement comes first, followed by the function name. Anything that makes the purpose of the function clear is suitable for a name. The name cannot include any spaces or non-alphanumeric characters.

If the function has arguments, list their names in parentheses following the function name. For example, a function to calculate sales tax might require two arguments: the dollar amount, and the sales tax rate:

```
function calculateTotal(amount, rate)
```

The names of the function and the arguments are arbitrary; the function definition could just as easily look like this:

```
function determineOrderTotal(orderAmount, salesTaxRate)
```

If there are no arguments, include empty parentheses:

```
function calculateTotal()
```

A function consists of one or more statements that do the work of the function. They must be enclosed in curly braces:

```
function calculateTotal()
{
   document.OrderForm.Total.value = subTotal +
(subTotal)*taxRate;
}
```

For additional information about functions, see the descriptions of the new, return, and this statements.

new

Use this statement to create an instance of an object. Creating an instance of an object is done in two steps:

➥ Define the object type by writing a function

➥ Create an instance of the object using the new statement.

For example, if you were writing JavaScript for a form that deals with students, you might want to create an object type for a student. The object would contain various properties of a student:

```
function student(gradeLevel, major, name)
{
  this.gradeLevel = gradeLevel;
  this.major = major;
  this.name = name;
}
```

You could use this object type by creating an instance of the object using JavaScript:

```
tempStudent = new student("Freshman", "Math", "John
Smith");
```

You can now refer to the various properties of the user-defined object directly: the value of `tempStudent.major`, for example, would be "Math".

return

The `return` statement specifies the value returned by a user-defined function. A function can return any kind of value — a string, a number, a Boolean (true or false) value, — or no value at all. For example, a function that simply carries out some action need not return a value. In such cases, however, you might want to return a true or false value, indicating whether the function succeeded at its task.

One example of a function that must return a value is one that calculates the tax on an order. If we suppose that the sales tax is 7.9 percent, the following function takes the order total, and calculates the tax on it:

```
function calculateSalesTax(orderTotal, discountAmount)
{
  netTotal = orderTotal − discountAmount;
  return netTotal * 0.079;
}
```

The following function checks to see that the value passed to it is within the allowed range of values, and then performs its task, returning true. If the value is not okay, it does not perform the task, and returns false. Note that this function calls the `calculateSalesTax` function. If the JavaScript code that calls this function gets a value of false back, it can display a warning to the user.

```
function displayTotal(orderTotal)
{
  orderDiscount = document.form1.orderAmount * (1-
document.form1.discountPercent);
  if ((orderTotal − orderDiscount) < 10.00)
    {
      // Order total is too small.
      return false;
    }
  else
    {
      salesTax = calculateSalesTax(orderNet,
orderDiscount);
      document.form1.orderTotal.value = orderNet +
salesTax;
      return true;
    }
}
```

Whether you create a function that returns a value, or a function that returns a true or false value, be careful to make sure that every possible path through the function returns a value. Otherwise, you will get an error when the function is executed.

this

The keyword this refers to the calling object, and is used frequently in functions. For example, if you call a single functions from three different text fields, you can use this to refer to whichever object called the function.

The following three text items all call the verifyItem() function:

```
<INPUT TYPE="text" NAME="Item1" onClick="verifyItem()">
<INPUT TYPE="text" NAME="Item2" onClick="verifyItem()">
<INPUT TYPE="text" NAME="Item3" onClick="verifyItem()">
```

The verifyItem() function checks to see that the user has entered a valid item description, and uses the this keyword to refer to the current item calling the function. If the user has entered some text in the text box, the function updates the order total with the price of the item. If the user did not enter text in the box, the function displays an alert and does not update the order total.

```
function verifyItem()
{
   if (this.value != "")
   {
      // User entered an item description.
      if (this.name == "Item1") {orderTotal += 99.95} else{
      if (this.name == "Item2") {orderTotal += 8.95} else{
         if (this.name == "Item3") {orderTotal += 79.95}}}
   }
   else
   {
      alert "No item entered for "+this.name;
   }
}
```

Using the this keyword is much more compact than referring to every object with the full hierarchy, such as document.OrderForm.Item1.value.

if

```
if (condition) {
    statement
    statement }
[else {
    statement
    statement }]
```

Figure 7-20: The syntax of the if statement.

The `if` statement (see Figure 7-20) is used to control program flow. There is an excellent example of the `if` statement in the preceding example for the `this` keyword. You can use an `if` statement anywhere in a program where you want to create alternative branches based on some condition.

For example, you can use the `if` statement to verify entry in form fields:

```
function checkEntry(someData)
{
    if (someData <=100 && someData > 0)
    {
        // Value is in correct range.
        return true;
    }
}
```

You will find many, many uses for the `if` statement. The examples here and in Chapter 5 are peppered with `if` statements and should give you plenty of ideas for how to make good use of the statement.

while

```
while ( condition ) {
    statement
    statement }
```

Figure 7-21: The syntax of the while statement.

A while loop (see Figure 7-21) is used to repeatedly execute a block of statements until the specified condition is no longer true. The condition is tested before the statements are executed — if the condition isn't true the first time the while loop is encountered, then the statements are not executed at all. The while loop is useful when you can't predict how many times you might have to perform a group of statements. The for loop is better when you know how many times to loop through the statements. For example, if you have a form that allows the user to add any number of student test scores, a while loop is a useful way to iterate through the group of scores. If you have a form with seven text fields, a for loop is a better choice for iterating through those text fields.

In the example of student test scores, the following function uses a while loop to determine the average text score:

```
function averageScore(numberOfScores)
{
   if (numberOfScores > 0)
   {
      currentScore = 1;
      while (currentScore <= numberOfScores)
      {
         scoresTotal +=
document.Form2.elements[currentScore].value;
         currentScore+=;
      }
      averageScore = scoresTotal/numberOfScores;
      return averageScore;
   }
}
```

The above example makes use of the elements array to step through the form's elements. Note that the first element reference is to element 1, not element 0. I am assuming that the first element on the form is *not* a score! I am also assuming that the remaining elements on the form are scores. Such a form might be defined like this:

```
<FORM ACTION="" METHOD="post">
Enter name of this class: <INPUT TYPE="text"
NAME="className"><BR>
Score #1: <INPUT TYPE="text" NAME="score1"
onChange="validateScore()"><BR>
Score #2: <INPUT TYPE="text" NAME="score2"
onChange="validateScore()"><BR>
Score #3: <INPUT TYPE="text" NAME="score3"
onChange="validateScore()"><BR>
Score #4: <INPUT TYPE="text" NAME="score4"
```

```
onChange="validateScore()"><BR>
Score #5: <INPUT TYPE="text" NAME="score5"
onChange="validateScore()"><BR>
Score #6: <INPUT TYPE="text" NAME="score6"
onChange="validateScore()"><BR>
Score #7: <INPUT TYPE="text" NAME="score7"
onChange="validateScore()"><BR>
Score #8: <INPUT TYPE="text" NAME="score8"
onChange="validateScore()"><BR>
Score #9: <INPUT TYPE="text" NAME="score9"
onChange="validateScore()"><BR>
<INPUT TYPE="button" VALUE="Calculate Average"
onClick="displayAverage()"> 
Average score: <INPUT TYPE="text" NAME="average">
</FORM>
```

To complete this web page, you would need to write two additional functions. The first, validateScore(), would check to make sure that the score is in the correct range (between 0 and 100). The second, displayAverage(), would use the averageScore() function to calculate the average score (don't forget to write a loop to determine the value for numberOfScores!) and then display the result in the last field on the form. I leave these two functions to you, to write as an exercise. If you want to check your work against mine, look at the JavaScript code in the file \tutorial\chap07\javasoft\Jscript06.htm. Hint: check out the code example for the for and break statements below.

break

The break statement terminates the current while or for loop. Program control is transferred to the first statement following the loop. You can use the break statement to leave a loop early, or to exit a loop because of a problem.

For example, in evaluating the average score (see sample code for while statement), you could break out of the while loop if you encountered an invalid test score of zero:

```
while (score <= numberOfScores)
{
   scoresTotal +=
parseInt(document.Form2.elements[score].value);
   score++;
   if (parseInt(document.Form2.elements[currentScore].value)
== 0)
   {
```

(continued)

```
      // Scores of zero are not allowed; may be invalid
      data.
      alert("A score of zero may be invalid data.
      Aborting.");
      break;
   }
}
```

The code example for the for statement also illustrates use of the break statement. See also the continue statement, which is sometimes a better choice than the break statement.

for

```
for ([initialize;] [condition;] [increment]) {
    statement
    statement }
```

Figure 7-22: The syntax of the for statement.

The for statement is a looping statement, and is often used when you know exactly how many times you need to loop. In the example cited in the description for the while statement, I suggested that you create a loop to determine the number of valid test scores before determining the average of all test scores. A for loop is perfectly suited for this job. You know that you have nine possible test scores, and you can scan them one at a time in a for loop to see if they are valid. In the following example, a function that displays the average scores first uses a for loop to see how many valid scores there are:

```
function displayAverage()
{
    // Initialize number of scores to zero.
    numberOfScores=0;
    // Determine the number of valid scores with a for loop.
    for (i=1; i < document.Form2.elements.length-4; i++)
    {
        // See if the value is not null.
        if (document.Form2.elements[i].value != "")
        {
```

```
        // Valid score; increment counter by one.
        numberOfScores++
    }
    else
    {
        // Invalid score; stop scanning.
        break
    }
}
// Get the average of all scores.
average = averageScore(numberOfScores);
// Display the result on the form.
document.Form2.average.value = average;
}
```

This function will work in most situations, because it does not include invalid test scores in the calculation. However, if additional test scores were on the form following the blank, they will be omitted. If you want to have some fun with JavaScript, revise this function so it omits blank test scores, and still includes all valid test scores. Hint: you will also need to revise the averageScore() function.

for...in

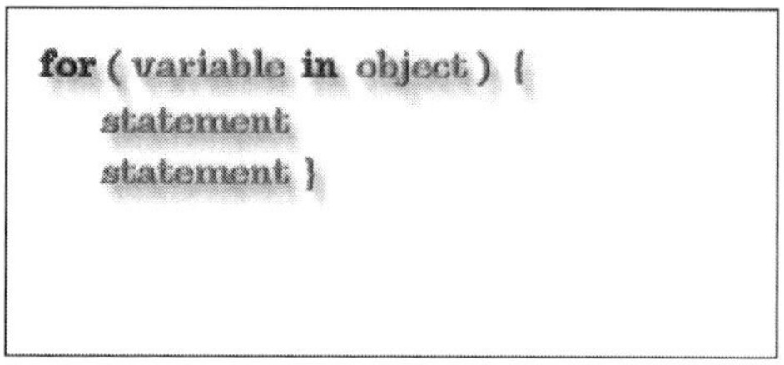

```
for ( variable in object ) {
    statement
    statement }
```

Figure 7-23: The syntax of the for...in statement.

The for...in statement (Figure 7-23) allows you to iterate through the properties for an object. The following function, for example, uses a for...in loop to display all of the properties for a text box on a form:

```
function getProperties(obj, objName)
{
    var result = ""
    for (var i in obj)
    {
        result += objName + "." + i + " = " + obj[i] +
"<BR>"
    }
```

(continued)

```
    result += "<HR>"
    return result
}
```

I have included a sample web page that uses this function; you can find it in `\tutorial\chap07\Jscript07.htm`. The above function generates the following output when you view the form in Browse mode:

```
document.Form1.input1.type = text
document.Form1.input1.name = input1
document.Form1.input1.form = [object Form]
document.Form1.input1.value = Some text.
document.Form1.input1.defaultValue = Some text.
document.Form1.input1.length = null
document.Form1.input1.options = null
document.Form1.input1.selectedIndex = null
document.Form1.input1.checked = null
document.Form1.input1.defaultChecked = null
```

The page displays this information because I included a line of JavaScript at the bottom of the page that calls the `getProperties()` function:

```
<script>
    document.write(getProperties(document.Form1.input1,
"document.Form1.input1"));
</script>
```

continue

The `continue` statement, like the `break` statement, terminates execution of the current loop. However, execution continues with the next iteration of the loop. This allows you to set a condition with an `if` statement for which the balance of the loop will not execute. The `continue` statement is a better choice than a `break` statement for the task I assigned in the description of the `break` statement. If you encounter an invalid test item, use a `continue` statement to avoid adding it to the number of valid scores.

with

```
with (object) {
    statement
    statement }
```

Figure 7-24: The syntax of the with statement.

The `with` statement (Figure 7-24) establishes a default object for a block of statements. You can then reference the objects properties in the block of statements without prefacing the property with the object name. For example, if you wanted to refer to a number of properties of a user-defined object:

```
function student(name, subject, test, score)
{
   this.name = name;
   this.subject = subject;
   this.test = test;
   this.score = score;
}
function validateStudent(student)
{
   with (student)
   {
      if (name == "") {
         document.form1.student.name.value = "invalid
         name";
      }
      if (subject == "") {
         document.form1.student.subject.value = "invalid
         subject";
      }
      if (test == "") {
         document.form1.student.test.value = "invalid
         test";
      }
      if (score <= 0 || score > 100) {
         document.form1.student.score.value = "invalid
         score";
      }
   }
}
```

More JavaScript Clocks

Earlier in this chapter, you saw one example of how to create a JavaScript clock. There are other ways to create a clock using JavaScript. The nicest feature of the earlier example is that the clock updates itself. However, the limitation is that the clock must appear in a text box on a form. If you do away with the form and the text box, you can use graphics to construct your clock. The down side is that the clock will not update itself; you'll need a button to update the clock by redisplaying the window.

For example, consider the web page shown in Figure 7-25. It contains two versions of a clock written in JavaScript. A text-based clock displays the current time using normal text. Also, a graphics-based clock uses images to display the current time. The images at the bottom of the page in Figure 7-25 show what the individual images look like. In both cases, once the time is displayed, it does not update.

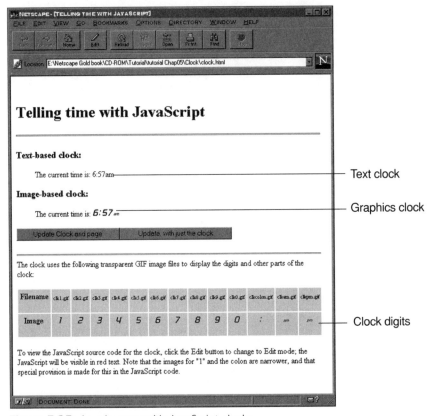

Figure 7-25: A web page with JavaScript clocks.

The web page with the clocks can be found on the CD-ROM at `\tutorial\chap07\clock\clock.html`. Double-click on this file and then view the page in Edit mode. You'll see something like Figure 7-26. Notice that a lot more JavaScript code is used in this example!

When working with such a large chunk of JavaScript, it is usually safer to add the JavaScript code in Notepad, rather than in Netscape Gold. The key is to add `<SCRIPT>` and `</SCRIPT>` tags before and after the JavaScript functions (see Figure 7-27). If you want to look at just the JavaScript functions, you can find them in the file `\tutorial\chap07\clock\clock.txt`.

```
<!-- Variable declarations -->
var Tm1;
var Tm2;
makeClock();
<!-- The following functions sets the value of the two global   -->
<!-- variables above. These variables are then called from the  -->
<!-- document proper, later in this file.                        -->

function makeClock()
{
        <!-- All images start with the same preface, so the ImgStart and -->
        <!-- and ImgEnd variables are used to avoid needless repetition. -->
        var ImgStart = '<IMG SRC="'+justPath(location.href)+'clk';
        var ImgEnd = '.gif" HEIGHT=16 WIDTH=12 ABSBOTTOM>';

        Tm1 = "";  <!-- Variable for image-based clock. -->
        Tm2 = " "; <!-- Variable for text-based clock. -->
        now = new Date();
        var theHour = now.getHours();
        var theMinute = now.getMinutes();
        now = null;

        <!-- Adjust for 12-hour time, and determine whether AM or PM. -->
        if (theHour >= 12)
        {
                suffix = "pm";
                theHour = theHour - 12;
        }
        else
        {
                suffix = "am";
        }

        <!-- Check for midnight. -->
        if (theHour == 0)
        {
                theHour = "12";
        }

        <!-- Add "0" before single-digit minutes. -->
        if (theMinute < 10)
        {
                theMinute = "0" + theMinute;
        }
        else
        {
                theMinute = "" + theMinute;
        }

        <!-- Build the clocks. -->
        theHour = "" + theHour;
        for (i = 0; i < theHour.length; i++)
        {
                <!-- Build hour. -->
                if (theHour.substring (i, i+1) == "1")
                {
                        Tm1 += ImgStart + theHour.substring (i, i+1) + '.gif
                        Tm2 += theHour.substring (i, i+1);
                }
                else
                {
                        Tm1 += ImgStart + theHour.substring (i, i+1) + ImgEnd;
                        Tm2 += theHour.substring (i, i+1);
                }
        }

        <!-- Add colon between hours and minutes. -->
        Tm1 += ImgStart + "colon" + '.gif" HEIGHT=16 WIDTH=7 ABSBOTTOM>';
        Tm2 += ":";

        for (i = 0; i < theMinute.length; i++)
        {
                <!-- Build minutes. -->
                if (theMinute.substring (i, i+1) == "1")
                {
                        Tm1 += ImgStart + theMinute.substring (i, i+1) + '.gif
                        Tm2 += theMinute.substring (i, i+1);
                }
                else
                {
                        Tm1 += ImgStart + theMinute.substring (i, i+1) + ImgEnd
                        Tm2 += theMinute.substring (i, i+1);
                }
        }
        <!-- Add AM or PM. -->
        Tm1 += ImgStart + suffix + ImgEnd;
        Tm2 += suffix;
}

<!-- Function for getting path without filename. -->
function justPath (InString)
{
        finalSlash=InString.lastIndexOf ('/', InString.length-1)
        OutString=InString.substring (0, finalSlash+1)
        return (OutString);
}
```

Telling time with JavaScript

Text-based clock:

The current time is: `document.write(Tm2);`

Image-based clock:

The current time is: `document.write(Tm1);`

The clock uses the following transparent GIF image files to display the digits and other parts of the clock:

Filename	clk1.gif	clk2.gif	clk3.gif	clk4.gif	clk5.gif	clk6.gif	clk7.gif	clk8.gif	clk9.gif	clk0.gif	clkcolon.gif	clkam.gif	clkpm.gif
Image	1	2	3	4	5	6	7	8	9	0	:	am	pm

To view the JavaScript source code for the clock, click the Edit button to change to Edit mode, the JavaScript will be visible in red text. Note that the images for "1" and the colon are narrower, and that special provision is made for this in the JavaScript code.

Figure 7-26: The web clock in Edit mode.

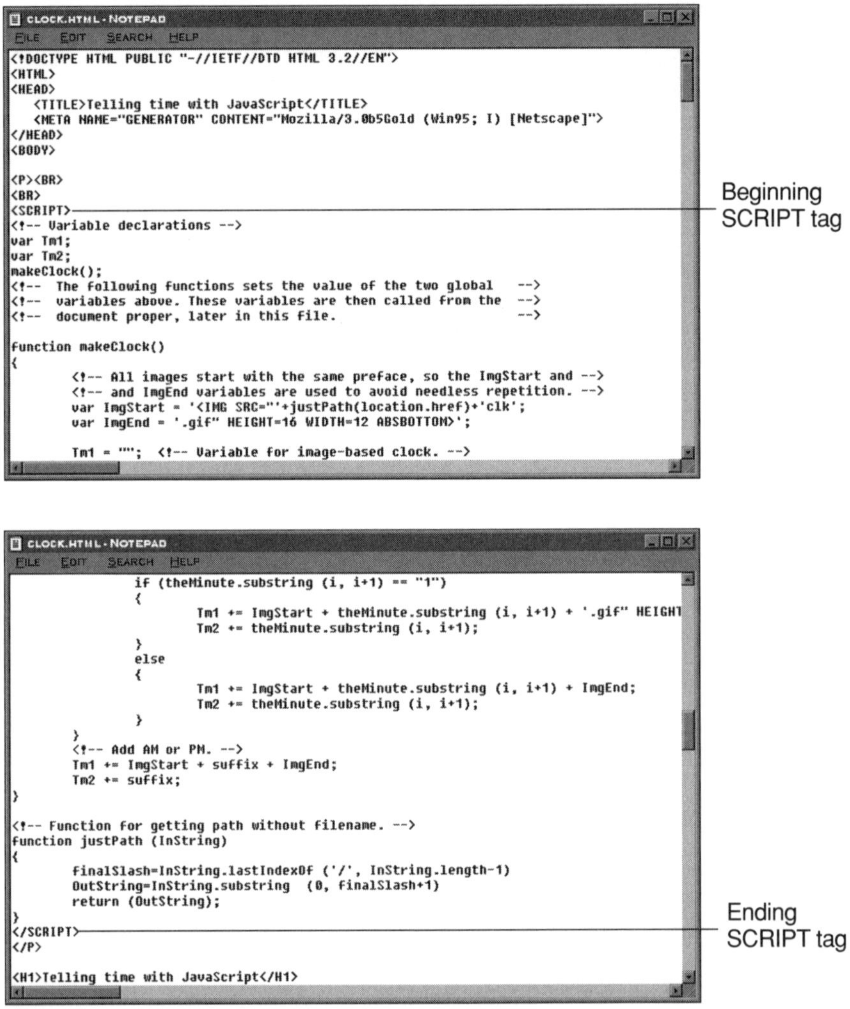

Beginning SCRIPT tag

Ending SCRIPT tag

Figure 7-27: Beginning (top) and ending (bottom) SCRIPT tags for the JavaScript functions.

The block of JavaScript code contains two functions. The first constructs the text- and image-based clocks, and the second is a simple utility function that extracts the path from a fully qualified filename. The clock function executes automatically one time when the page loads, putting the text-based time into the variable `Tm2`, and the image-based time into the variable `Tm1`. To display the time on the page, use the `write` method:

```
<P>The current time is: <SCRIPT>document.write(Tm2);
  </SCRIPT></P>
<P>The current time is: <SCRIPT>document.write(Tm1);
  </SCRIPT></P>
```

To add the JavaScript statements, simply type them in, select just the JavaScript statement (for example, `document.write(Tm2)`), and use the Properties | Character | JavaScript (Client) menu selection to tell Netscape Gold this is JavaScript.

You can use the basic method shown in this example — storing a value in a variable, and then writing the variable on the page — for many web page tasks. For example, you could create a calendar for the current month, or display a random image for advertising purposes each time the page is loaded.

 I have included another JavaScript clock that displays a late-breaking Netscape 3.0 feature: spacer bars. Double-click the file `\tutorial\chap07\clock\clock.htm` to see the effect, and check the source code for information on working with spacers.

NetKey #7: JavaScript Quick Reference

The JavaScript language seems to change with every new release of Netscape Navigator, and there is a good reason for that: The language is changing just that fast. Vendors are competing vigorously to have the best web scripting language. Microsoft's Visual Basic Script, for example, is an alternative scripting language for the web. For now, VB Script only works with Microsoft's browser; JavaScript is much more widely accepted. That may change.

What is guaranteed to change, however, is the language itself. The more pressure there is from scripting alternatives, the more likely that similar features will crop up in JavaScript.

I have included a language reference on the CD-ROM that you can use to learn much more about JavaScript. It includes example after example of real JavaScript code. This is the easiest way to learn how to work with JavaScript.

Using NetKey #7

 To begin, double-click on the file

`/tutorial/index.htm`

on the CD-ROM, which will automatically start Netscape Gold in Browse mode. As usual, if you do not want to connect, click the Cancel button when the connection dialog box appears. The appearance of the file `/tutorial/index.htm` is shown in Figure 7-28.

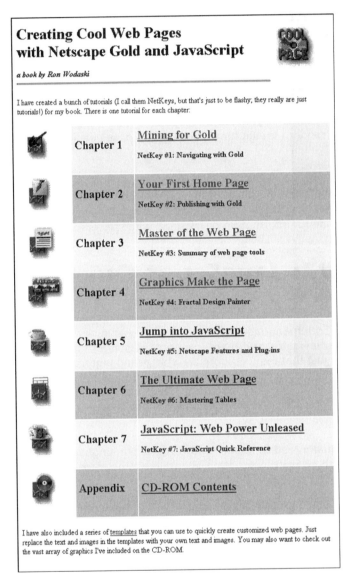

Figure 7-28: The web page for access to NetKey pages.

The file /tutorial/index.htm contains hyperlinks to the NetKeys for every chapter in the book. To learn how to create a complex image with Painter, click the hyperlink for Chapter 7, *JavaScript Quick Reference*. The first NetKey page for this chapter is shown in Figure 7-29. To explore this NetKey, simply click on any and every hyperlink (usually underlined text) that strikes your fancy. Note that I have included a hyperlink to Netscape's definitive (and frequently updated) official JavaScript reference on the NetKey web page.

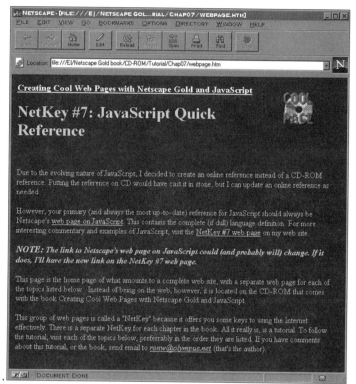

Figure 7-29: The NetKey page for Chapter 5.

To access the NetKey page for Chapter 7 directly, double-click on the file
`/tutorial/chap07/webpage.htm`.

About the CD–ROM

Appendix

In This Chapter

This is the most feature-packed CD-ROM that I have ever included with one of my books. The focus is on materials that are useful for two things, and two things only:

Learning how to create web pages

Creating great web pages

To access the material on the CD-ROM, you can simply insert the disc into your CD-ROM drive and wait for the self–starting menu (see Figure A-1) to run. If you have turned off self–starting of CD-ROMs, you can open the root folder of the CD-ROM and double-click on the file `autorun.exe`. This displays the window shown in Figure A-1.

To access any area of the CD-ROM, simply click on the appropriate button. The CD-ROM includes:

➡ Extensive *tutorial support* for the book

➡ *Web page templates*

➡ *Goodies*

➡ Web *utility software*

➡ Complete *sample web sites*

➡ *Freeware and shareware* products

➡ *Sample graphics* from four great vendors

➡ *Bonus files* added at the last minute

Details on the various areas of the CD-ROM are covered in this appendix.

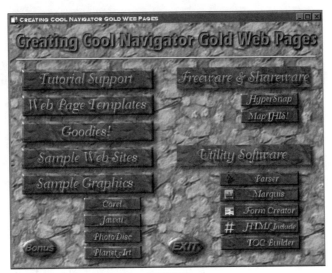

Figure A-1: Accessing the CD-ROM.

TIP The CD-ROM was completed after the book. You can find special treats and late-breaking news on the CD-ROM. Double-click the file `viewme.htm` in the root folder of the CD for more information. You'll also find extensive references to material on the CD-ROM throughout the book

Tutorial Support

I have included a large number of files on the CD-ROM to support the various tutorials included in each chapter, as well as to provide additional material that did not fit into the chapters. These are called NetKeys throughout the book. You can access the NetKey tutorial support files directly, as instructed in each chapter, or you can browse them by clicking the *Tutorial Support* button on the self-starting menu.

You can also view the tutorial support materials by double-clicking the file `\tutorial\index.htm`.

Web Page Templates

Templates make it easier to create web pages by providing an example you can modify to suit your needs. I have included a wide variety of web page templates, which you can access by clicking the *Web Page Templates* button on the self-starting menu. This displays a web page like the one shown in Figure A-2. The main page shows lists of the available templates.

Click on the template names at far right to jump to the template itself. To view thumbnail images, click on the template category (Background, Brochure, Calendar, and so on). Figure A-2b shows an example of template thumbnails. Click on the thumbnail to jump to the actual template.

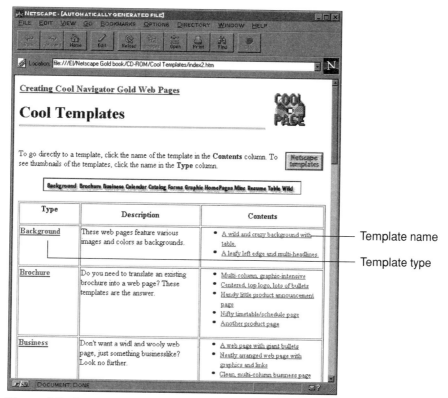

Figure A-2: *Accessing web page templates.*

To view thumbnail images, click on the template type (Background, Brochure, Calendar, and the rest). Figure A-2b shows an example of template thumbnails. Click on the thumbnail to jump to the actual template.

The actual template page will be different from what you see in Figure A-2, as the templates were still being created at the time this Appendix was written. However, the basic operation of the template page will remain the same.

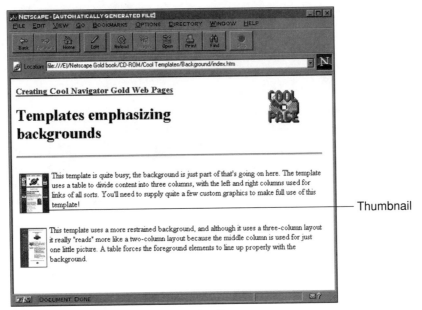

Figure A-2b: Viewing template thumbnails.

You can view the templates directly by double-clicking the file
`\Cool Templates\index.htm`. However, the best way to view the
templates is directly from Netscape Navigator Gold. To set the CD-ROM
templates as your default template source, click the Options | Editor
Preferences menu selection to display the dialog box shown in Figure A-3.
Make sure the General tab is active (click it to make it active). The middle
section of the dialog box allows you to specify the source for templates. My
CD-ROM drive is drive G:, so I added the following to the Location text box:

```
G:\cool templates\index.htm
```

Substitute your actual CD-ROM drive letter for G:. Click OK to save the
change. Now, whenever you use the File | New Document | From Template
menu selection, you'll automatically start from my cool templates.

If you still want to work with the Netscape templates, I have included a link
at the top of my main template page — simply click the link to jump to the
Netscape Templates. This allows you to have access to a large number of
templates from one source.

If you do not want to keep the CD-ROM disc in your CD-ROM drive all of
the time, you can put the following URL into the Location text box:

```
http://www.olympus.net/biz/mmad/ng/cool_templates/index.htm
```

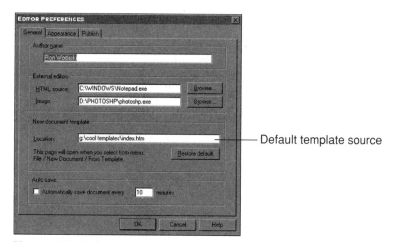
Default template source

Figure A-3: Setting the location for default template source file.

I will be adding additional templates to this location, so it may be your best choice! It includes most of the templates from the CD-ROM, as well as new templates that strike my fancy. If you have a template of your own that you want added to the online templates, send it to me via e-mail at ronw@olympus.net. All submissions are subject to editing, of course, if I can think of a way to improve them! All submissions are free for anyone to use in any way that they wish.

Goodies

Goodies is a very general term, and I use it on purpose. No one word describes the kinds of neat things I've managed to stuff into this area of the CD-ROM. Among the things you will find are an exhaustive collection of buttons in a wide range of colors, horizontal lines, vertical lines, backgrounds, and much more. There is only one cure for your curiosity regarding this part of the CD: Get thee out there and click away! Click on the *Goodies!* button on the self-starting menu, or you can view the various goodies directly by double-clicking the file \goodies\index.htm.

Web Utility Software

I have included a handful of Visual Basic applications that I hope will enhance your work with web pages. Each application offers something unique that I could not find anywhere else on the web.

Magic Parser

The Magic Parser (Figure A-4) allows you to receive form data in its typical nerdy format and convert it to something we mere humans can understand. Operation of the parser is explained step by step in Chapter 5, and complete instructions are provided in the online documentation file (\parser\readme.htm).

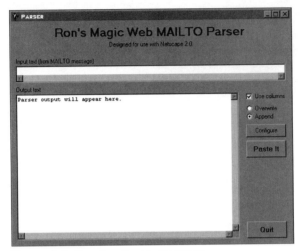

Figure A-4: Running the Magic Parser

You can start the Magic Parser directly by double-clicking the file \parser\parser.exe.

To install the Magic Parser to your hard disk, double-click the file \parser\disk1\setup.exe.

Marquis

The Marquis allows you to manage your list of URLs outside of Netscape Gold. The program has four major divisions (see Figure A-5). At top is the list of groups. Click the small arrow at the right of the drop-down list to see the current groups available. You can add new groups whenever you add a new URL to the list of URLs.

The largest division is the list of URLs or their names (toggle which is displayed with the View menu). This displays the URLs in the current group, or all URLs if you choose All as the current group in the list of groups.

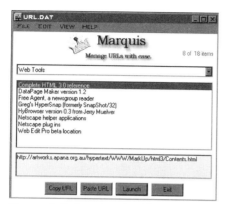

Figure A-5: *Running the Marquis.*

The third division displays either the URL or the name of the currently selected item in the list of URLS, depending on what is displayed in the list. If the list displays names, then the third division displays the actual URL. If the list displays full URLs, then the third division displays the name.

The fourth division is the row of buttons at the bottom. From left to right, these buttons are:

Copy URL   Copies the URL of the currently selected item in the list of URLs to the clipboard. From there, you can paste it into e-mail, a web page, and so on.

Paste URL   Identical to the Edit I Add URL menu selection, but copies the contents of the clipboard as the URL.

Launch   Launches your browser and goes to the currently selected URL in the list of URLs. Only works if your browser is not already running.

Exit   Exits the program.

You can save lists of URLs to disk, open lists of URLs from disk, extract the URLs from an HTML file, and perform many other tasks with URLs. See the online documentation file (`\marquis\readme.htm`) for details.

You can run the Marquis directly by double-clicking the file `\marquis\marquis.exe`.

To install Marquis to your hard disk, double-click the file `\marquis\disk1\setup.exe`.

Form Creator

The Form Creator allows you to specify the contents of a form, and then generate a web page (HTML file) containing the form. Basic operation of Form Creator is described in Chapter 5, and complete instructions are provided in the online documentation file (\form creator\readme.htm). Figure A-6 shows the appearance of the Form Creator.

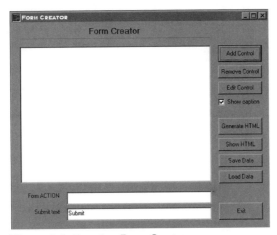

Figure A-6: Running Form Creator.

You can run the Form Creator directly by double-clicking the file \form creator\formcreate.exe.

To install the Form Creator to your hard disk, double-click the file \form creator\disk1\setup.exe.

HTML Include

The HTML Include program allows you to generate a web site using standard subfiles. For example, if every (or most) web page(s) is going to have a standard footer, you can create a master file that HTML Include uses to generate all of the web pages. You can create a subfile containing the footer information, and HTML Include will neatly add that information to the web pages it generates.

Figure A-7 shows the appearance of HTML Include. For complete information about using HTML Include, refer to the online documentation file (\HTML include\readme.htm).

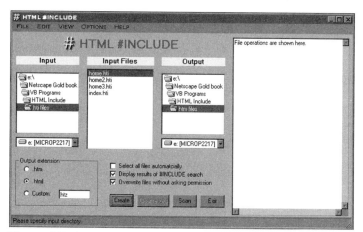

Figure A-7: Running HTML Include.

You can run HTML Include directly by double-clicking the file
`\HTML include\htmlinc.exe`.

To install HTML Include to your hard disk, double-click the file
`\HTML include\disk1\setup.exe`.

TOC Builder

The Table of Contents Builder (TOC Builder for short) will scan a web page or a web site and generate a table of contents in the form of a web page. You can select the kinds of web page objects that TOC Builder will add to the table of contents. These include:

➥ URLs found

➥ Local files referenced

➥ Bookmarks

➥ Filenames

➥ Headings up to and including a specified level

In addition, you can specify how TOC Builder will format the output. Output options include:

➥ Use a table to format output. The first column describes the type of item, and the second column contains the item itself.

➥ Include all local files on the web site in the table of contents

➡ Strip out HTML codes, such as <CENTER> tags, that might cause problems in layout of the table of contents

Figure A-8 shows the appearance of the TOC Builder. Consult the online documentation file (`\TOC builder\readme.htm`) for more information.

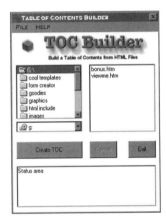

Figure A-8: Running TOC Builder.

You can run the TOC Builder directly by double-clicking the file `\toc builder\buildtoc.exe`.

To install the TOC Builder to your hard disk, double-click the file `\toc builder\disk1\setup.exe`.

Sample Web Sites

In addition to the many web pages included as templates and tutorials, I have included two more or less complete sample web sites on the CD-ROM. You can access these web sites by clicking the *Sample Web Sites* button on the self-starting menu.

You can view the Diamondback sample web site directly by double-clicking the file `\website\default.htm`.

You can view the Fanny's Fun Farm Products sample web site directly by double-clicking the file `\tutorial\chap06\fanny\index.htm`.

Freeware and Shareware

I have included two key programs on the CD-ROM, but in most cases you will want to download the latest versions of these programs using the links provided. The two programs included on the CD-ROM are covered in the book, and I included them so you would have instant access to the software for working the tutorials. Check the CD-ROM for any last-minute additions.

MapTHIS!

MapTHIS! is a program that allows you to create image maps for your web pages. Use of the program is covered in Chapter 4, and documentation in the form of a help file is supplied with the program.

You can run MapTHIS! directly by double-clicking the file
`\shareware\mapthis\mapthis.exe`.

To install MapTHIS! on your computer, create a folder for it on your hard disk (for example, `C:\My Programs\MapTHIS`) and copy all of the files from the CD-ROM folder `\shareware\mapthis`, including the subfolder `\shareware\mapthis\examples` and its contents.

To download the latest version of MapTHIS!, visit the URL at

`http://galadriel.ecaetc.ohio-state.edu/tc/mt/`

HyperSnap

HyperSnap is a utility for capturing Windows 95 screens/windows/regions. However, it also has excellent built-in support for image transparency and interlacing. This makes it a great tool for web images. See Chapter 4 for information about working with HyperSnap.

You can run HyperSnap directly by double-clicking the file
`\shareware\hypersnap\snap32.exe`.

To install HyperSnap on your computer, create a folder for it on your hard disk (for example, `C:\My Programs\HyperSnap`) and copy all of the files from the CD-ROM folder `\shareware\hypersnap`.

To download the latest version of HyperSnap, visit the URL at

`http://www.nb.net/~gregko/snap32.htm`

Sample Graphics

I have included sample clip art graphics from four vendors on the CD-ROM. Each vendor has graciously agreed to allow you free use of the sample images on your web pages. Click the large *Sample Web Graphics* button on the self-starting menu to open the Visual Basic application shown in Figure A-9, or click on the name of a vendor on the self-starting menu to view that vendor's graphics directly.

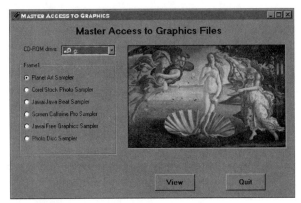

Figure A-9: *Accessing sample graphics.*

To access the graphics for a vendor, open the folder for that vendor's files on the CD-ROM:

Corel	\graphics\corel
Jawai	\graphics\jawai\freepc
PhotoDisc	\graphics\pdisc
Planet Art	\graphics\planet

You will find various image formats on the CD-ROM, including PhotoCD (.pcd), bitmaps (.bmp), GIF, and JPEG. Some of the images are provided in multiple sizes, and some are available only in one size.

Symbols

home page creation, 280–283

links, 266

product pages, 291–293

rough sketches, 265–268

home page, 265

for multipage layout, 268

for single-page layout, 267

translating into web pages, 267

for web pages, 266

teaching pages #1, 284–287

teaching pages #2, 287–291

web site plan, 264–265

web site requirements, 264

file compression, 179–180

file sizes and, 180

Photoshop options, 179

See also JPEG images

File menu

Edit Document command, 84

New Document submenu

Blank command, 36, 108, 160

From Template command, 80

From Wizard command, 56

New Web Browser command, 95

Open File in Browser command, 95, 141

Open File in Editor command, 41

Save As command, 27, 47, 96, 184

Save command, 37, 127

File menu (MapTHIS!)

Exit command, 194

New command, 188

Save command, 194

File Transfer Protocol. *See* FTP

filenames

backslashes in, 109

image, 116

path specification, 108, 109

saving pages and, 78, 108

in URLs, 16

Windows 95, 108

files

copying, 110

FAQ, 100

image

adding hyperlink to, 97

inserting, 115

locating, 89

placing, 109

selecting, 37, 116

JPEG, 171

text, 111

See also filenames

fixed width text, 30

folders

author's web site, 153

for graphics, 151

for images, 109

for saving web pages, 18

O

IDG BOOKS WORLDWIDE, INC. END-USER LICENSE AGREEMENT

4. **Restrictions on Use of Individual Programs.** You must follow the individual requirements and restrictions detailed for each individual program in this Book and on the CD-ROM. These limitations are contained in the individual license agreements recorded on the CD-ROM. These restrictions include a requirement that after using the program for the period of time specified in its text, the user must pay a registration fee or discontinue use. By opening the Software packet(s), you will be agreeing to abide by the licenses and restrictions for these individual programs. None of the material on this CD-ROM or listed in this Book may ever be distributed, in original or modified form, for commercial purposes.

5. **Limited Warranty.**

   (a) IDGB warrants that the Software and CD-ROM are free from defects in materials and workmanship under normal use for a period of sixty (60) days from the date of purchase of this Book. If IDGB receives notification within the warranty period of defects in materials or workmanship, IDGB will replace the defective CD-ROM.

   (b) IDGB AND THE AUTHOR OF THE BOOK DISCLAIM ALL OTHER WARRANTIES, EXPRESS OR IMPLIED, INCLUDING WITHOUT LIMITATION IMPLIED WARRANTIES OF MERCHANTABILITY AND FITNESS FOR A PARTICULAR PURPOSE, WITH RESPECT TO THE SOFTWARE, THE PROGRAMS, THE SOURCE CODE CONTAINED THEREIN, AND/OR THE TECHNIQUES DESCRIBED IN THIS BOOK. IDGB DOES NOT WARRANT THAT THE FUNCTIONS CONTAINED IN THE SOFTWARE WILL MEET YOUR REQUIREMENTS OR THAT THE OPERATION OF THE SOFTWARE WILL BE ERROR FREE.

   (c) This limited warranty gives you specific legal rights, and you may have other rights which vary from jurisdiction to jurisdiction.

6. **Remedies.**

   (a) IDGB's entire liability and your exclusive remedy for defects in materials and workmanship shall be limited to replacement of the Software, which is returned to IDGB at the address set forth below with a copy of your receipt. This Limited Warranty is void if failure of the Software has resulted from accident, abuse, or misapplication. Any replacement Software will be warranted for the remainder of the original warranty period or thirty (30) days, whichever is longer.

(b) In no event shall IDGB or the author be liable for any damages whatsoever (including without limitation damages for loss of business profits, business interruption, loss of business information, or any other pecuniary loss) arising out of the use of or inability to use the Book or the Software, even if IDGB has been advised of the possibility of such damages.

(c) Because some jurisdictions do not allow the exclusion or limitation of liability for consequential or incidental damages, the above limitation or exclusion may not apply to you.

7. **U.S. Government Restricted Rights**. Use, duplication, or disclosure of the Software by the U.S. Government is subject to restrictions stated in paragraph (c) (1) (ii) of the Rights in Technical Data and Computer Software clause of DFARS 252.227-7013, and in subparagraphs (a) through (d) of the Commercial Computer — Restricted Rights clause at FAR 52.227-19, and in similar clauses in the NASA FAR supplement, when applicable.

8. **General**. This Agreement constitutes the entire understanding of the parties, and revokes and supersedes all prior agreements, oral or written, between them and may not be modified or amended except in a writing signed by both parties hereto which specifically refers to this Agreement. This Agreement shall take precedence over any other documents that may be in conflict herewith. If any one or more provisions contained in this Agreement are held by any court or tribunal to be invalid, illegal, or otherwise unenforceable, each and every other provision shall remain in full force and effect.

CD-ROM Installation Instructions

Insert the attached disc into your CD-ROM drive and close the drive. The startup screen shown in Figure Z-1 should appear automatically. If the startup screen does not appear automatically, start AUTORUN.EXE in the root directory of the CD-ROM.

Figure Z-1: The startup screen for Creating Cool Navigator Gold Web Pages.

IDG BOOKS WORLDWIDE REGISTRATION CARD

RETURN THIS REGISTRATION CARD FOR FREE CATALOG

Title of this book: **Creating Cool™ Navigator Gold Web Pages**

My overall rating of this book: ❑ Very good [1] ❑ Good [2] ❑ Satisfactory [3] ❑ Fair [4] ❑ Poor [5]

How I first heard about this book:

❑ Found in bookstore; name: [6]   ❑ Book review: [7]

❑ Advertisement: [8]   ❑ Catalog: [9]

❑ Word of mouth; heard about book from friend, co-worker, etc.: [10]   ❑ Other: [11]

What I liked most about this book:

What I would change, add, delete, etc., in future editions of this book:

Other comments:

Number of computer books I purchase in a year: ❑ 1 [12] ❑ 2-5 [13] ❑ 6-10 [14] ❑ More than 10 [15]

I would characterize my computer skills as: ❑ Beginner [16] ❑ Intermediate [17] ❑ Advanced [18] ❑ Professional [19]

I use ❑ DOS [20] ❑ Windows [21] ❑ OS/2 [22] ❑ Unix [23] ❑ Macintosh [24] ❑ Other: [25]_____
(please specify)

I would be interested in new books on the following subjects:
(please check all that apply, and use the spaces provided to identify specific software)

❑ Word processing: [26]   ❑ Spreadsheets: [27]

❑ Data bases: [28]   ❑ Desktop publishing: [29]

❑ File Utilities: [30]   ❑ Money management: [31]

❑ Networking: [32]   ❑ Programming languages: [33]

❑ Other: [34]

I use a PC at (please check all that apply): ❑ home [35] ❑ work [36] ❑ school [37] ❑ other: [38] _____

The disks I prefer to use are ❑ 5.25 [39] ❑ 3.5 [40] ❑ other: [41]_____

I have a CD ROM: ❑ yes [42] ❑ no [43]

I plan to buy or upgrade computer hardware this year: ❑ yes [44] ❑ no [45]

I plan to buy or upgrade computer software this year: ❑ yes [46] ❑ no [47]

Name: Business title: [48]   Type of Business: [49]

Address (❑ home [50] ❑ work [51]/Company name:)

Street/Suite#

City [52]/State [53]/Zipcode [54]:   Country [55]

❑ **I liked this book!** You may quote me by name in future
IDG Books Worldwide promotional materials.

My daytime phone number is _____

IDG BOOKS

THE WORLD OF
COMPUTER
KNOWLEDGE

❏ YES!
Please keep me informed about IDG's World of Computer Knowledge.
Send me the latest IDG Books catalog.

COMPUTER
BOOK SERIES
FROM IDG